FROM VIENNA TO MANAGUA

This is the autobiography of one of the most remarkable women of our times. Marie Langer (1910–1987) was a psychoanalyst whose political commitment led her through some of the century's most dramatic political events both in Europe and Latin America. A clandestine Communist in 1930s Red Vienna and a medical volunteer in the Spanish Civil War, she went into forced exile in Argentina and later in Mexico. In both countries she influenced the development and direction of psychoanalysis, always stressing the need to combine the insights of analysis with those of Marxism and feminism. At the end of her life she was working as a group-therapy organizer in Sandinista Nicaragua.

In this much acclaimed autobiography, she traces her life odyssey and reassesses Freud's concepts of 'reality', the death instinct, the Oedipus complex and femininity, as well as the contributions of Klein, Lacan and Reich. The introduction by Nancy Caro Hollander of California State University describes how Marie Langer's involvement with revolutionary Nicaragua provided the exhilarating opportunities that she had lost after the defeat of Republican Spain. *From Vienna to Managua* demonstrates the possibility of surviving even the most heinous political repression, whilst maintaining one's understanding of the human condition and one's optimism for the future.

Marie Langer is the author of *Sexuality and Maternity* (Virago, forthcoming) and the editor of *Cuestionamos* (Free Association Books, forthcoming), a collection of radical Latin American writings on psychoanalysis. Margaret Hooks is a writer and journalist living in Mexico City.

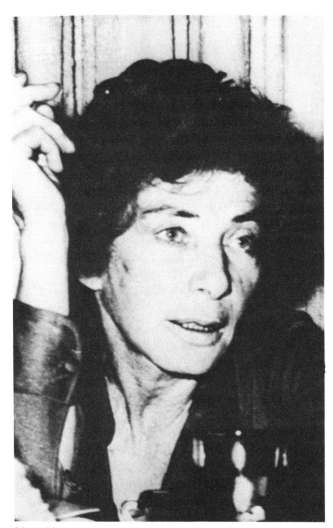

Marie, Mexico, 1975

FROM VIENNA TO MANAGUA
JOURNEY OF A PSYCHOANALYST

Marie Langer
with Enrique Guinsberg
and Jaime del Palacio

Translation by Margaret Hooks
Introduction by Nancy Caro Hollander

'an association in which the free development of each
is the condition of the free development of all'

Free Association Books / London / 1989

First published in Great Britain in 1989 by
Free Association Books
26 Freegrove Road
London N7 9RQ

Originally published in Spanish under the title
Memoria, historia y diálogo psicoanalítico
by Folios Ediciones, Mexico City © 1981

Published in German under the title
Von Wien bis Managua: Wege einer Psychoanalytikerin
by Kore, Verlag Traute Hensch in Freiburg © 1986

English-language translation © Margaret Hooks 1989
'Psychoanalysis and revolution in Latin America' © Arturo Varchevker 1989
Photographs © Veronica Langer 1989
Reproductions assisted by Liba Taylor
This edition was greatly facilitated by
the good offices, care and persistence of Judith Valk,
Librarian of the Zurich Psychoanalytic Seminar.

British Library Cataloguing in Publication Data
Langer, Marie
    From Vienna to Managua: journey of a psychoanalyst.
    1. Psychoanalysis – Biographies
    I. Title   II. Guinsberg, Enrique   III. Palacio, Jaime del
    IV. Memoria, historia y dialogo psicoanalitico. *English*
    150.19'5'0924

    ISBN 1-85343-056-0
    ISBN 1-85343-057-9 pbk

Typeset by MC Typeset Limited, Gillingham
Printed and bound in Great Britain by
Short Run Press Ltd, Exeter

EDITOR'S NOTE

The original Mexican edition of this book was produced by editing a series of tape-recorded interviews, into which Marie Langer inserted quotations from various works; some were referenced with footnotes, usually without page numbers given, and many were not referenced at all. Moreover, the English-language translator did not have access to the English-language publications quoted (in Spanish) in the Mexican edition; in any case, such access would have been of limited value, given that the citations lacked page numbers.

For the English-language edition, we have compiled a bibliography by using information from the Mexican and German editions, as well as from many other sources; to the extent that the references could be found, we have inserted conventional bibliographic references into the text.

CONTENTS

LAS VOCES EN LOS RECUERDOS

A Marie Langer

Nació judía como otros nacen negros o mestizos o chinos.
La desapercibida marca para la inmolación o el abandono
a la hora del reto y el miedo y descubrir la raza para
cargar con ella como un castigo.

Así se juntan los detalles de la Viena de los 30. La
República fugaz e inestable, en la confusa hora de la
invasión y a cada quien su sitio y su suerte. O sea el
campo de concentración o el exilio, el acorralamiento o
la salida airosa y triste; al fin que para algo trágico
o feliz se nace, ante la guerra, ante la vida; ante la
España pasionaria o ante el mar en busca de otras fronteras.
El exilio es un laberinto de cuidades como huellas.
Lo que nos guarda y nos retiene es la memoria.
Las voces en los recuerdos de la vieja casa rural y acogedora,
donde crece la niña Verónica y los otros niños
corriendo alocados desparramando objetos. Pero no sólo es
el pasado, sino su fuerza de mujer. El paso es el vuelo
sobre las gradas que se elevan y van ascendiendo con
sus alas blancas, pájaro que conoce lo alto, lo difícil
del vuelo en una noche de tormenta. La identidad
feliz de ser mujer, primero y último, la solitaria lucha
del amor contra el tiempo, y vivir y olvidar las calles
de Montevideo y México, en un tejido de ideas como inútiles
cosas que salen a poblar páginas y a llenar mentes –
que se interrogan de esos mundos inexplorados, talvez
inexistentes, pero que ayudan a vivir.

MANUEL MARTINEZ
Managua, 1986

Voices in Memories

To Marie Langer

Born Jewish like others are born black or halfcaste or Chinese. The imperceptible brand which marks you out for immolation or abandonment in the hour of defiance. The fear. And the discovery of your own race, borne as a punishment.

The story takes shape in the Vienna of the '30s. The fleeting and unstable Republic, in the confused hour of the invasion. Each to her place and destiny: concentration camp or exile, the round-up or the sadly fortunate departure. Ultimately one is born for tragedy or joy – in war, in life, in passionate Spain, or in the open sea, in search of new horizons. Exile is a labyrinth of cities, like footprints. What anchors us and keeps us is memory. Voices in memories of the friendly old house in the countryside, where little Veronica grows up and the other children run wild, scattering objects everywhere. Not only the past, but also her strength as a woman. The path means scaling the heights, soaring upwards, rising on white wings, becoming a bird inured to altitude and the trials of flying through a stormy night. The happiness of being a woman, first and foremost the lonely struggle of love against time; living and forgetting the streets of Montevideo and of Mexico, in a web of ideas like useless items populating pages and filling minds – minds which wonder about those unexplored, perhaps non-existent worlds which nevertheless help us to live.

Translated by Arturo Varchevker
assisted by Denise De Rôme, Peter Hulme
and Ann Wright

INTRODUCTION

I FIRST LEARNED about Marie Langer in the summer of 1983, when an Argentinian colleague sent me a copy of *Memoria, historia y diálogo psicoanalítico*. An autobiographical journey, created in concert with two collaborators, the book weaves together an analysis of individual life experiences with a description of some of this century's most dramatic political events in both Europe and Latin America. It is at once a singularly personal document and a social history.

What emerges from her autobiography is the portrait of a complex woman who lived her life with extraordinary coherence and integrity. Born in 1910 to a wealthy and progressive Jewish family, Marie grew up in the politicized culture of 'Red Vienna'. She engaged in her first political act when she was just nine years old. Still in primary school, she organized her twenty classmates to create a parliament during recess in order to denounce the tattletales among them. She later attended the Schwarzwald Schule, where her early political and feminist sensibilities were formalized by Marxist and feminist instructors who introduced her to a critical vision of the world. After graduation from medical school, Marie entered Freud's Wiener Vereinigung Institut in Austria, where she studied with Helene Deutsch and Jeanne Lampl de Groot and underwent her training analysis with Richard Sterba. She also joined the Communist Party, convinced that it was the only party on the Left that understood the cataclysmic threat represented by European fascism.

Psychoanalysis was already under attack as a subversive ideology by the Nazis in Germany. In a misguided act of self-protection, the Institut in Austria passed a ruling that prohibited analysts and analysands from participating in clandestine organizations. Since Austro-fascism had declared all political opposition illegal, the ruling virtually obliged the members of the Institut to refrain from anti-fascist political activity. This was the first time that Marie experienced what would become one of the more dramatic themes in her life: the conflict between her professional commitment to psychoanalysis and her political commitment to revolution. She believed that the Institut's ruling only served to delegitimize it, and she soon left to become engaged exclusively in the struggle against fascism.

Eventually she and Max Langer, a physician whom she would later marry, joined an International Brigade in order to contribute to the effort to save the Spanish Republic. Following Franco's victory, Marie was forced to flee Europe. She and Max emigrated to Latin America and ultimately settled in Buenos Aires, the cosmopolitan capital of Argentina. Shortly thereafter, Marie resumed her psychoanalytic work; and in 1942, she and five psycho-analytic colleagues founded the Argentinian Psychoanalytical Association (APA).

During the next several decades, Marie helped to build Latin America's most prestigious psychoanalytic training institute and society, one that eventually was recognized internationally as an important centre of Kleinian thought. From the early 1950s on, Marie developed a professional identity as the most prominent female psychoanalyst in Latin America. Through her own experience as a mother of four children and her appreciation of the unconscious conflicts of her female patients about bearing and rearing children, she developed a special interest in the psychosomatic disorders of reproduction and mothering. Her pioneering work was unique within psychoanalysis because it situated female psychiatric problems within a Marxist and feminist framework.

Beginning in the late 1960s, internal ferment within the APA reflected a growing political crisis in Argentinian society. The country's repressive military government ruled over a dependent capitalist economy in crisis and was confronted by militant political movements demanding a radical restructuring of political and economic institutions. Within Argentinian psychoanalysis Marie assumed a leadership role in a movement that excoriated institutionalized psychoanalysis for its complicity with an exploitative class system. The participants in this dissident movement argued that the Argentinian Psychoanalytical Association had lost sight of the liberating potential of psychoanalysis, instead mirroring the bourgeois order it served through its rigidly hierarchical structure and intellectually repressive atmosphere.

In 1971, at the annual meeting of the International Psychoanalytical Association, Marie gave a paper entitled 'Psychoanalysis and/or social revolution'. This was the first time that the International had met in Vienna since the end of the Second World War, a fact of special significance to Marie. In what turned out to be her farewell address to the International, she criticized the bourgeois ideology of the organization and argued that both

Marxism and psychoanalysis contained views of the repression and potential liberation of human beings that could be integrated. She asserted the inevitability of profound structural change in contemporary society, and urged her colleagues to use their psychoanalytic knowledge to facilitate rather than oppose progressive social movements. She admonished them not to follow in the regressive footsteps of the analysts who had left Cuba after the 1959 Revolution or those who were about to leave Chile in the wake of Salvador Allende's election as President of that country. 'Now', she proclaimed, 'we will renounce neither Marx nor Freud' (1971, p. 268). Marie and many colleagues left the APA and created a revolutionary mental health movement in Argentina. It aligned itself with other sectors of society that opposed the severe economic decline and increasing political repression which were the symptoms of a system in crisis.

In June 1974, the infamous right-wing death squad, the Argentinian Anti-Communist Alliance, targeted Marie for assassination. Her name joined others on its death list because of her commitment to democratize the mental health system and to denounce the atrocities committed by the Right as it moved to defend a social structure that benefited a small élite class at a rising cost to the majority of working people. Marie was forced to seek political exile in Mexico on the eve of the military's draconian seven-year 'Dirty War' against the civilian population, during which untold numbers of Argentines were jailed, tortured, murdered, and disappeared.

Along with many of her colleagues and thousands of other political refugees from Argentina who shared the same fate, Marie began the painful process of rebuilding her life in a new and unfamiliar environment. Determined to retain her professional and political identity, she taught and supervised in the graduate training programme at the National University of Mexico and became affiliated to a variety of Mexican psychoanalytic and psychological institutes. In response to the widespread need for therapeutic treatment among the exile community, she and other Argentinian mental health professionals established the Mental Health Commission, which functioned as an integral part of the Committee of Solidarity with the People of Argentina. By the late 1970s, the Mental Health Commission was extending aid to exiles from the Conosur (Argentina, Uruguay and Chile) and to refugees from Central America. Thus Marie was able to offer therapeutic aid to others while continuing to share the anguish of those in the exile community who had sustained massive losses – family, friends, comrades and a political movement that had promised the possibility of a new social order.

For Marie, the act of writing her autobiography was surely one of assessing the meaning of her life. It was also the opportunity to bring together in a single volume some of what she had thought and written about over the years. Perhaps it was also a way of capturing the images of the lost political movement and of honouring those individuals who had helped to define and implement it – those who had died and those who had lived to continue some form of the struggle in exile. Her book demonstrates the possibility of surviving even the most heinous political repression while sustaining one's understanding of the human condition and one's optimism about the future.

CHALLENGE OF NICARAGUA

But Marie's story did not end with the publication of her autobiography. At the age of seventy-one, she began a new chapter in her life, one in which she would finally have the opportunity to integrate her feminist convictions, her Marxist commitment and her psychoanalytic practice in an environment that valued rather than repressed this endeavour. Marie and other Latin American psychiatrists and psychoanalysts living in Mexico during the 1970s had avidly followed the Nicaraguan people's struggle to overturn fifty years of the brutal Somoza dictatorship. They knew some of the leadership, like Ernesto Cardenal, who had spoken about the Nicaraguan Revolution at a meeting of the Committee of Solidarity with the People of Argentina (COSPA). Marie and her colleagues in the Mental Health Commission of COSPA had aided the revolutionary Nicaraguans in the autumn of 1978 by providing psychotherapy to a group of combatants exiled in Mexico.

When the Sandinistas triumphed in their successful struggle to overturn the Somoza dictatorship on 19 July 1979, Marie's enthusiasm was like that of so many progressive Latin Americans who saw this triumph as a people's victory over a repressive military machine that had been engineered and fuelled by the USA. People from all over the world – physicians, nurses, teachers, agronomists, engineers, film-makers – went to help the war-damaged revolutionary country initiate its social and economic reconstruction. Marie was elated by the prospect of joining these international efforts to help the Nicaraguan people take control of their own country. In 1981, she became the Co-coordinator of the Internationalist Team of Mental Health Workers. This group of twelve Latin American psychiatrists and psychologists live in Mexico and travel monthly to Nicaragua to train a variety of professionals who provide direct health and educational services to the people of Nicaragua.

From Marie's perspective, this was the first time in history that the Marxist and psychoanalytic dialogue had risen from intellectual debate to political practice. The young revolutionary Nicaragua was thus the first country undergoing radical social transformation to endorse a psychoanalytic psychology as a foundation of the mental health programme for all of its citizens. For the last six years of her life, Marie became passionately involved with the social experiment initiated by the Sandinista Revolution in 1979 through her central role in the development of Nicaragua's first national mental health care system.

It was at this moment in her life that I met Marie. I wanted to write her biography and she agreed to work with me on the project. Several months after our initial contact, I saw her for the first time in autumn 1983, in Berkeley, California, where she and two colleagues from the Internationalist Team came to speak about their projects in Nicaragua and to raise funds for their continuation.

That weekend in Berkeley gave me the opportunity to observe Marie's magnetic impact on audiences. Hundreds from the politically progressive community of Berkeley came to hear about Marie's labour in Nicaragua. During the first evening's gathering they listened intently to her description of the challenge represented by the underdeveloped conditions of Nicaragua. She spoke of the legacy of poverty of the tiny dependent capitalist country, whose population of 2.7 million had suffered from a 60 to 70 percent illiteracy rate before the 1979 Revolution. The people still endured a minimal standard of living, reflected in a per capita annual income of only US $897. She described the multiple effects of almost fifty years of political repression by the Somoza dynasty, as well as the economic impact of decades of misappropriated state budgets that had resulted in a pitifully small social welfare system with appallingly few trained mental health professionals. She went on to portray the Nicaraguans as victims of the US-funded Contra war, whose main target was the civilian population. And she related the joy of working with the Nicaraguans. Despite the Contra terror and the economic privations of the US blockade, they were inspirational because they believed in a better future and they were committed to building a peaceful and just society to bequeath to future generations.

Marie's physical presence belied her seventy-four years: she was slim, lithe and often dressed in jeans and a Latin American peasant shirt, with a shock of white hair framing a tanned and lined face. Her startling blue eyes alternated between direct confrontation and sidelong coquettish glances, lending a captivating blend of strength and charm to her personality. As she spoke, her hands gesticulated for emphasis, while the smoke from her eternally lit cigarette swirled around her. I was struck by her energy, her easy manner as she carefully chose the words in her rusty English that could convey the nuances of her experience in Nicaragua.

At her second public appearance the following day, Marie spoke at the University of California to scholars and students about the work in Nicaragua. A lively dialogue about the possibility of integrating the basic tenets of Marx and Freud was followed by a discussion in which the viability of Melanie Klein's psychoanalytic concepts was questioned. Marie asserted that important Kleinian concepts, such as unconscious phantasy and reparation, were useful in her work. She demonstrated their clinical application among patients from the Central American refugee population in Mexico and among victims of the pre-revolutionary period in Nicaragua. She then spoke of the widespread phenomenon in Nicaragua of what she called 'frozen grief'.

She explained that a large number of individuals have experienced losses in the revolutionary struggle and the Contra war and have not had the opportunity or the appropriate conditions in which to mourn. She pointed out that a person who has not grieved the loss of loved ones may suffer many apparently unrelated symptoms, such as psychosomatic illnesses or interpersonal conflicts. The person cannot acknowledge the loss or carry on life in the present and remains fixed to the past. Once the death of a loved one is unconsciously denied, one's ability to maintain healthy relationships may be impaired. Marie described how mental health professionals working in Nicaragua had to be aware of this problem as a possible factor in every patient's history.

Later that evening, while sitting on the edge of the stage in La Peña, Berkeley's Latin American cultural and political centre, she spoke with community and solidarity activists about the Internationalist Team and their social projects. She spoke with feminists about the notable participation of women in the revolutionary struggle and described some of the exceptional female Sandinista commanders, whom she knew personally. And she urged us to intensify our political activity to help bring an end to the atrocities committed by our government in Nicaragua.

Throughout the weekend, Marie and I met to discuss the biographical project. When she left Berkeley, she invited me to come to Mexico to begin our work together. I had no idea then how much my life would change. In the next four years, I visited Marie often in Mexico to do research and record almost seventy hours of interviews with her. I travelled with her to Nicaragua in order to observe the work of the Internationalist Team and organized several fund-raising events in Los Angeles for the Internationalist

Team's efforts in Nicaragua. During that period, I grew to understand the many aspects of her complex personality and to appreciate her impressive willingness to be vulnerable and share her psychoanalytic understanding of her own abilities and limitations.

When I listen to some of the taped interviews I did with Marie between 1983 and 1987, I momentarily forget that she is dead. Our taped voices bring the past into the present, and I react spontaneously to our conversations as if they were occurring today. In a discussion about the volatile political conditions of Argentina in the early 1970s, I find myself smiling as I hear us laugh about our similar experiences, long before we knew one another, with the politically contradictory Peronist movement during those years. I feel slightly tense as I listen to another tape in which I challenge her assertion that women in the First World have gained sexual liberation and we enter into a heated debate about sexual politics.

Listening to another tape, I laugh out loud at one of her typically ironic remarks about her own contradictions, and frown at the sound of one of her chronic coughing spells, hearing my voice chide her as one would a defiant child about the harmful effects of her constantly lit cigarette. I shudder listening to the tension that suddenly erupts between us after she has fallen ill and we are trying to discuss her major book on women; she mentions a review written in 1952 criticizing its class bias, and when I excitedly ask her if she has a copy, she angrily snaps back about my naïvety to think she would have included such extraneous papers among the precious items she hurriedly packed when she was forced to flee her home in Buenos Aires. And I relax as I listen to the way we find of repairing the tension by acknowledging the deep conflict and distress we both feel in the face of her inoperable cancer.

I conjure up the image of the living room of Marie's house in the old colonial section of Mexico City. It is snuggled up against one of the massive walls enclosing the enormous grounds of the family home of her dear friend and colleague, the other Co-coordinator of the Internationalist Team, Ignacio (Nacho) Maldonado. It seems far removed from the hustle and pollution of Mexico's congested streets and overcrowded barrios, a refuge that creates a sense of external peace for the activist who never stops. It is in this room that Marie and I spend hours discussing her personal history, her political commitments as a feminist and Marxist, and her work as a psychoanalyst. In this room, people have come from Central and South America, the USA, England, Austria, France, Italy and Spain to have coffee or Nicaraguan rum and talk with Marie. It is in this room that every Monday evening since 1981, from 10 p.m. to midnight, the twelve members of the Internationalist Team have met to organize and co-ordinate their work in Nicaragua.

The walls are colourful with Marie's pictures and posters, many of which reflect the folk art and revolutionary politics of Mexico, Guatemala, Nicaragua and Argentina. Scattered here and there are visual remnants of Marie's European past, and, since December 1985, a photograph of Marie and Fidel Castro hangs right at the head of the stairs. It is a colour photograph, and, in spite of her age, Marie looks youthful and demure alongside the large frame of the famed revolutionary leader, who is chatting with her about the timeliness of introducing psychoanalysis to Cuba. The shelves of the fireplace are stacked with correspondence – some answered, some not – amidst books and xeroxed articles reflecting the many interests of her life, often sent by colleagues and comrades who wish to share their thoughts and concerns with her. Downstairs, the tiny guest-room has been converted to an office, where the volunteer secretary maintains the files of the Internationalist Team. There is still a small bed and sofa to accommodate the visitors who come from everywhere, many to collaborate with the endeavour in Nicaragua. During the times I spend with Marie in this house, I feel honoured to be numbered among those who have slept in this simple room where so much important work takes place.

I see Marie as I listen to our taped discussions. She always sits in the same spot on the couch with its back to the big bay window that looks out on to the beautiful garden filled with large trees of every green hue imaginable. She curls up her youthful body, absent-mindedly arranges the loose shirt hastily put over her jeans and says: 'OK, *compañera*, what do we speak about today?' Her voice carries a mixture of urgency and irony – as if she feels the importance of recording her life, but is unable to overcome entirely her sense of personal modesty. During the conversation, her sky-blue eyes are a clear barometer of the meaning of the subject at hand, and I grow to view the lines in her tanned face as positive signs of a life fully lived. Often a wry comment in her Argentinian Spanish is made disarmingly appealing by its tenacious Viennese accent. After a while, I begin to kid her about the coquettish demeanour that suddenly emerges in personal exchanges and in public appearances from her generally competent and straightforward posture. Acknowledging its existence, she accepts this stereotypically feminine behaviour as a benign reminder of the persistence of her early Viennese upbringing.

No matter what we discuss, Nicaragua is always present. The subject pulls at her like a magnet, and again and again we return to speak about her work there. The fact that Marie can be useful to Nicaragua signifies the recovery of the lost political project of progressive social change begun in Argentina. Her engagement in Nicaragua has yet another meaning. She tells me that it represents a profound continuity with her past. 'I realized on my second trip to Nicaragua what the experience is for me,' she says. 'I realized that there I am not old nor young . . . I am atemporal . . . and I live it as if the Spanish Republic, the old Republic, had won, and I am collaborating in the reconstruction. It is . . . a continuity . . . and finally, and suddenly, I am there' (Langer, 1984; n.d., p. 27).

INTERNATIONALIST TEAM

When Marie and her colleagues began their work in collaboration with the Nicaraguan government, the new Ministry of Health (MINSA) was developing a bold and humane strategy to meet the mental health needs of the Nicaraguan people. MINSA had inherited a mental health system that reflected the inequitable class relations of pre-revolutionary Nicaragua. A single psychiatric hospital in Managua had serviced the entire country, and its patients had survived passively in its appalling conditions, controlled by drugs and electroshock treatment. While the poor and middle classes had found little recourse but to send mentally disturbed family members to this deplorable institution, the wealthy had sent family members in need of psychotherapeutic attention to Costa Rica or the USA (Ortiz, 1979; Ministerio, 1981).

In contrast to the abysmal mental health system under Somoza, the revolutionary Nicaraguan state declared its political commitment to invest an impressive percentage of its limited resources to develop universally available mental health programmes. MINSA has emphasized a strategy of preventive care, which it plans to offer through a network of hospitals, community clinics and the 'Centres for Psychosocial Attention' (CAPS). According to MINSA, mental health is the product of a dialectical relationship among the biological, psychological and social aspects of life. Thus, psychology should play a central part in the development of people's health and, as such, should have a relationship with all the health services and programmes and be taught as an aspect of all specialized trainings (Langer and Maldonado, 1983). The people's direct involvement in health programmes of all kinds has been encouraged through the Sandinista mass organizations, which function to mobilize people to participate in reconstructing their society. This psychological model and political perspective of the Sandinistas were shared by Marie and the other members of the Internationalist Team.

In August 1981 the team of twelve was formed. All the members wished to contribute their skills to Nicaragua, but none of them could leave their families and professional commitments to move there for a substantial period of time. So they created the group which, through its weekly meetings in Mexico, would assure continuity and consistency in the work of its members, each of whom travels to Nicaragua two or three times a year for ten days. Marie shared the responsibilities of co-ordinating the group's efforts with Nacho Maldonado, a psychiatrist who had also been active in the dissident movement within Argentinian psychoanalysis. They and six other Argentines were joined by three Mexicans and one Chilean. All had a psychodynamic orientation within their specialties of psychiatry and psychology. Formally under contract to the Nicaraguan National Autonomous University, the Mexican Metropolitan University and the Mexican National University since their formation, they have developed projects at the psychiatric hospital and children's hospital in Managua and the university hospital in León. They have initiated programmes through MINSA in other regions of the country as well.

The work has been varied. They have taught physicians to appreciate the psychological dimension of the doctor–patient relationship. They have trained and supervised Nicaraguan mental health professionals in family and brief psychotherapy and offered classes in psychoanalytic theory and technique at a variety of sites. The Internationalist Team has also been integrated as the mental health component of the unique work-study programme at the medical school in León, where the curriculum is organized around a specific theme each year and students pursue research and community service related to the thematic focus of the year. The Internationalist Team also participates in joint research projects and works with MINSA to evaluate government programmes.

The strategy of the Internationalist Team has been to shift gradually from a much-needed focus on treatment of symptoms and rehabilitation to the prevention of mental illness. They have chosen brief and group therapy as the preferred treatment model, not only because of the few numbers of trained personnel and limited resources in Nicaragua, but in accord with Sandinista political ideology. As Marie and Nacho have written,

We work in groups, not only because in a society that desires the integral development of all, individual psychotherapeutic attention is insufficient, but because problems and mental suffering are generated in groups and it is in group situations that they can best be resolved. Group activity is in total accord with Nicaraguan ideology: it strengthens solidarity and teaches people to view their pain in social terms and to alleviate it together. (Langer and Maldonado, 1983)

While by no means the exclusive orientation among Nicaraguan mental health professionals, the Internationalist Team's psychodynamic approach has enjoyed a warm welcome, particularly because of its members' sensitive application of basic psychoanalytic principles to Nicaraguan cultural, social and economic circumstances. In 1985 Marie was invited to give a talk while in Cuba at the Casa de las Americas about her work in Nicaragua. She thought that the invitation was a significant event, since the Cubans, like so many on the Left, have tended to view psychoanalysis as a bourgeois, decadent and idealist practice. But, at least partly in response to the large numbers of Latin American psychoanalysts who have been identified with struggles for progressive social change, Cuban mental health professionals and intellectuals have recently become interested in psychoanalysis.

In her Havana talk, 'Psicoanálisis sin divan' (Psychoanalysis without the couch), Marie described and critiqued the historical antipathy expressed by Soviet psychology towards psychoanalysis. She asserted that psychoanalysis is a science of human subjectivity in which the psychoanalyst attempts to clarify the relationship between immediate, subjective experience and the objective conditions that belong to the general contradictions of society. Stressing the importance of understanding unconscious mental functioning and of interpreting symbolic meaning in dreams, fantasies and delusions, she gave examples of how her work in Nicaragua reflects the application of these and other psychoanalytic concepts. In this paper, as throughout her recent work, Marie was particularly interested in adapting psychoanalytic theory and technique to the economic, cultural and political conditions of Nicaragua.

When the Internationalist Team began to work in Nicaragua, these conditions were complex, and the fervent optimism of many thousands of political activists existed side by side with the ravages of war and revolution. At the time of the 1979 Triumph, the Nicaraguan people had lived through fifty years of brutal political repression and over a decade of violent revolutionary struggle. During the Revolution, approximately 35,000 people, or 1.5 percent of the population, had lost their lives. Between 88,000 and 110,000 people had been wounded, of whom 48,000 to 68,000 required continual medical attention. More than 150,000 had been forced to abandon their homes, some 48,000 children had been orphaned and one million people needed food in order to survive. Many hospitals and medical centres had been damaged or entirely destroyed during the war. Nearly half of the entire population had been directly and adversely affected by the conflict. The psychological impact of the Revolution was even more extensive. Thousands suffered from panic disorders because of the terror and repression of Somoza's fearsome National Guard. Many were affected by severe depression in response to multiple losses of loved ones. Traumatic neuroses and psychoses were commonplace, with symptoms that included listlessness, emotional withdrawal, anxiety, intellectual impairment, paranoia and damaged self-esteem.

With the Triumph, some of the more transient nervous disorders diminished. This was especially true among individuals who suffered from reactive depression, post-traumatic stress disorders or frozen grief. For them, the triumph of the Revolution and their participation in implementing the ideals and values for which many had died was a form of psychological reparation. But revolution does not automatically resolve psychological problems. On the contrary, in significant ways it stimulates them because of the profound alteration it causes in the social relations of class and gender. For example, the emphasis that the Nicaraguan Revolution placed on the struggle for women's equality often exacerbated tensions among people. In the process of challenging traditional gendered arrangements, the Revolution added stress to the most intimate emotional relationships of those whose energies were required to take on the challenge of building a new society.

Because the Sandinista government recognized the importance of attending to people's psychological needs as well as the necessity of mobilizing them politically to tackle the enormous problems of underdevelopment, Nicaragua was the perfect environment for Marie to actualize her unique psycho-political perspective. Her theoretical understanding of social structure and social change and her practical experience as a political organizer in Argentina helped her guard against the danger of viewing politics in exclusively psychological terms. At the same time, her psychoanalytic perspective, accumulated over years of working intensively in clinical settings, permitted her to comprehend how human beings committed to even the most radical political programmes might fail to achieve them for psychological reasons.

MANAGUA

In order to appreciate Marie's experience in Nicaragua fully, I went with her and Nacho in June 1984, when they travelled first to Managua and then to León, where the work of the Internationalist Team was concentrated that month. Nicaragua was lush green and often suffocatingly hot and humid; the natural beauty and peaceful landscape of the small Central American country were often painfully distorted by the physical devastation of war. The centre of Managua remained flattened from the destructive 1972 earthquake; except for a beautiful children's park built since the Revolution, entire blocks were overgrown with weeds and wild flowers. Overcrowded buses, old cars running on inventions gerry-rigged by their creative owners and local mechanics made transportation an uninviting prospect. Family-owned stores in working-class neighbourhoods and supermarkets in the bourgeois sections of Managua were lined with half-filled shelves. In all these aspects of life, there was vivid proof that the US destabilization policy towards the Nicaraguan economy had a debilitating impact on Nicaragua's daily life. Dramatically rendered revolutionary billboards lined the major roads alongside vulgar ads pitching products of multinational companies, a visual index of the pluralistic political and economic model chosen by the Sandinistas.

Everyone seemed on the move, their busy days filled with the long hours of work required to sustain themselves and their families. Political activists went from their work to meetings of the unions, the women's movement, the neighbourhood defence committees and church organizations. *Compañero* (companion or comrade) was the familiar greeting and affectionate term used among everyone identified with the Revolution. The term indicated closeness and respect; it was a linguistic signpost of values and goals shared in a difficult and exhilarating political process.

In Managua, Marie and Nacho quickly adjusted themselves to the intense rhythm of work. The days were divided among meetings with MINSA staff and hospital administrators, consultation with mental health professionals associated with the Internationalist Team's projects, and teaching and supervision responsibilities at several different sites. Lengthy midday meals and late evening dinners with friends and colleagues included energetic political discussions, whose content ranged from the difficulties of realizing the goals of their various projects to the future of Nicaragua's ability to survive under the US economic and military assault.

Let me give you several examples of what I observed that illustrates Marie's psycho-political perspective in her work. At the psychiatric hospital, the Internationalist Team was offering a course on psychoanalytic theory and another course on psychotherapeutic technique, and Marie and Nacho taught classes for several days as part of these courses to psychiatric residents, social workers and psychologists who worked at a variety of sites in and around the city. Several participants in the courses presented cases for supervision, and one case in particular revealed an interesting conflation of personal and political issues. Dora, an astute young social worker, discussed her treatment of a seventeen-year-old girl who had become agoraphobic after suffering two serious psychotic episodes. Dora had begun family therapy with her patient and the patient's mother and sisters. The mother occupied a dominant position in the family, and all of her daughters, including the patient's married sisters, lived with her. The daughters all claimed to be devoted to their mother and spoke about themselves as having an ideal and loving family. The therapy sessions occasionally included the father, who had another common-law wife and children with whom he currently lived. One of the patient's older brothers had died in battle about a month before the Triumph. Not only had his death gone unrecognized publicly by the community, but the family's street had been renamed to honour another combatant who had also been killed by Somoza's forces.

In the supervision, the meaning to the family of the patient's psychotic episodes was examined. Marie suggested that it was important to think of them as a possible container for the otherwise unexpressed aggression of the mother and daughters, who maintained the idea that they were a perfect family with no conflict whatsoever. Although the daughters had husbands and children, they had been unable to separate from their mother in order to establish their own households. They were equally unable to express any aggressive feelings towards the mother, whose failure to maintain a relationship with her husband drove her to rely on her children for fulfilment of her emotional needs. The patient's symptoms justified her mother's overprotective attitude, one which kept the patient regressively dependent on her. At the same time, the patient's agoraphobia and fear that something might happen to her mother should she leave the house permitted her to protect her mother from her unconscious aggression by never leaving her side. The patient's illness had also been successful in drawing the father back into the primary family unit through his visits to see his daughter at home and his participation in the treatment. The patient's psychotic episodes and her agoraphobia might, Marie went on, be a manifestation of frozen grief related to the death of the brother. Just as the identified patient could not go outside, none of the members of her family could 'come outside' themselves to mourn their loss. Marie concluded by suggesting that the therapeutic work needed to address both the feelings of the mother towards her husband, who had abandoned his responsibility towards her and their children, and the unconscious conflict between the mother and her daughters, now related to the unexpressed desire of the daughters to attain psychological independence from the mother. Attention would also need to be focused on the death of the brother in order to help the family mourn.

This, then, was Marie's psychoanalytic interpretation of the case. But Marie also understood the social dimension of the family's difficulties. She knew that in Nicaragua this family could rely on, in addition to psychotherapeutic intervention, political resources like the Association of Nicaraguan Women (AMNLAE) – an organization with a special interest in education, child care, family life and employment for women – which has spearheaded the struggle for women's legal and political equality. The patient's family was typical of the almost 60 percent of the households in Managua that are female headed and centred. AMNLAE has successfully fought for the legal obligation of men who abandon their children to pay child support and has also secured a new law that calls on all family members, regardless of sex, to participate in household and child-rearing tasks. From Marie's point of view, through involvement with the multifaceted activities offered by AMNLAE, the mother and daughters could develop increased self-esteem and relations of mutual support with other women.

Returning to the issue of frozen grief, Marie indicated that in revolutionary Nicaragua, the neighbourhood Committees for the Defence of the Revolution (CDS) and the popular Church were both arenas in which private mourning could be facilitated through community rituals. In the case of this particular family, the possibility had not been realized and the community had failed to respond to their need. The family's ability to mourn for the dead brother would be enhanced by public acknowledgement of his death and of his importance to the Revolution. Thus, Marie believed that, in a society where the state, political ideology and mass organizations encouraged people's involvement in social struggles to improve the quality and substance of their lives, psychologically disturbed individuals could benefit from political activism.

In another setting, Marie and Nacho held a class with psychologists and psychiatrists whose work focused on war trauma among soldiers. These psychotherapists were interested in discussing problems related to several patients who had had psychotic breakdowns following experiences in battle. On two separate occasions, each patient had panicked and given orders to retreat, thereby permitting Contra attacks against undefended villages. Following an elaboration of Freud's view of trauma and the importance of interpreting responses to current traumatic situations in light of possible prior traumatic experiences or constitutional vulnerability, Marie dealt with the difference between regression and fixation in a patient suffering from a current war-induced trauma. She then explored the meaning of an act motivated by fear and interpreted by the super-ego as cowardice. Several of the Nicaraguan mental health workers then asserted their belief that it might be best to reinforce the ego defences (by telling the errant soldiers that good soldiers don't panic and retreat and increasing the super-ego guilt expressed by their patients).

Marie responded by reminding them that conflict is always present in the human psyche, and that everyone, even the bravest soldier willing to die for his or her country, suffers conflict in some way. She argued that, in the case of their patients, the conflict was manifest in a very obvious way through the psychotic episodes. The conflict had to be identified, examined and resolved in order to prevent the recurrence of the psychotic episodes. Marie strongly advised against any attempt to use political ideology to secure compliance from individuals who suffered from emotional conflicts that impaired their ability to perform. To do so, she argued, would be to treat psychological problems with political nostrums and would succeed only in intensifying the conflicts that produced the psychotic behaviour in the first place. Thus Marie suggested to her Nicaraguan colleagues that only a psychodynamic understanding and treatment of their patients' psychological problems would achieve the political goal of rehabilitating soldiers to enable them to continue to defend the sovereignty of their country.

LEÓN

On the fifth day, we travelled to the provincial city of León, where Marie and Nacho continued their work. We were driven there by Tania, a French psychiatrist who had been in Nicaragua for several years and at the time was the only psychiatrist serving a population of 500,000 in the region of León. The trip seemed interminable, because Tania's car repeatedly broke down. The fuses, which could not be changed because of the lack of replacement parts due to the US economic blockade, blew every fifteen to twenty minutes. A trip of two hours took over five, with periodic recovery stops along the side of the road. Given the heat and lack of roadside comforts, the situation threatened to try even a saint's patience. But Marie was in grand form. She seemed perfectly content to take things as they came, to live with the inconvenience, to be happy just to be in Nicaragua. Her mood was infectious and I began to use our frequent pauses to interview her for the biography. Periodically, young armed soldiers would drive by in trucks patrolling for possible sabotage. When they stopped to check on us, they addressed us with the familiar *compañero*, and, in marked contrast to civilian reactions to the military in other Central American countries, we were not bothered at all by this close contact with the soldiers.

We finally arrived in León at dusk and went to the Internationalist House. We would be staying there for the duration of our work in the sweltering heat of this city, whose famous stoic colonial style admitted few trees to the endless stone of its sun-blanched buildings and streets. Through the Internationalist House the Sandinista government provided room and board to volunteers from all over the world who came to assist Nicaragua. Behind its massive front door, the entryway was plastered with photographs of Pierre Grosjean, a French physician who had come to study and treat mountain leprosy. Emotional poems in his honour told of how he was killed in a Contra attack against a small village where he was participating in a vaccination campaign. Inside the building, a large square central patio with a kitchen and dining area was surrounded by a maze of rooms. Some were new additions, rooms created out of tarpaulins hanging over clothes-lines. Most of these innovative spaces contained a bed, a small bookcase, a political poster and sometimes a portable radio. The entire place was in sad disrepair. We were taken to our room, which was a large dilapidated area with about six randomly arranged beds and one small, glaring light bulb hanging from its high ceiling. I wondered how we could live in this discomfort and continue our intense work schedule. I noticed that Marie was smiling. Unperturbed, she threw her suitcase on one of the beds and cheerfully went out to greet some of the other *internacionalistas* she knew. By the following day I would understand how one could forget about the modest conditions of our lodging. The spirited political exchanges at mealtime amongst its inhabitants, their intense commitment to purposeful work and their clear belief in the possibility of building a new society, all served to create a lively and exciting ambience.

In León the work of the Internationalist Team was varied. Marie and Nacho met with the staff at the university hospital to plan the mental health component of the third and fourth years of the work-study programme. They provided Tania and three Nicaraguan psychotherapists with supervision of cases at the university hospital. And they helped to develop a strategy to respond to the demand for psychotherapy, which was increasing as a result of the availability of the service. Marie and Nacho strongly urged Tania and her Nicaraguan colleagues to establish a series of brief treatment groups, composed of patients waiting to be placed (admission groups) or of patients suffering from similar symptoms or problems. The groups would meet for six to ten sessions and the therapist would provide a focus for the patients' work. The Nicaraguans closely associated with the Internationalist

17

Team were strongly in favour of the shift. Cristo, a bright young psychologist and a dedicated Sandinista activist, was especially frustrated by his patients' meekness, which he interpreted as a symptom of what he called 'the culture of passivity' imposed on his people through Nicaragua's tradition of dependency on the USA and its history of repression under Somoza. Cristo was excited about the suggestion of moving towards a brief therapy model that would focus patients on specific group goals.

One theme to emerge in Marie's clinical work in León related to the role of women and men in the family. Like other feminists, Marie was aware that the oppression of women had produced a strong female presence in the Nicaraguan Revolution and the many militant women who were now combating the manifestations of traditional male privilege in the political economy of Nicaragua. But the other side of the legacy of a male-dominated society was reflected in the many women who suffered from low self-esteem and troubled relationships with their children. Marie responded to the pathology of the Nicaraguan family in both psychological and political ways.

Several examples will illustrate the point. She participated in a session of a group whose co-therapists were Tania and Marta Lorena, a Nicaraguan social worker. One woman complained bitterly about her husband's mistreatment of her, and the other women launched into an emotional critique of men, berating them for maintaining two or three families simultaneously and being undependable or abusive in their treatment of women in general. All of the female patients were taking potent tranquillizers which were prescribed for them by physicians trained in pre-revolutionary Nicaragua. The women complained bitterly about their drug dependency. Marie commented wryly, 'So, instead of a bad man in the house, you have bad tranquillizers!' Everyone laughed in acknowledgement of the sad truth. Afterwards, Marie advised the co-therapists to convert this group, which had met for some time without a focus, into a brief treatment group that would meet for ten sessions and focus on drugs as a symptom of their problems. The patients would be encouraged to work on the conflicts underlying their addictions. The task of the group would be to identify several things in each patient's life that could be changed. Later, in a conversation with me, Marie emphasized that, in Nicaragua, these patients had political organizations that could help them by turning their passive victimization into active resolution.

Another aspect of the psychological problems that developed when families were abandoned by fathers was evident in the classes with paediatricians on the doctor/patient relationship. Marie lectured on the transference dimension of the child's relationship to the physician. She and Nacho spoke of the developmental stages from infancy through adolescence and the different techniques of interacting with the child and her family required by each stage. They encouraged the paediatricians to be aware of their psychological motivations in their professional choice and their feelings about the profession as important resources in managing their emotional reactions to patients. The physicians identified a general pattern encountered among their patients by noting that physical symptoms were often displaced psychological problems. They indicated that a high percentage of their patients suffered from psychosomatic illnesses, such as asthma. They also specified the ways in which maternal over-involvement inhibited the development of self-reliance in young children and adolescents. Afterwards, Marie and I discussed these issues in more detail because I noted that she seemed to focus on an exclusive psychological discussion with the physicians. She answered by saying that in these classroom settings, the particular emphasis was on teaching skills to improve the quality of the physicians' psychological interventions with their patients. I recognized that this was the purpose of the class, but I wondered if she had any other thoughts about the matter. She responded by pointing out that many cultural and economic factors had produced an historical pattern of male abandonment of families, resulting in problematic relationships between men and women. Female-headed and -centred households often caused mothers to establish their closest affective ties with their children. Understandably, in such circumstances mothers would be threatened by their children's strivings for independence. She asserted that, although the psychological problems identified with this social phenomenon required intervention by mental health professionals, a complete resolution necessitated the continued political struggle by women to win equality with men in every domain.

Our last day in León was a special treat, for it marked the fifth anniversary of the Sandinista liberation of León. We arose early to the sound of drums and guitars and much commotion in the streets. It was a happy day, a celebration that brought thousands of women, men and children into the main plaza to hear speeches, sing songs and noisily commemorate the Sandinista victory. The day was sweltering, but Marie seemed to have the stamina of a teenager. When she wasn't observing the merrymaking from the half shade of the bleachers or under the umbrella of one of the many vendors hawking sodas and Nicaraguan sweets, she was snaking her way through the dense crowds to get close enough to hear a speech or see a theatre group perform political satire for the joyous audience. What better way to leave the work in León than with such affirmation.

One of the speakers to be heartily applauded was Comandante Dora Maria Tellez, a slight, pretty woman with short, bobbed hair whose diminut-

ive stature was deceptive. She had been one of the *commandantes* responsible for the daring occupation of the National Palace in August 1978 and
later for the final assault on León. A medical student before she became a
full-time revolutionary, Dora Maria had maintained a special interest in the
health system. She was soon to become the Minister of Health of Nicaragua.
The Internationalist Team would continue to work with MINSA, and they
would be especially proud of the establishment in León of a Centre for
Psychosocial Attention, where many brief treatment groups, CDS meetings
and a variety of occupational classes and cultural activities offers people the
opportunity to engage actively in their own psychological and political
growth.

TRIBUTE TO A REVOLUTIONARY

In the three years following our trip to Nicaragua, Marie continued in her
role as the Co-coordinator of the Internationalist Team. She returned to
Nicaragua many times and travelled to Europe, where, because of her
reputation, she was able to draw progressive mental health professionals to
hear her speak about her work in Nicaragua. She believed this activity was
important because it allowed her to combat the disinformation campaign
against Nicaragua, and it also allowed her to raise money to support the work
of the Internationalist Team.

In December 1985, Marie was honoured in a very special way. She was
invited to present a paper in Havana at the annual meeting of an organization
called the Encounter of Intellectuals for the Sovereignty of the People of
Our America. This organization brought together prestigious figures from
the arts, literature and science to engage in a dialogue about strategies for
Latin American economic and cultural liberation. Marie was one of the few
mental health professionals present at the meeting. In an emotional moment,
Marie learned that she had been elected to the twelve-person permanent
commission of the organization. She was the second woman to be elected to
the commission and the only one to represent the sciences. Marie felt much
personal satisfaction to be so highly esteemed by the members of the
commission. She interpreted her inclusion in the permanent commission as
an indication that psychoanalysis had been recognized not only as a part of
the intellectual movement for Latin American independence but as a scientific tool in that endeavour. For Marie, this public honour was a recognition
of having achieved a synthesis of her political and professional commitment
to human emancipation.

But this personal victory was clouded by the discovery, shortly after her trip to Cuba, that she was suffering from inoperable cancer. During the following two years, she struggled to continue the work that so enhanced the value of her life. Experimental cancer treatments gave intermittent hope to her family, friends, colleagues and comrades that Marie would be able to survive the illness that was consuming her. She alternated between her wishful desire to live and her rational acceptance of death. When she felt physically strong, she worked. When she was tired and weak, she rested. In the summer of 1987, Marie returned to Buenos Aires to finish her life in the home that she had been forced to leave thirteen years earlier. Surrounded by her family, she died on 22 December 1987.

Long before she knew that she had cancer, Marie talked with me about ageing and death:

> I don't want to die without meaning – I want to live until the end. So when the dangers of the Nicaraguan work become undeniable, I always remember an article by Mao . . . in which he argued that there was an important difference between a worthwhile death and one that has no value . . . I believe this very much, and I believe that my life has been worthwhile, within my own limits. (Langer, 1986)

Among the posthumous memorials that took place in Argentina, Mexico and Nicaragua, the one that she might have most appreciated was the new name chosen by the *compañeros* of the team whose efforts she so resolutely nurtured. As the team continues to facilitate the growth of Nicaragua's new mental health system, it is known as the Marie Langer Internationalist Team of Mental Health Workers.

NANCY CARO HOLLANDER
California, October 1988

PROLOGUE: A FEW WORDS

WE HAVE FINISHED WRITING this book for which I haven't wanted to write a prologue until now, perhaps because of an inability to extricate myself from it. I want to recount, from my perspective, its how, its why and its history.

For a long time, young women – like Marta Lamas and Diana here in Mexico or Marielena in Venice, women who are really friends in spite of our age difference – have been asking me, 'How did you manage to turn out so different from my mother, or my grandmother?' They have also remarked, 'We're scared of getting old, of being forty or fifty. Sixty doesn't matter: by then one knows that one is an old woman, but you are a lot older and you don't seem old, one can talk to you. How did you do it?' These young women, vibrant and intelligent, are none the less afraid of ending up like their mothers. How many middle-class mothers, well-preserved and well-cared-for, at fifty or sixty are already old women who lead sadly bitter or sweetly submissive lives?

To these young women, in search of an alternative model, I will address myself in the coda on the subject of women.

I dedicate what I have written in the coda to these young women; not only to them but also to the young men who are their partners, men who don't want to be *machos* and who are in search of a real camaraderie with their wives. Also to my daughters and sons, daughters-in-law and sons-in-law and to my husband who sustained his restless wife, thanks to which I had the necessary respite to have a stable, virtually old-fashioned family. And, of course, to my analysands, from whom I've learned so much.

In parenthesis: I like my profession, I continue to like it, and even today a good session or supervision absorbs me, releases me from my daily preoccupations and can make me content. My dedication is a little long, but there are many I must mention. Without them, and of course, without Jaime and Enrique, this book would not exist.

Effectively, the book began to write itself in my head after long talks with

Marielena on feminism. I mention feminism but we talked about many other things: childhood, psychoanalysis, political militancy and literature. The interest Marielena had in Austrian writers between the two wars . . . in Schnitzler, in Roth, in Karl Kraus . . . When we began talking about them, the writers of my adolescence, there suddenly welled up in me, along with nostalgia, memories buried by my long stay in Latin America, memories of my childhood and youth in Vienna.

Later, back in Mexico once again, my daughter Veronica suggested that I put together my life story through recorded interviews. Veronica is my youngest daughter, whom I had when I was forty-three. We were able to fill three cassettes with sincere, relaxed conversations between an old mother – I refuse to use the word elderly, it infuriates me – and her young daughter. But at the end of the third interview Veronica said to me, 'It's not working, Mama, I don't know enough about history or psychoanalysis in order to have a real dialogue with you.' What's more, Veronica is not in fact a writer but an actress.

Enrique Guinsberg had already proposed that we write this book. He explains his 'why' in the pages that follow. However, I can add that Enrique insisted that I should communicate my experience and account for my ideology to young mental health workers; that we should discuss the role of the mental health worker in society and of the psychoanalyst committed to the Left. I agreed with him and we began work. But, faced with his first question about my childhood and social background, in place of Marxist analysis I poured out anecdotes, the ones I had told to Veronica and others I had nearly forgotten. I realized that when I wasn't deeply involved in my story, the rest lost interest for me. I read the texts of our academic discussion and complained to myself, 'I don't recognize myself in any of these, they're too abstract'. And also, 'I wasn't so important, or heroic; that's why I'm still alive.'

It was through this need to recognize myself that I realized I wasn't only writing for the others carefully mentioned here but also that putting together my personal and professional history responded to a need of my own which became more pressing as I neared seventy. I had to summarize my life. While the professional-ideological had its importance, it wasn't enough for me to understand myself.

This is where Jaime came into the picture. After reading the transcribed texts of the conversations with Veronica, and the many others with Enrique, he convinced me that the material was worthwhile and offered to put it in order, to rewrite what was necessary and finish it off as well. 'I've only just finished reading a history of Austrian social democracy in the 1930s,' he commented. The book was under way.

Writing this book has been at times both hard work and pleasure. Remembering previous experiences, I missed the three of us really being a team. Only now, at the end, the reason has become clear to me. Each of us had in mind a different book and a different audience. Enrique is the most serious of the three and he asked for seriousness from me too: long dialogues on themes important to the young psychologist and psychoanalyst who doesn't belong to the Psychoanalytical International (not to be confused with the Second, Third or Fourth International; nothing to do with it). We spoke of theories, of Marxism, psychoanalysis and the need for a real praxis. We attempted to remember and clarify old polemics. These conversations were very useful. They helped me recover the language of the 1970s in Buenos Aires. It was easy for us to understand each other when we talked about this era in which we had shared a lot without knowing each other personally. It was more difficult when we discussed my clinical experience, as an older teaching analyst, since we came from different backgrounds. Faced with my fickleness in not wanting to enter into certain polemics with Marxist critics of psychoanalysis who, of course, had never been in analysis themselves, like Schneider for example, Enrique functioned as my professional super-ego. And I discovered that his readers, at times imaginary opponents, were his students, certain colleagues and past and present mental health workers. We worked hard for a year and a half and I think that we achieved a good text. It was Jaime who ordered and polished our innumerable pages, read and commented upon in lucid and friendly co-operation with Horacio. (Horacio Skornik died of a heart attack before the Spanish-language edition of this book was finished. He was the book's principal supporter and collaborator. However, as he had intended to return to Argentina before the fall of the dictatorship, he asked not to be named for security reasons.)

The audience Jaime desired is, simply, people interested in history and literature and also in analysis, although not from a professional point of view. Jaime has had years of experience in individual and group analysis and the subject interests him from this point of view, the personal rather than the theoretical. While Enrique and I could be guilty of a certain 'ideological terrorism', Jaime isn't like that. I believe, although we still haven't discussed it, that the political line of the book didn't interest him as much as the human and historical aspect. Moreover, he was in charge of the literary/aesthetic aspect. Jaime is a writer and his audience is his generation. But why did other things interest him in taking part in this undertaking? The raw material of my autobiographical discussions with Veronica and Enrique tempted him,

I suppose, putting myself in his place, in order to better understand the cultural and emotional origins of his wife, my daughter Ana.

And myself? I spent my childhood and youth in Austria, my mature years in Argentina and my old age I spend here in Mexico. Without realizing it, I think indiscriminately in German and Spanish, sometimes adding a graphic expression from another language. As I pointed out, I turned seventy practically as the book was finished. I needed to reflect, to find myself and my identity. It was productive for me to get involved in this project. It had the value of a daily self-analysis. I could see myself, from outside, with a certain objectivity although also through very narcissistic glasses, but this is inevitable when one spends so much time on oneself. (Is this the *transference* of self-analysis, as Emilio Rodrigué claims?)

I was able to make some discoveries – how, for example, the sexual rebellion of my adolescence was the first step towards the Left (to Reich it would have seemed I had discovered the obvious). However, while in the long run sex located me in the 'feminine sphere' – that is to say, in love, in the couple and in becoming a mother – it did not exclude fulfilment in other areas. Aline Furtmüller, my high school teacher, whom I have quoted many times in my narrative, once explained to us that to be living in a *republic* and not a monarchy obligated us to assume a responsible role in the *res publica*, in other words in the common cause.

My desired audience is young women, as I've already said. And fears, there are those as well. What will some of my colleagues say? What would I have said years ago of an analyst who displayed her intimate life even though they were intimacies of forty to seventy years before?

It's hard for me to say goodbye to this book, the undertaking of the three of us. I regret that as a result of geographical distance we were not able to include Emilio Rodrigué in our dialogue. That would have been spectacular. Fortunately, Armando Bauleo, passing through on professional visits, made some pertinent political suggestions. And, once more, I mourn the loss of Horacio.

MARIE LANGER
Mexico, January 1981

MORE WORDS

WHY THIS BOOK? Marie Langer has already indicated why in her prologue. She also rightly says that we three participants were never a team and each of us had a different idea of the book. It is therefore necessary to point out what *my* desired book was.

The answer rests in an idea which developed through my contact with Marie Langer – 'Mimi' to her friends, in spite of her preference for Marie which few respect – at first through her works, then later as a result of her practice of breaking with the morbidity of the psychoanalytic institutions, and eventually in person in Mexico through friendship, in attending her seminars and in our common projects with many Argentinian mental health workers.

I was familiar with her frank and critical attitude and her clinical and ideological brilliance through her published work, her militant dissidence and her search for challenging, alternative, non-alienating work in mental health. All this and more was evident in her seminars, in our conversations and joint projects. Not to have rescued this experience and lucidity in some way would have meant a great loss.

Such was my intention in suggesting this book to her; to rescue a personal history and experience in which, as well as a theoretical knowledge neither pseudo-intellectual nor out of books, there exists a notable and constant coherence between past and present, between words and action, things which on their own mean a lot in a professional arena often so conformist and lacking in criticism as are important sectors of mental health workers.

I was also interested in understanding how this particular product came about in concrete history, that is, how Marie Langer came to be what she is and was: that she should have had this life in which, coming from a Jewish family in imperial Vienna, she would end up with Communist and feminist positions and practices, would participate in Spain in the International Brigades and would have to go into exile first in Argentina and then in Mexico. That she would co-found the Argentinian Psychoanalytical Association and then leave it decades later without abandoning psychoanalysis. A personal history interwoven with a social history which both embraces and contains it, wherein Marxism and psychoanalysis – these two great bodies of theory that she said she would never abandon – permit a two-fold approach.

I did not know Mimi while I was studying and working in Argentina, although, as she says in her prologue, we had in fact a lot in common. To me, as a psychology student in Rosario, the second largest city in Argentina, Marie Langer was a brilliant analyst – virtually a 'sacred monster' – famous for her indispensable and required text books. But I understood her true and most important capabilities in Buenos Aires when I saw her as one of the leaders in the cleansing process – also necessary and indispensable – that began to take place among mental health workers at the beginning of the 1970s.

It was a process which we shared, although in different forms and from different positions. Hers is known and, what's more, is recounted in this book in our conversations; mine is (too), only approximately. While we shared ideological positions in general as well as those related to the process taking place among mental health workers, my area of struggle was essentially political – work which prevented me, in those combative years, from taking part in the actual professional struggle. I was working as a psychologist and carrying out a study which I never finished. However, political praxis and the resulting situation prevented me from approaching the institutions and taking the professional courses which taught alternatives considered to be valuable and important to mental health workers, who sought not to alienate themselves in orthodox and conventional practice. My position was not dissociation – since I carried out my political and professional practice in a manner I considered to be consistent – but separation in spite of my wishes. I managed to write a book clearly based on this line but was unable to act concretely in the political-professional area.

Marie Langer, I repeat, was virtually a paragon at the time, as much for her practice of breaking with orthodoxy as for her works on the same theme in the two volumes of *Cuestionamos* (We Question, Langer, 1971, 1973), and, above all, at least to me, for her position in which the political-ideological and the professional were areas largely united in theory and practice, differing from many to whom the two areas should not be mixed in order to avoid a 'dangerous' contamination of an objective and pure science.

Our meeting in Mexico facilitated an understanding, already personal, which among other things demonstrated the continuation of an important common vision which, in spite of our different professional backgrounds, made this book possible, necessary to us both, from different but coinciding perspectives.

But this prologue is not an attempt to eulogize or summarize all the individuals and ideas that appear throughout its length, with their truths, their contradictions, their doubts and their limitations, these expressions of a wide sector of mental health workers among whom Marie in some ways emerges as a brilliant figure.

How was the book made? The original intention, which was discussed in mid-1979, was to put it together using dialogues on different themes as a basis, taking the idea from *Conversaciones con Enrique Pichon Riviere* which was published in Buenos Aires years ago (Lema, 1976). The idea was accepted with a few reservations which reappeared throughout the project, although these were later replaced with conviction and hard and interesting work. This work, with virtually weekly meetings, lasted till the end of 1980.

The book's development consisted of taped conversations based on the pivotal themes of Marie Langer's life, her theoretical perceptions and her experience – outlooks which, while difficult to separate in many cases, were respected as far as possible. In every case only aspects that Marie Langer had direct experience of in her practice were touched upon, sidestepping those which were not part of her experience. It must surely be because of my insistence that we discuss subjects I consider of great value to *my* concept of the book that Mimi describes me as 'the most serious of us' and as her 'professional super-ego', concepts which I don't know if I should take as a compliment or as something else.

The dialogues in this final version are not literal versions of the conversations: they went through a correction process, as much because of the fact that spoken discourse is different from written, as because of the difficulty in maintaining coherent sequence in an intentionally unstructured conversation. However, there are no major changes: the vast amount of material collected was only put into order a little, repetitions were taken out, ideas were clarified, quotations from other authors were given textually rather than from memory and the work of many hours in front of the tape recorder was synthesized.

Finally, what appears here as *prologue* is really, for me, the *epilogue* to a difficult, complicated but highly satisfactory project. It is hoped that the original objective has been fulfilled and that this book is used so that the magnificent experience of its protagonist becomes known and discussed and serves as an expression of unity towards a practice in which the purpose of psychology will be to liberate and not to act as an instrument of oppression. A goal which for me, for us, is a challenge we strive to meet and to which we devote our endeavours.

ENRIQUE GUINSBERG
Mexico, January 1981

Marie's father, Leopold Glas, during World War I.

PART ONE
Remembrances

NOTE

The editor has added subheadings to the text of Part I, in order to signpost major themes and periods, even though the text was not originally compiled according to such categories.

Marie Langer has used Social Democrats and Socialists interchangeably, though the party did not call itself Socialist until after World War II. She also uses Christian Socialists and Catholics interchangeably, the latter term referring to the party's social composition and outlook.

Marie's parents, Margareth and Leopold Glas, Austria, 1920s.

The four children (from left to right): Lizzi (Marie's cousin), Marie, Gucki (Marie's sister), Geo (Marie's cousin)

FROM VIENNA TO
BUENOS AIRES

I WAS BORN IN 1910. What does that mean? That I virtually belong to the century.

It means that I experienced an imperial Oedipus complex, if one can call it such. Behind my father was the old Emperor of Austria, Franz Josef. I'm the youngest of two daughters and according to my mother should've been a boy. When I was four years old, the First World War broke out. It was the first historical upheaval of the century and my father, who was a reserve officer, had to go to the front. I didn't take it tragically, it seems. As my parents laughingly told me much later, I had very drily asked, 'But if Daddy goes to war, who's going to kill him, a Russian or a Frenchman?' None the less, I think this was how I covered up my anxiety about my father and my desire to go to war with him. Was it merely to be with him, or for us to die together? Yet I knew this wasn't possible, not only because I was a child but also because I was a girl, and girls didn't go to the front. The only women who went to war with the soldiers were the nurses. From then on I knew I wanted to have a career. I wanted to be a nurse.

In 1917, the year of the Bolshevik Revolution, I turned seven, and the Emperor Franz Josef died. I couldn't believe it: it was as if someone had told me that God had died. I was a believer at the time and prayed every night for the war to end. That I, a pretty bright child, should have believed the Emperor to be immortal (even though nobody had told me so) indicates that for my family, and perhaps the whole Austrian bourgeoisie, the Empire – despite its social, political and national conflicts and contradictions – was unchangeable. This belief lent the Emperor a halo of immortality. Besides, it was with his death that the collapse of the Empire began. Karl, his successor, was not only weak but had taken over an already-lost cause.

Karl fell from power in 1918 and we lost the war. The Empire was dismembered and there was revolution in Vienna. The Republic was declared. In the streets below our windows, people streamed past, shouting slogans I didn't understand but which frightened me. At first, I wanted to be loyal to the Emperor and all the patriotism I'd been taught. My cousins and I locked ourselves in my bedroom with the blinds down and played the national anthem on our His Master's Voice gramophone with its huge horn. We stood to attention and sang; we felt brave and exposed to grave danger, but this patriotism didn't last long.

My family were non-practising Jews, atheists in fact, and extremely wealthy, particularly on my mother's side. My father was a pacifist, polit-ically very sceptical, quite critical and – something I only realized as an adult – overwhelmed by feelings of guilt about his fortune, which, it should be added, diminished radically before 1929. To go back to the time of the war, I suppose it was his connections that allowed him to come home after less than a year at the front. The medical reason for his release was 'night blindness'; it gave rise to many jokes. The disease does exist, however; it's a vitamin shortage. He was later promoted to captain and the house was full of officers.

My mother was born in 1886. She was a lady, with all the awfulness of the ladies of that period, with all the awfulness of 'ladies'. She was younger than Alexandra Kollontai . . . Another kind of woman, unlike either my mother or Kollontai, existed at the time, although she too belonged to the middle and upper classes. She was conventional, submissive, Victorian and pure. Freud's patients were like my mother but perhaps also like the others. How could they get out of being like that? How could they stop being anything but ladies or submissive? On the whole, they didn't. They suffered from neur-osis, they were miserable but decent; mothers-wives, *comme-il-faut*. Some took refuge in love; others, very few, made revolution. Madame Bovary is from the previous century, but she still lived on in nearly all women, especially those from the upper and middle classes. Anna Karenina is another whose way out was love, dignified but equally tragic. At the other extreme there was frivolity. My mother, though she suffered for her subter-fuge, belonged to the group of women who were a bit frivolous.

But there were the exceptions, the women who made revolution, such as Alexandra Kollontai. As a child I read a beautiful book about some of these women. It was my first contact with the Left . . . When I went to Leningrad in 1971, I saw Vera Figner's cell in the Fort of St Peter and St Paul, where she was imprisoned for years. She was one of those who struggled for the revolution, but not for the Bolshevik Revolution, not yet, nor for the 1905 Revolution. It was long before that. They were closer to the Narodniks. They went to live with the people to incite them to rise up against the Czar, but there were very few of them. Oddly enough, they were raising the same issues, a century earlier, as are being discussed today in the Latin American Left. Do guerrilla groups and *focos* (revolutionary bases) raise the consciousness of the people or are they counter-productive because repression is increased simultaneously? An enlightened vanguard or a Left immersed in the masses? Insurrection versus reformism?

With respect to women, another of these Russian militants of the last century, Vera Zasulich, says that in her adolescence, before the revolution was even dreamt of, she had made detailed plans to avoid becoming a governess because she was a poor girl without a dowry. 'It would have been much easier, of course, if I had been a man, I would have been able to do practically anything . . . Then the distant spectre of revolution appeared and made me equal to boys; I too could dream of action, of heroic deeds', and of the great battle.

Yes, obviously, joining the revolution was once the appropriate way to escape the fate outlined for women.

MY PARENTS' MARRIAGE

My mother had a little wicker basket, all the ladies had one; in the basket there were probably twenty keys. Everything was locked; she opened and closed, opened and closed and gave things to the cook or the chambermaid, but she didn't work. In those days the house was an institution, much more complicated than it is today; it was a real enterprise. For a lady it was her official reason for being. My mother directed the staff of servants. There weren't many of us, so we didn't need a lot; my grandmother had many more. We had a cook, a chambermaid, a governess or a nanny and a chauffeur. There were four of us: my parents, my sister and me. My parents didn't want any more children because it was already considered vulgar, and my mother knew how to take care of herself with a silver suppository. All of the ladies did it; if they didn't, it was because they were too Catholic.

How did they preserve their marriage? There's a strange story with two sides to it. Supposedly my parents were very young and very in love when they got married after a two-year courtship. My mother was the second daughter. The first was Steffi, who wasn't engaged, so my mother couldn't get married. The eldest had to get married first. My parents conspired so that Steffi would marry Alfred, my father's brother. The two couples were married on the same day in the main salon of the Hauser Palais, my grandparents' house. Steffi and Alfred were married five minutes before my mother and father. In this version, my parents' marriage was a love match and my aunt and uncle's, which turned out to be excellent, wasn't. However, I think that both my father and my uncle got married because the dowries of the two sisters allowed them to expand greatly the small factory they had inherited.

The unofficial version which my mother later told me – when I turned fourteen I became her confidante – was that she had been very much in love with a famous scientist who was a friend of my grandfather's, but he disappeared before declaring his love, so she had decided on my father. Years later, the scientist justified his disappearance as a result of his having eczema or something like that on his face, which had embarrassed him. When they met again my sister had been born. They fell passionately in love . . . Later came all the rest of my mother's affairs . . .

My parents got married in 1904; at that time marriage was the only acceptable fate for a woman. I remember having an old French governess, who must have been pretty once; when I knew her she was still attractive and kind. We asked her why she had never married and she replied, quite naturally, because she hadn't had a dowry. She was poor and for her it was indisputable: no one got married without a dowry.

In the second year of high school I had a literature teacher called Aline Furtmüller. She was a Social Democrat Member of Parliament and very progressive. She used to read us a poem of which I remember a few verses. It's a poem written at the end of the century in which a girl tells her parents that she's in love with a man whom she wants to marry. Her father tells her she has to marry another man that he has chosen. 'Not him,' she says. 'I don't love him or admire him.' And her father turns to his wife and says:

> Weisst du, was es Neues gibt?
> Haben wir uns je geachtet?
> Haben wir uns je geliebt?

('Do you see the changes in the world?/Have we ever admired each other?/Have we ever loved each other?') And he says so in total indignation, with total self-righteousness. What an idea, love in marriage! The poem is from the previous century. At the beginning of this century people were swearing love for each other but I think it was a necessary invention in order to get married, to keep the woman in her appointed role without feeling guilty and for her to be able to accept it.

How married couples reacted when confronted with adultery depended on the code of honour. I'm thinking of Anna Karenina. There's a very sad novel, *Effie Briest*, which I liked a lot. It's the story of a girl from the lower echelons of the nobility who marries an officer, also from the nobility, whom she doesn't love and whom no one thinks she ought to love. They have a daughter. At one point they go to live in a garrison in northern Germany. She leads a very sad life there: the snow, the cold, the isolation. Some of the officers organize a theatrical production in which she plays the main role, with a supposed lover, one of the officers. Outside of the production, Effie falls in love with the officer and ends up having sex with him.

Then the husband is transferred somewhere else. Effie forgets the lover and begins to love her husband and her only daughter. One afternoon Effie faints; her husband looks for the remedy in her sewing box, a little basket with coloured ribbons, and in it he finds some letters that the lover had written her years before. He thinks, 'My God, it's better not to read them.' But he reads them anyway and finds out that she had betrayed him. Five or six years had already passed but the code of honour in the army is insurmountable. 'I love this woman,' he says to himself. 'What happened in the past doesn't matter . . . But, no! I am a Prussian officer.' He shows her the letters and throws her out of the house, keeping the child. He kills the man who sullied his honour in a duel, without hate, even with some compassion. Effie lives a miserable life in her parents' house, where she was not welcomed, and gets tuberculosis. Before she dies she has a conversation with a friend and says she wants to see her daughter. The friend takes her to the child's school but Effie Briest's daughter turns her back on her when she sees her. 'What a shame you are dying so young,' her friend says. And Effie answers, 'It's not important. Life is like a banquet. It's not so serious to leave before the end.'

JEWISH ATHEISTS

Yes, in short, I come from the sceptical, atheistic, Jewish bourgeoisie. Although I am ashamed to admit it, I say so with a certain pride.

My family history: my maternal grandfather was born in a wagon in which my great-grandparents travelled throughout the Austro-Hungarian Empire. My great-grandfather sold trinkets and my great-grandmother sewed for farmers. She used her apron strings to take their measurements. They were doing this not because they were gypsies but because in those days Jews could not own property or have fixed dwellings. After the unsuccessful bourgeois revolution in 1848, there were some improvements which included the 'emancipation' of the Jews. This meant that they could have a fixed address, even own their own house, and, perhaps most important, the right to a higher education.

My grandfather started out as a horse trader, an occupation frowned upon because it was full of trickery and fraud. He quickly became a very rich man. He won the concession to supply the whole of the imperial city of Vienna with trams, horse-drawn in those days. Something for which he was severely reproached at the time was providing the British Army with horses in the war against the Boers, the South African settlers who were fighting for their independence from England. Today I think he did the right thing, but he didn't do it for ideological reasons. His economic position would have allowed him to buy himself a title, as many Jews did at the time, but he didn't, as he thought it was nonsensical. On that point my grandfather and I are in agreement.

My mother was brought up with governesses and every luxury. She was cultured and could sing, she had a lovely voice. There were always little volumes of the complete works of Schopenhauer scattered on the coffee tables at home. He was her favourite author. He said awful things about women, but she believed he was right. Mama smoked a lot. One of the images I have of her is in blue: the Kedive cigarettes she smoked came in little blue boxes, the volumes of Schopenhauer were bound in blue. It was her favourite colour. The novel she liked best was *Buddenbrooks* by Thomas Mann. 'Poor Tony Buddenbrook,' she would say to me when we discussed children from good families. But her own family was not 'good', being Jewish, and because of the horses and Boers affair.

My mother's side of the family was completely atheistic. My grandfather paid no attention at all to religion but still my mother suffered for being a Jew. She used to tell me how on her first day at school they asked the children, 'What are you?' When it was her turn she didn't understand. The teacher got annoyed and said to her, 'Don't be silly. Answer! What are you?' My mother came home crying and told her father what had happened. 'Daughter,' my grandfather said, 'they were asking you if you are Jewish or Catholic – you are a Jew.' This piece of information created a trauma which lasted her whole life.

I was lucky because neither my surname nor my physical appearance is Jewish, and my name, Marie, is above suspicion. One day I asked my mother why she had given me such a common name. 'I didn't venture to have you christened,' she replied, 'so I resigned myself to giving you the most Catholic of names.'

She wanted to save me from a Jewish fate, as her brothers and sisters later tried, in vain, to save themselves when they got baptized as adults. My sister

38

was baptized before she got married for the first time. In 1955, when my mother, already an old lady, returned to Vienna, the Jewish municipal organization tried to charge her an enormous sum for the taxes she hadn't paid during her years of exile. She refused, and lost her 'rights' as a Jew; she couldn't, for example, be buried in a Jewish cemetery. 'The kind of tram you arrive at the terminal in doesn't matter,' she wrote to me when she was seventy-five.

No, my mother's family was not at all religious. My father's was slightly; even so, his brothers and sisters also got baptized when they were older. While he lived with his parents, my father had to fast during Yom Kippur and go to the synagogue at least a couple of times a year. He told me about the slap his father gave him when he caught him with a ham sandwich during Yom Kippur. However, as soon as he got married he gave up even these customs. But Jews, religious or not, suffered equally from discrimination. Emil, my father's very respected brother, who was an assistant professor at the university, had to get baptized in order to get a professorship. My parents were Viennese and that was sufficient (to save them from some of the stigma of being Jews). Freud, who was from Moravia, had much more of a struggle. *The Interpretation of Dreams* contains all the material related to what he went through to become a professor.

Why am I mentioning all of this? Because, although we were rich, I was always aware of my two disadvantages: being a Jew and a woman. To these I later added another: to be divorced. That's why joining the Left seemed to me to be the only logical solution. I was sure that Communism would put an end to this marginalization.

I cannot deny that being born Jewish affected me. I recently read some interviews with exiles from the Nazi era, the majority the founders of what is usually referred to as the 'Frankfurt School' in sociology and psychology. Reading these interviews with people just a few years older than me – mainly German Jews, all 'progressives', not one a Zionist or a religious Jew – I could see once more how German and Austrian anti-Semitism impacted upon our lives much more than National Socialism. How do you explain that to Jews born in Argentina, for example, or Mexico? In Argentina anti-Semitism is a kind of snobbishness among the upper classes, where they refer to the Jews as 'Moishes'. Of course, they would never have allowed a Jew to belong to the Jockey Club, but the Argentinian middle and lower classes were not anti-Semitic. In Austria and Germany they were. Even the Social Democrat workers were anti-Jewish, although they wouldn't consciously admit it. In the Communist Party they always made sure that there were no Jewish surnames in the executive, as it would have been bad for propaganda.

When I started school at a private academy, where there were a lot of Jewish girls, I'd look at my Catholic classmates one by one and think, 'On that forehead they also drew a cross with holy water.' I knew about holy water through our cook, who was very Catholic and whom I loved a lot. I went with her to evening Mass every day and she gave me some little pictures of the saints and martyrs. The torture they'd gone through terrified me but at the same time I came to understand that you have to be able to suffer or die, for an ideal. For many people, this is related to being militant, especially in Latin America, where so many of the militants come out of Catholicism.

When I was sixteen I had a religious crisis. At first, I attempted to take up the Jewish religion but met with opposition at home. Later, during a long and painful Good Friday, I tried the Catholic religion. Afterwards I became a definite atheist and later a Communist.

WARTIME CHILDHOOD

To go back to my mother. She had a lot to do with my vocation. She could have been Freud's Dora. Fortunately, in spite of everything, she was less repressed. My mother and my maternal grandmother, who was nicknamed Taifun after the Chinese hurricane, were very strong women. They needed to fulfil themselves in some sphere, but, as their husbands had money, they couldn't work, so they lost themselves in trivialities. My mother was from the Victorian era, but like Madame Bovary she thought about love. It was easy in Vienna, as a 'lady' had much more right to commit adultery than to do serious study or work. Adultery entailed lying; my mother argued, 'Us poor women, always subjected to men, what else is left us but lying?'

Nevertheless, when my father went to war and the refugees began to arrive from the Russian border, my mother and aunt opened a canteen for children. We all lived in the same house, in the Palais which had once belonged to a count. Each family had half a floor and my grandfather had one enormous floor all to himself. The canteen for refugee children was set up on the ground floor. My mother worked constantly, to collect the food, to attend to the children; she forgot about her clothes and her appearance. When my father came back from the front, however, she dropped everything and took up her role as a lady once again. My father would never have asked her to because he wasn't that demanding; he wasn't in the least bit *macho*. But the natural thing for my mother was that once her husband was around she couldn't work. I vaguely remember a time when lots of officers came to the house and that there was one I called uncle. Afterwards my mother told me that he had been her lover and that he was a hero, a nationalist who had fought for the independence of Czechoslovakia. So my mother gave up work and went back to her love affairs.

The majority of the refugee children were Jews, but very different from us. Their parents were religious with beards, ringlets and kaftans and they were poor, from the ghetto. My best friend from high school arrived at this time. Her family spoke Yiddish and their German was heavily accented. (I don't speak Yiddish, as my mother would never have allowed me to learn it, but I understand a lot of it from the German.) The 'nice' assimilated Jews (half of my family had converted to Catholicism) were such snobs, but also so afraid of anti-Semitism and that they might be confused with these Jews, that they themselves became anti-Semitic towards these poor fellow-Jews who had escaped from the Russian front. Hitler would later take charge of putting an end to this discrimination.

I remember a story which was humiliating for my mother. When my uncle wanted to be a professor he had to be baptized. At the time my mother had broken off with her first lover, the famous scientist friend of my grandfather, with whom she had had another relationship after her marriage. My father, none the less, asked her if she would go and see him to get him to support my uncle Emil's nomination at the university . . .

This famous scientist, Doctor Eugene Steinach, was supposedly my father. I have two conflicting memories. One day when I was small, Mama – who could get very angry, even come to blows, although I never took her blows very seriously – screamed a word at me in Viennese slang, *bankert*. I didn't know what it meant at the time, but it stayed engraved on my mind and it was only later that I found out she had called me a 'bastard'. It's a bit much that a mother should say that to her daughter but Mama would yell anything when she was angry. Sometimes she would say that I was my father's daughter and sometimes that I was someone else's. What I don't know is whether she resumed her relationship with the scientist after my sister's birth or mine.

Physically I am very like my father. On occasions he would put his glasses on me and say, 'See how much she looks like me.' My mother would answer jokingly, but all jokes have some degree of truth in them, 'No, that one's not yours.' I never took it very seriously, at least not consciously. A lot of years have passed and I still don't take it seriously. I think that my mother fantasized too much. She needed her fantasies because she lacked so many other things. My mother had sexual relations with other men during the time she was married to my father. 'You can cheat on your husband but never deny him yourself in bed,' she used to say. She didn't really know who she was. In the same way, on a different level, she didn't know who I was. This doubt, which was torture for many women, served to fuel her fantasies. For her the doubt belonged to a beautiful memory, and that's why she revealed it, for better or for worse, in a jolly joke or in an insult . . . I'm sure that I am my father's daughter; I resemble him too much.

One day I saw my supposed father; my mother pointed him out at a holiday resort. In my subsequent reconstruction, which must be very fantasized, he's a short man – like a gnome – with a long red beard and yellow eyes, attractive but very strange looking, much older than my mother. He was very famous and dabbled in rejuvenating people with hormones. When I decided to study medicine, I thought at first that maybe I wasn't intelligent enough. But then I told myself that I was either the daughter of a great medical researcher or the niece of a professor of medicine; whichever way you looked at it, I had the heritage.

My mother never forgave Frau Mutter, as she called her mother (one day when I called her that she replied angrily, 'Don't say that, I say it because I hate her'), for having interrupted her education. Despite this interruption Mama was very cultured. After primary school she went to a private school, something like a Lyceum, where she was taught literature and languages. When she had just a year to go, my grandmother decided to take a trip to the Riviera and Egypt and she made my mother go with her. In Paris, Mama became seriously ill with rheumatism and as a result had a vague heart problem. She later used this ailment as a pretext for many things, but she believed herself to be much worse than she really was. When she was angry she got a pain in her heart, she said, and nobody dared contradict her. She was a sensitive and intuitive woman. To some extent she was aware of the importance of sex; let's say her scientist lover had transmitted this 'hormonal' preoccupation to her. 'The glands do it all,' she would say. 'Hormones do it all.' She was sure that she had become ill with rheumatism, from which she suffered for the rest of her life, for psychosomatic reasons, and that it was her mother's fault. She only became frivolous later when she had no other outlet for her talents.

Between the wars Vienna and Berlin became places full of misery for some and frivolity for others. Frivolity was a way of life. It's not the same as now; perhaps today we would describe it as 'snobbishness'. But no, it's not that either . . . The real frivolousness came after the war. In that era my mother cut her long hair along with her long skirts. She and my father started going to a dancing school to learn the Charleston and the foxtrot, all of that. She freed herself of her corsets. Women had acquired the right to have a body and show their figures. Books belonging to a new literature began to appear in the house. *La Garçone* by Victor Margarite is about a young emancipated woman who nevertheless finally accepts her traditional fate as a woman. There was another novel, *Ariane*, very controversial at the time; I've forgotten who the author was. The heroine hides her virginity from her lover and confesses, much later, that what he'd interpreted as rejection in their first sexual encounter ('Don't close up like that . . . perhaps you don't love me?') had in fact been because she was a virgin. Virginity had begun to lose its value.

In the theatre, it was possible to put on Arthur Schnitzler's *La Ronde*, whilst outside the Deutschnationalen, the forerunners of the Nazis menacingly chanted something which roughly translates as: 'We're going to give it to these Jews who are once again going to this filth.' *La Ronde* had fallen foul of the censor during the monarchy for being pornographic. However, when I reread it last year in Zurich, I realized that it was a formidable criticism of the Victorian, Viennese hypocrisy which Freud so fitly denounced. It also clearly showed the double standards and the degradation of women. Perhaps it was Schnitzler who best captured the decadence of imperial Austria as did Roth the decline of its army and ruling class.

The Perfect Marriage by Van der Velde also appeared at that time. It tore the veil of mystery from sex with graphs and curves which crudely illustrated the differences between sexual climax in men and women. Women were no longer ashamed to feel pleasure; they even had to learn to achieve orgasm. Meanwhile, from Berlin, Magnus Hirschfeld was reclaiming the 'third sex', homosexuals.

But my mother loved in the romantic sense. I think she was frigid. As she communicated it to me, it was love with a capital 'L' that interested her, the love that Alexandra Kollontai criticized because it impeded women in the revolutionary struggle and also in their own development.

When she was an old woman, my mother wanted to write her life story. Yet, like all the women of her time, so socially restricted and forced into deceit and falsehood, I don't know if she would have written the truth. She didn't write anything anyway. Perhaps I talk about her so much because, in referring to my life, I also want to refer to hers. It might seem that I criticize her a lot, but I see her as the result of a certain social situation, unchangeable at the time.

If I want to reclaim women through feminism it's because I also want to reclaim the woman that existed in my mother. When she was dying, Effie Briest spoke of a banquet: it was the metaphor of a bourgeois lady that occurred to her even at the moment of death. My mother causes me sorrow because she wasted a good part of her life being a lady.

This is the first dream I remember. It was night. The street was wet and dirty from the rain. The omnibus stop below my window was deserted. The ground was covered with *Povidltaschkerl*, a kind of ravioli stuffed with a black plum paste much thicker than ordinary plum jam, and I was one of them. The omnibus appeared and was going to flatten us all. Only my screams prevented it because I woke up; my mother opened the venetian blinds a little and the light calmed me down. I could sleep again. *Povidltaschkerl* are part of Viennese cuisine, a mixture of Czech and German cooking, and I really liked them a lot.

Our flat was very large with a balcony in front and a conservatory. There was also a playroom for the children. It had been designed by one of the best architects of the day. My mother had a special talent for decorating, but the custom in those days was that if you were going to live in a place for a long time, maybe a lifetime, then an architect did the interior decorating. It wouldn't have been proper for my mother to do it. My sister and I had a white bedroom, full of sunlight, with a decorated border around the four walls. I slept by the window and Gucki said to me before I went to sleep, 'Turn the light out.' 'No, you turn it out.' 'Then I'll turn into a ghost.' Generally I ended up turning it out and it was total darkness because the blinds were closed. That's why I had that nightmare.

I was four when my father, who was a reserve officer, left for the front and I asked, 'Who's going to kill him, a Frenchman or a Russian?' Just recently I realized that this question was not jingoism but the most logical response to the bloodthirsty slogans that were heard day and night in the streets:

> Jeder Schuss, ein Russ
> Jeder Stoss, ein Franzos

which meant, a dead Russian for every bullet and a Frenchman for every swordthrust – it rhymed. The worst thing was that they wouldn't let me go to see him off. The soldiers paraded through the city and the women went with the children and sang songs and gave them flowers. 'You'd get very tired, you can go to meet them when they come back victorious,' my mother consoled me. Our house was near a railway station. At the end of the war the soldiers arrived from the East, not victorious, but with their heads down, their uniforms torn and their tails between their legs. One day in 1915, on a Saturday afternoon, I was in bed eating my favourite dessert, chocolate pudding, when a man I didn't recognize came in: it was my father.

The war was also my mother and my aunt Steffi's refugees, the children that ate in the canteen on the ground floor. A ludicrous recollection: One lovely Christmas, the top of the tree reached the ceiling of the highest room.

A girl played 'Silent Night' on the piano. But she had no hands; she played with a prosthesis.

Everything was strange in the imperial army. There were many jokes about it because nobody was ever given the post they were suited to. When he came back from the front, my father, exceedingly mild mannered and kind, was made a public prosecutor. He had studied a type of textile polytechnics. His brother, on the other hand, was a lawyer and ran our textile factory, for which he was exempted from military service. A lot of military men came to the house then, particularly my father's superior, who was poor. Many army officers would have been poor if it had not been for their wives' dowries. They had a taboo against marrying a woman without a dowry. They had a lot of taboos. They couldn't travel on trams because they had to maintain a way of life which appeared upper class. I vaguely remember an officer who had two single daughters whom he couldn't marry off because he had next to nothing for their dowries. They came to our house for a good meal. At that time we had a Russian servant, a prisoner of war, assigned to my father because he was an officer. (He had been promoted to captain during his time as public prosecutor for his fight against the black market.) I really loved this servant-prisoner, whom my parents treated very well. He was an excellent painter and did portraits of all the family and of our friends. He gave me wooden toys; I don't know where he got them from because they were Russian.

'Ah, *que la guerre est jolie!*' a friend of my mother's was able to say when she could finally have a lover in peace because her husband was at the front. I adored the yellow bread that crumbled because it was made of corn and, I suspect, a little sand. There was no white or black bread, and this yellow bread was fun. We never lacked for anything; my father was a prosecutor against the black market, but we always ate black-market food. My grandparents had an automobile but they could no longer use it because they had to hand over the tyres. They went back to the horse-drawn carriage. Later the electric light went and we had to use lamps which burned a horrible-smelling paraffin. There was very little gas and as a result very little hot water, so that Gucki and I had to bathe together and then only two or three times a week. We had to take coal to school and if it was extremely cold for a long time, then the school simply closed down. Nevertheless, behind-the-lines was secure.

But no, the war was not lovely, particularly not for those at the bottom. The restrictions that it brought might have been entertaining for us rich children, but for the poor and the refugees they were terrible. We did absurd things, whose usefulness gives an idea of the shortages there were. Women unravelled old rags to make a kind of cotton wool which went to the hospitals at the front. They also wove wrist covers (not me because I was too small) for the soldiers to wear on their wrists so the cold air couldn't get in through their sleeves.

One day my mother announced that she had to go to Budapest to look for her sister, who was pregnant and had been widowed. 'You are crazy,' my father replied. 'The Bolsheviks have taken over.' (Bela Kun had taken power in Hungary in 1918.) But my mother went anyway and brought back her youngest sister so she could have her daughter in Vienna. My aunt's husband had died of influenza; in fact, more people died of influenza than in the war. I had it and can still remember being delirious, going from the taps in the kitchen to the taps in the bathroom, opening the faucet and no water coming out. In those days they didn't give people who had influenza water. I don't know why not.

Then the revolution and fear. 'They are going to socialize the dwellings and we have a very big flat,' my father said. There was an easy remedy. The Russian prisoner had disappeared, so my father brought an employee from the factory to live with us. He behaved very politely and was very shy. We pretended we were two families and now they couldn't socialize the flat. Really the employee had only come on his own because my parents never invited his family to live with us . . . And the people demonstrating and shouting.

'You who are always thinking about clothes,' my father said to my mother and my sister Gucki, 'now you'll see what'll happen when the Bolsheviks come.'

And my cousins Geo and Lizzi and I locked up with the windows closed and the blinds down playing the anthem on the gramophone.

My father spoke of the Bolsheviks jokingly, as a sort of threat. Really, he was defending the Left when he told off my mother and Gucki for their silly preoccupations when people were suffering from hunger. I myself ended up identifying with the threat. But the revolution didn't come to Austria; it was only the fall of the Empire, and maybe that was best. We didn't have any possibility of ending up better than the Hungary of Bela Kun or the Bavaria of 1918. Today we know that if Vienna had attempted a Bolshevik revolution it would've been cruelly suppressed. The Communist Party had no strength. It had just begun to exist a short time before, formed by the prisoners of war who had come back from the Soviet Union. Hans Koplenik, our Party Secretary, the 'Old Man' as we used to call him, had been a prisoner of war for a long time in Czarist Russia. During the revolution he had fought with the Reds against the interventionists. He was proletarian.

In Austria, the Social Democrats won, at least in the city of Vienna. It was the most left of the Second International parties. They tried to create a decent municipal government, always held in check by the conservative and clerical governments of the rest of the country. Vienna had about half of the total inhabitants of Austria, the tiny Austria that remained after the dismembering of the Empire. Even though Vienna had a 'red' majority, the remainder of Austria was 'black', as they put it then. The Social Democrats really took democracy seriously. They faced great difficulties in keeping the city supplied with provisions, because the farmers were often opposed to selling their products to Vienna, and the other countries no longer helped. Yet, despite everything, the Social Democrats' government brought about great social advances in education, housing, social security and health. At that time everybody, Left and Right, was in favour of an 'Anschluss' of German–Austria), in other words, the formation of a single nation with Germany. But this was prohibited by the Treaty of Versailles.

SCHOOL DAYS

In those days I was going to a ridiculous, elegant school. We recited a psalm every morning. It was a school for nice girls. But somehow or other I understood a bit about politics, because in my final year I organized a kind of parliament (that's the name we gave it) during the 11 o'clock recess. It might have had something to do with my father being a prosecutor, but also in solidarity with our new Republic, in which we were all united. If anyone accused or informed on a classmate ('Miss Adela, she's copying', for example), then they were punished. No one would speak to them for a couple of days, a week or a month. The parliament was a sort of popular assembly. I don't know where I got the idea from but it was a total delight.

I finished the fourth year and enrolled in the Lyceum, from which I would not be able to go to university. It was the start of an ongoing battle with my mother. She had a great dread of my getting tuberculosis, perhaps because her younger brother, my uncle Franzi, had spent his youth in Switzerland – on the magic mountain, as he called it. My mother had this idea fixed in her mind, in spite of my being stronger than my sister. When I got bronchitis she took me out of school and bought me a dog and sent me to the park with it every day to get some sun. It's true that I had a private teacher, but I was a very bad student.

At one point, I announced to my mother that I'd decided to enrol at another school, a Lyceum from which I'd be able to enter the university.

That's when the battle really began. She started to look for schools nearby but there were only boys' schools. Even when they would have accepted me, as occasionally they took girls, my mother decided against it in the end: the bathrooms were dirty and I might get ill. There was a very demanding state college for girls only, but it was too far away; I would have to get up very early in order to arrive on time and I might get ill as a result. This was also discarded. The truth was, she had a lot of objections to my going to any college whatsoever. The loss of this school year was costly because it meant that I received my medical degree in 1935, when Austro-fascism made it impossible for me to enrol in the hospital service because I was Jewish. A year earlier it might still have been possible for me to have become a real doctor.

Finally, I ended up at the Schwarzwald Schule, one of the most important events in my life. It was a private Realgymnasium from which one could go to the university. The headmistress was a feminist. I didn't realize how important she was until a trip I made to Vienna three or four years ago. On that occasion, a writer contacted me – and all the other ex-students that he was able to find – to ask about the principal, Frau Doktor Schwarzwald, and my experience as a pupil at the school. He was writing about her and the cultural and political influence she'd had on the Vienna of that era. She was about forty in 1922, and had studied in Switzerland because in those days she wouldn't have been able to get a higher education in Austria. In Zurich she studied at the first university in Europe that admitted women, where the Russian women revolutionaries were also educated. In Vienna she founded this private school which was very expensive for those who could afford it, not too costly for those of moderate means and had lots of scholarships for those who couldn't pay anything. The Schwarzwald Schule had a feminist line *a priori* and was Marxist as well. Frau Doktor Schwarzwald was a liberated woman, with short grey hair, married to a bank manager. She used to bring her lovers to the school and hired some excellent, politically committed Marxist teachers.

Unfortunately, I didn't get to enjoy all the benefits of the school to the full because my parents didn't let me. I could never go to the holiday camps where they gave all the Social Democratic cultural and political training. When this man, who was writing about the Schwarzwald Schule, interviewed me recently, he was puzzled to find out that I became a Communist because the school (which was closed by the Nazis, of course) was a totally Social Democrat nucleus. With reference to feminism, I think one anecdote is enough to describe the feminist ideals upheld in the school. At fifteen, I fell in love, and my boyfriend became my lover. Peter was a very bad student at an elegant Catholic school. He was from the lower ranks of the nobility, but he had a title, Freiherr von. One day we made a date for midday at the ice rink, which meant we both had to get out of school. I pretended I wasn't well and the teacher asked me what was wrong. Feigning modesty, I told her I had my period so she sent me to the headmistress. I told her what was wrong and she said, 'This time you can go. But remember, if you want to have the respect men have, if you want to study and work just like men do, then don't ever again complain of this kind of malaise.' I never again used being a woman as an excuse to say 'I can't.' I think it's strange, that, of all the thousands of things that are said to you in school or during your life, there should be one that affects you as much as this affected me.

On another occasion she called my mother. 'Please,' she said, 'don't ever allow your chauffeur to park in front of the school again. Also, do not send your child to school in a fur coat. It is very disagreeable for the students who cannot afford these luxuries,' she added. Our French and German tutor, who was also our *Klassenvorstand*, that's to say, directly responsible for the students, was a Social Democrat Member of Parliament for the municipality of Vienna. The history teacher gave his classes from the dialectical materialist position, and the Latin professor was also a Marxist. To sum it up, it was a very special school.

My best friend, Ruth, was extremely poor, always on the edge of hunger. She belonged to one of those Jewish families that had been driven from the Russian–Polish border after the war and had come to Vienna, one of the families whose children my mother and aunt had been involved with. Ruth lived in a building which had eight tiny flats to a floor. There were four children and the parents, and they only had two rooms and a kitchen. The water tap was in the hallway and there was only one per floor. We went to the same school because she was one of the many poor scholarship pupils. We took the tram or else I went to pick her up with the chauffeur.

I was not aware at the time how much the school and the atmosphere there were influencing me. On the conscious level I was wrapped up in my love for Peter. I don't know if it was really love or a result of my mother's embargo on my studying seriously. That's why I was always in the next-to-last place in class until my final year. I remember when I was about fourteen and in my third year, Tommy Schwarz, whom I knew because he was in his last year at the same school as my cousin Geo, wrote on the blackboard during recess, 'Professor Tal can lick my ass.' It sounds awful, but it was the most common insult in Austria and Bavaria. It wasn't at all original and, as it turned out, extremely foolish.

Mr Tal read it and got Tommy Schwarz expelled without respecting any

49

of the formalities, that is, without calling all of the teachers to a *Concilio Abeundi*.

Tommy went up to the fifth floor, tied his hands together and jumped out of the window. I didn't know this boy well enough to understand his character and his suicide; today I wouldn't attribute it wholly to this incident. But outwardly it was the reason. The first demonstration of high school students in Austria was organized as a result. We were given the Vienna town hall for a huge rally. There were red flags and much indignation and anger on the part of the speakers and demonstrators. Nothing like it has occurred since. After this protest, delegates were elected for each student body; I was elected in my final year.

I am an old-fashioned mother, but I could understand my children's militant and sexually liberated adolescence because I belonged to a similar era. It only surprises me that it happened in Austria in the early 1920s and in Argentina fifty years later, yet it still hasn't come to Mexico. It's true that both experiences ended in tragedy, but not totally. Perhaps the wonderful May Day parade I saw in Vienna three years ago is a result of that era. It's not the revolution, nor the liberation of the proletariat, but at least one can breathe freely in Austria.

CHILDHOOD FRIENDS AND FANTASIES

I've often been asked: How was it possible that, as a young woman in such a distant era, I was able to leave my family circle to study and become a left-wing militant? I think it was thanks to my school and to my father's support. There were four of us in this generation of my family: two cousins (children of my father's brother, Uncle Alfred) and Gucki and me. Genetically speaking we were brothers and sisters. We lived in the same house and virtually grew up together. Geo, my oldest cousin, had a very strange and tragic history, due in good part to the violent contradictions in the Jewish, bourgeois, Viennese environment. He was my little childhood sweetheart. Much later, when I was around seventeen, I read Freud's *Interpretation of Dreams* (1900) and began to analyse my own. To my consternation, I realized that, in spite of being in love with Peter, my incestuous interest in Geo still remained.

George (Schorschi, as he was called as a child in Viennese) was five years older than me. He hated and despised his little sister Lizzi, who was younger than me, and was not very close to my sister Gucki, who was the same age as him. Gucki and her friend Milli, who later died in a concentration camp, played interminably at dolls. She had lots of very elegantly dressed dolls, both big and small. What's more, Gucki knew how to handle the spinning top with a lot of grace and dexterity. Geo was excluded, obviously. But he played with me. I helped him line up his little lead soldiers. I can still remember a huge, splendid, impregnable castle we made out of papier mâché to resist a siege or to be taken by Napoleon's army. I was five, and I didn't know anything about Napoleon, but I admired my big cousin who knew about history and explained everything to me. One day we would get married, in spite of being first cousins: like Lorca's pilgrims the Pope would give us a dispensation.

On long afternoons Geo would read to me from the three volumes of Felix Dahn's *Der Kampf um Rom* (The Battle of Rome). I still know by heart the sad words of the funeral hymn sung by the defeated Goths as they carried the body of their last king in its oak coffin towards the north in search of far-off Tule. We were on the side of these honest, barbarian warriors. I wonder if it wasn't then that Geo began to feel the morbid admiration that he later expressed for the modern-day Germans, the National Socialists, whom he could never belong to because he was a Jew with dark curly hair and black eyes. By an ironic, perverse coincidence Geo was precisely the only one of the four of us who didn't have the blue eyes and the blond or chestnut hair demanded by the Nazis and the Austrian ideal of beauty.

One day, when we were at a holiday spot, I heard groans and went to see what was causing them. Geo and his friends were playing cowboys and Indians, and they had tied him to a tree and were tormenting him. He was crying, more out of fear than pain. Twenty-five years later when I heard they had taken him to Auschwitz, this scene came back to me like a nightmare.

I think it was the absurd upbringing of the heir-prince his parents gave him that ruined this talented boy who had every opportunity within his reach. It made him 'unsuited to our century' and caused him to disregard the danger and stay on in Austria; he was the only one of the four of us to be trapped by the Nazis. School had been very difficult for him because he wasn't interested in studying. When he was just about to finish his degree, his parents gave him a beautiful jumping horse: Tarquinus Superbus. (It was given the nickname Prelick because the stable hands were, predictably, Czech.) The examination day coincided with the horse-jumping competition and, of course, Geo went to the competition. A year later he got his degree and began to study law; he lasted six months. He was later impressed by the elegance of a surgeon he had seen operate, so he decided to study medicine; but he only put up with it for a year.

One Christmas I asked Ruth, my poor Jewish friend, to help me decorate the tree. Geo found us doing it and threw my friend out of the house. 'How could you allow a Jew to decorate *my* Christmas tree?' he asked me later. Viennese Jews could be like that. But Hitler ignored these variations. As soon as the Anschluss happened, the Nazis took first his wife, a very pretty young Jewish woman, and then him. In Auschwitz she managed to save herself by making friends with an SS officer. After Geo was captured, his wife found him among the line of recent arrivals and told her friend, 'That's my husband. If anything happens to him I'll kill myself.' Geo left Auschwitz unharmed but he could no longer live with his wife. In the end they divorced and, after the separation, he committed suicide. 'I am unsuited to this century,' he wrote in the note he left. That was my cousin Geo, the flower of Viennese youth.

My cousin Lizzi, who was my best childhood friend, didn't finish her education either. The first money I earned in my life, my aunt paid me for giving Lizzi classes, even though I was such a bad student. Lizzi accepted only because we had agreed beforehand to divide the money between us.

It still saddens me that Lizzi wasn't happy, that she should have later died of a ridiculous cerebral cancer, handled carelessly by the family and negligently by the doctors. I regret that I couldn't help her much. But at least I could give her a last burst of life when she came to Buenos Aires, a short time before I left. Already a semi-invalid but still self-sufficient, she would go out on her own to buy things for her daughters and grandchildren. We went to the theatre together and when she left she told me that it was the last time that she had been almost happy. This cancer, very slow but dangerous because it increases the pressure of the cerebral fluid, destroying valuable nervous tissue, was diagnosed too late. Yet it appears that it began just after the death of her mother, just when she was ready to start living again.

When we were girls we loved each other more than sisters. We were very alike although she was prettier than I was, with a Greek profile, fuller lips and brighter colouring. I was the 'intelligent one'. I would call myself Mizzi and when we were with strangers, who sometimes got us confused, we pretended to be twins.

Lizzi and I grew up alternately in the tense environment of sex and repression in my home and in the cold, formal, refined atmosphere of hers. I preferred her home and her mother to mine. There was no hysteria; everything proceeded in a calm and rational way. I later realized that Lizzi suffered at home because of her parents' total preference for Geo, the eldest and the boy. That's why we spent more time in my house (the two flats occupied one floor of the Hauser Palais), joined in the bond of childish innocence, without realizing the erotic content of our friendship. We liked to hide under the baby-grand piano and spy on the outside world through the fringes of the Spanish mantilla which covered it. We enjoyed knowing that my mother in turn was spying on us to keep us from doing undefined 'ugly things'. But we didn't do anything except talk and make plans. It was under the piano that we decided to run away with a circus because we wanted to be acrobats. We admired their agility and courage.

We liked to play at being afraid. In the smoking room there was a very tall fireplace. We climbed into it and in the darkness played at scaring each other with hallucinations. 'D'you see them? Here they come,' Lizzi would say. 'Yes! I see them, a strange army of girls. Now I can hear them as well. Listen, ratatata, ratatata.' 'Of course I can hear them, but they frighten me.' 'Me too.' 'Now it's changed. Now it's a green dragon that's coming past . . .' And the physical agility. I leapt off the highest wardrobes without batting an eye. It was a bit more difficult for Lizzi and she sometimes got down without jumping, but she could climb to the top of the birch trees and swing in the wind. We liked trees a lot. We spent one summer in a chestnut tree. We converted it into a 'house' and drew up an outline of a book on how not to educate children that we were going to write as adults. We minutely recorded all the errors our parents, governesses and teachers made. As I said, Lizzi didn't study but she both read and wrote French better than German, not out of choice but because of Tante Steffi's ideas.

When we were about twelve years old we wanted to find out about alcohol so we went to Dachboden, to a hotel where we often spent the summer, and drank a bottle of egg liqueur between us. The result is that to this day I can't stand the taste of eggnog. At thirteen or fourteen, love began. We found mutually agreeable boyfriends, of course, but my aunt and uncle and my parents didn't approve of them because they were poor and 'surely interested in our dowries'. We held a black magic ceremony, which was great fun but not so magical because its effect was only felt years later. We knew that if we were poor we would be free to marry Peter and Erich. So we invented some complicated, mysterious prayers and shared some bread and salt, symbols of poverty. With this spell we hoped our parents' factory would go bankrupt. A few years later our parents started to have economic problems and Lizzi and Erich got married.

When I came back from Germany, already separated (from my first husband), Lizzi had had her first daughter and was living with her husband in the small Czech–German town where the factory was. Feeling bored, she'd decided to become an apprentice in a handicraft workshop. We'd practically lost contact. Lizzi got divorced and married a manufacturer much older than her, whom I couldn't stand. But she loved him; she had finally got the father she wanted. The war took them to Norway, then to Sweden and finally to Peru. We saw each other again in Lima. It was my last trip with my husband Max and my daughters. We went with Lizzi to Cuzco and Machu Picchu. Her husband claimed he'd never taken her there because he couldn't stand buildings that had been erected at the cost of the suffering of slaves. Obviously, he didn't know much about pre-Hispanic culture; what's more, he himself paid his workers a salary which wouldn't even feed a slave. We followed an ancient Inca route which would've taken us to Ecuador if we had carried on. Lizzi and I talked and talked. She told me how sad she was because her husband, although already an old man, had another woman, who was with him for his money; that her mother, who was ill with a mysterious form of cancer, took up all her time. She had to feed her meals of chicken and asparagus and play *chicaneuse*, a type of solitaire we had played as kids, with her for hours.

'Mama won't live much longer,' she told me, 'and then I'll do something, I'll go back to pottery or study something new. Something will have to happen.' Steffi lived on in a cloud of morphine for five more years and when she died Lizzi got cancer. She died in Mexico.

Gucki and I got on very badly. She was jealous of me and put me down. 'If I had a mouth as big as yours, I'd keep it shut,' she would say. It was the era of the tiny, painted, heart-shaped mouths. Gucki had a little mouth, blue eyes and blonde hair. My eyes were grey, they only became blue with age. She corresponded perfectly to the Viennese physical ideal. Yes, she scorned me and terrorized me. And I, who years later wouldn't allow anybody at school to be a tell-tale, went and told on her to my mother.

We sometimes played together, especially on holidays, when we didn't yet have any other children to play with. They were strange games; we played at being scared and invented a sadistic teacher we called Cochicoch. I suppose these games were related to our reading the famous, wicked Bibliothèque Rose, particularly *Les Malheurs de Sofie*, of which I still have horrifying memories. In another game we exchanged fear for provocation. It consisted of betting on who could annoy my mother most to make her lose her head, and be the first to get a slap.

Nevertheless, Gucki was very tied to my mother and was more docile than me. She married very young, when she was still a virgin. When she was separated two years later, she became a 'playgirl', although the term didn't exist then. A long time afterwards, when she was living modestly in a small village near Buenos Aires as 'Miss Gucki', the English teacher, she told me how the transformation had come about. My uncle Emil, the medical professor and my father's idol, had married Deli, a beautiful woman and, what fascinated my sister, an authentic *cocotte* or *demi-mondaine*. Gucki became Deli's friend and confidante; she often visited her and admired her jewels and furs. 'When she showed me her ring,' Gucki told me in Buenos Aires – 'do you remember, with the emerald and the enormous diamond? – I decided I wanted to be like her, to have rich, affectionate lovers who would give me valuable jewels.'

Uncle Emil and Deli's marriage didn't last long. The drama that ensued was similar to the plot of the film *Blue Angel* (based on the novel *Der Untertan* by Heinrich Mann), which had caused such a sensation at the time and was the beginning of Marlene Dietrich's fame. Deli went back to her former ways and Uncle Emil, who didn't want to give her up, patiently accompanied her on her long sleepless nights through the nightclubs of Vienna. My father predicted that he was going to lose his patients because nobody would trust a surgeon whose hands might start shaking during the operation after spending his nights drinking in dubious establishments. But Uncle Emil was stronger than the hero of *Blue Angel*, or else Deli was weaker. She did eventually leave it all, only to poison herself a short time later. She'd had enough of life. On her deathbed – it took days for her to die – she told Emil that she'd even gone to psychoanalysis to try to solve her problems. 'Psychoanalysis finally gave me the courage to kill myself,' she told him. Even her funeral was beautiful and had style. There were so many pretty young women, her friends, whom I watched with much curiosity. And Uncle Emil was weeping as he said goodbye to her, emphasizing in his speech in verse that she had left us on the twenty-first of March, precisely the first day of spring.

Exile was difficult for Gucki, even though we'd become closer since we were reunited in Uruguay and then later in Argentina. Gucki was not so young any more and she had never learnt a skill or profession, but she adjusted. In Montevideo, she worked as a chauffeur for Madame Morel, the owner of a pretty hotel on the Rambla. At that time, 1940, I suppose she was the first woman to become a professional driver. Afterwards in Argentina, she first lived with one Englishman and later married another one; that's how she learned to speak English perfectly. She changed little by little over the years and became Miss Gucki, the eccentric English woman who collected stray cats and dogs (especially after she was widowed) and was very respected in her village. She was very sickly for many years and died in 1978. Throughout her life she was symbiotically bound to my mother in a tie of love and hate, and I suppose this was why she never wanted to have children.

I am the only surviving one of the four us, which often makes me feel strange and alone. If my mother was still alive today she would have her explanation for why my mental and physical health was better than my sister's, even though she never read Freud much less Melanie Klein. I repeat what she told me many times, 'I got pregnant with your poor sister at an unfortunate time in my life, and I didn't even breastfeed her. That's why she's the way she is. Meanwhile, you were wanted. I was happy when I was pregnant with you and I breastfed you for a whole year. You were so strong we called you the baby lion. That's why you know how to organize your life.'

She was right. But it was also true that on the paediatrician's advice she stopped that lovely suckling from one day to the next. She went away on a trip so that I would 'forget her' and take the bottle. I believe that this brutal method left me feeling very resentful towards my mother, but it also saved me from a symbiosis with her.

How did I break out of my family environment? What saved me from becoming a 'lady'? I think it was the Oedipus complex. My father went to war precisely at the point when I would have most liked to have him close by. The only way to go with him was to become a nurse, or a doctor. In fact I did go to war as a doctor, but another war and twenty-two years later. Another factor that allowed me to free myself was that my mother was so busy with my older sister: Gucki had to be beautiful, elegant and sporty in order to marry well. I was left to my own wishes and resources. What's more, I chose medicine as a result of Vera Figner and her comrades, and my father fully supported my decision; he was proud of me.

In many aspects I made my life a negative identification with my mother and sister. I can't drive a car because they knew how to drive. (My mother drove when it was a total audacity for a woman to do so.) Gucki was an excellent dancer, and I'm terrible. She broke records at tennis and skiing and I lack style in spite of having been a good skier and mountain climber. I paid the price for wanting to have a different life from theirs. I renounced everything connected with them, the 'feminine', although I remember that when they asked me at school what I'd thought of studying, I answered, 'Medicine, if I don't get married first.' The teacher looked at me scornfully.

SEX AND ROMANCE

Marriage . . . sex. A well-brought-up girl like me had to be married even if she didn't know how children were born. I read Gucki's books, she was four years older. One day I asked my mother what the word *schwanger* (pregnant) meant. She answered with some quip, not the explanation. At ten or eleven years old, while on holiday, I fell in love, platonically, for the first time. I also found out how babies are made, thanks to some friends not much older but less sheltered than I was. I proudly told our servant, whom I liked a lot and who had denied me all information in this respect. She told my mother and my mother complained to the mother of the friend who had enlightened me. It turned into a scandal: my friend got a beating at home, as she had committed the crime of causing me to lose my innocence. The end result was that the group of friends stopped speaking to me, at least during that summer.

When I went to high school, I had my revenge. I would gather all the girls around me during the main break and 'enlighten' them. I had read everything about the birth of babies in the encyclopaedia, so I began to hold forth on the question of sex. Doubtless this is related to my psychoanalytic calling. I attempted to clear up the prevailing confusion. For example, we didn't know whether or not men menstruated. When I had my first sexual relations, I had only just stopped believing that you couldn't go with a man during your period without getting pregnant.

Once, after I had been having sex for a few months, we had to do free compositions in class. I gave mine the title 'Something which worries me a lot', and began to write a whole series of things which weren't true. I don't know why I did it, but I showed myself as being very affected by the existence of sexual relations. I said that I had been very shocked that my parents had had them. The German teacher, our academic supervisor, told me that I shouldn't dwell on the subject so much. 'If you hold one of your fingers very close to your eye,' she said, 'you'll virtually cover the whole of your vision. But if you hold it at a distance then you'll see the finger in its normal size in relation to the world.' She followed the Alfred Adler line. One shouldn't become obsessed with sex and neglect other interests as a result.

I had completely internalized the moral climate at home. In spite of the double morality, or maybe because of it, my father used to say that my mother was very good: she had come to marriage totally ignorant of everything about sex. She later commented to me that in her day her governesses had told her that the body existed in relation to the dress size and nothing else, and that one mustn't learn the names of the lower parts, not in German nor in any other language. In my childhood nobody mentioned the problem, apart from the child analysts and the Social Democrat teachers who talked about the importance of 'enlightening' children before they reached puberty. In my home, the most important thing was to get married and to be a virgin when you did so.

At thirteen I was in full rebellion and completely confused. I saw the boy I was in love with for the last time. He was French-Alsatian and four or five years older than me. He never realized that I was in love with him. I would see him at the lake where we usually spent our summer holidays. I was very excited when I went to meet him on that last occasion and he embraced me very warmly and told me that he wanted to tell me something. It was raining and we walked together under the one umbrella. I was wearing a lovely peasant dress.

'I had sex,' he said, 'and it is the most beautiful thing in the world. You must try it soon.' He told me about it like an older brother, and he had no intention of repeating the experience with me. As I listened my enthusiasm faded. I knew that our 'relationship' was over but I wasn't depressed; with his talk he succeeded in conveying to me that sex was worthwhile.

I believe that I never got good marks in history or geography in my eight years at high school because my head was full of sex and romance, due in part to the atmosphere at home. In this double morality, we had to be chaste and virgins when we married but we couldn't help but see that both my mother and my father had lovers. For their part, they also suffered as a result of this moral legacy because my mother, faced with the supposed innocence we had to protect at all costs, had a very good saying: 'Look, a girl's virginity is like a precious jewel: look after it well but if you lose it, don't get worked up about it.' At the same time, the problem concerned her enough to get us to read the very successful novel, *Mädchen die man nicht heiratet* (Girls Men Don't Marry).

Ambiguity and confusion . . . After the economic crisis the neighbourhood where we lived in the Hauser Palais had become run down and the streets were full of prostitutes. In front of the house there was a bar which I later frequented with a North American friend. We went there only to talk to the prostitutes. Around about nine o'clock at night we'd get together with one or more of them and buy them dinner and talk, just talk. Everything was complicated and bewildering. At school I still had some friends who were good, serious students, and others who were silly and whose heads were full of sex.

A schoolmate, also bourgeois, whose family was psychotic (they wouldn't speak to each other at the table, for example, because they were divided into groups that loathed each other) was able to use her house for parties; her mother was always inviting us. Sometimes we stayed away from school to go to Edina's house and help prepare for the evening's parties, to see if we couldn't finally win the affections of the boys we fancied and lose our damned virginity which, on the other hand, was not supposed to be lost. Much later, I realized that these parties were virtual orgies. When the Nazis entered Vienna, Edina's parents committed suicide. She managed to escape to Paris where she killed herself a few years later.

I was fourteen then and Lizzi, my cousin, was thirteen. Although it might sound strange, we were serious girls and deeply in love, she with Erich and I with Peter. We constantly asked ourselves if the boys would ever make up their minds. It was a challenge, we were in love and excited, but we also wanted to defy our families and the rules . . . I've already mentioned Peter Rodeck Freiherr von Roderbruck who went to the Schotten Lyceum and was a Catholic. He was a serious boy and was as much in love with me as I was with him. He wasn't bothered about my being a Jew, or not much anyway, but he was bothered by my incipient leftism. He wasn't a reactionary, more a conservative. He could have become a Nazi later on, but he didn't. Once when he saw me in a demonstration he came over and took my arm, but it was only to pull me out.

One of my happiest days was the day we went to bed together, in a room we had managed to get hold of. I had just had my fifteenth birthday. We arranged to meet in the same place the following week. He didn't arrive. I waited in the street in consternation that ended in desperation. 'It can't be! It can't!' I told myself. 'Is it like they say, that men only want women for that and then they leave them?' Later, his friend Kurt called me to tell me that Peter was in hospital dying, as he had crashed his motorbike on the way to our appointment. Kurt had said *agonie* (dying), but I had heard *onanie* (masturbating). I went to the bathroom and threw myself on the floor and cried and cried. This has never happened to me since. It was as if the crystal ball which had protected me had broken for ever. That evening, my mother had to call me to dinner three times because I refused to come to eat. I finally gave in and, as I approached the dining room, I heard my father comment, 'Poor boy, it's a great shame!' My mother answered him, 'Yes, it's a shame, but it's also fortunate that he's going to die because he was no match for her.' I never forgave her. Peter didn't have enough money to fit their criteria, even though he was an aristocrat and a Catholic. According to my mother he was only after my dowry.

I was in Vienna twelve years ago when my mother was still alive and I phoned Peter who came to pick me up in a luxurious Mercedes-Benz. 'Do you see the match you lost me?' I said to my mother. 'He wasn't after me for my dowry.' We left for the forest and ate in a tiny, deserted restaurant. 'Aren't you afraid that someone will see us and your wife will find out you went out with me?' I asked him a little coquettishly. 'My wife? No the problem is my mistress. She's very jealous.'

In the three years following the accident our relationship became very conflictive, although outwardly it appeared to be easy for me. I think that I must have been traumatized by the fact that he was nearly killed the week after we'd first slept together. On one occasion we were in a hotel making love and I got out of bed and knelt down in a corner of the room and began praying. I was out of my mind, in a state of terrible guilt and stupidity. 'I want to be with him, I want to be with him,' I repeated to myself all the time. At home they were up in arms. 'He's so ugly,' said my mother . . . I remember that years later I heard my mother saying to my father about Peter,' He was an attractive boy, wasn't he?' 'But you always told me he was ugly,' I interrupted. 'Well, we did it so you wouldn't get too enthusiastic.'

I behaved badly with Peter. I was wild, but he was Catholic and full of guilt about our relationship. One Christmas day we went to a hotel and I brought a Christmas tree and we lit little candles in the room; it was really lovely. But in spite of the many good things between us, during every holiday season, when we were separated for two months because I left Vienna, I always broke off with him because I reached the conclusion our relationship couldn't go on.

We often went out with Lizzi and Erich, and Kurt, our boyfriends' friend who didn't have a partner at the time. One time Lizzi phoned Kurt's house and thinking she was talking to him said, 'So your parents aren't at home. I'll come round this afternoon. Tell Erich not to forget the condoms.' It was only afterwards that she realized she'd been talking to Kurt's father. We had a terrible reputation. However, even though we were girls that men should not marry, Lizzi married Erich and if I didn't marry Peter, it was primarily because of my parents.

Then my paternal grandmother died. I was seventeen and in my seventh year at the Realgymnasium. Apparently, we still had money in 1927. My grandmother's death made my father very depressed. To cheer him up we decided to go to St Moritz for the Winter Olympics. My father and I went first because my mother had to stay with Gucki, who was divorcing her first husband. At the hotel there was an incident which gave me a lot of pleasure and filled me with pride. At the reception desk they asked us if we just wanted one room; they'd taken me for my father's lover.

Soon afterwards my mother and my sister arrived, all stirred up about the divorce, and the onslaught began again: 'You must get married, you have to get married', despite the fact that my sister had just got unmarried. And: 'There are interesting people here from good families.' They were more insistent with me (than Gucki) because in the end they recognized that Gucki had just got divorced. There were two foreigners there, Jewish landowners from Slovakia. One was ugly, but a nice person, whom I couldn't take seriously. The other was a 'good' man, as a husband should be according to the rules. He was twenty-five, eight years older than me, and a perfect gentleman. My parents persisted and I obediently began to fall in love. Within a short time everything was wonderful. My father came out of his depression over his mother's death, my mother out of hers over her eldest daughter's divorce and I out of mine over the break-up with Peter. I was in love with Micky (supposedly, of course).

Everybody was going to be content except for one thing: upon our return to Vienna economic disaster erupted. The crash of 1929 was getting closer. Failed speculation in the cotton market had brought the factory to the edge of bankruptcy. My father and my uncle had an enormous debt with the bank. Micky, unaware of the situation, continued to arrive once a week from where his family had their property. I'd confessed to him that I'd already had sexual relations and he had 'forgiven' me. In spite of the economic situation, everything seemed to be going along at full sail. I would leave school in the seventh grade, in other words, without taking my final exam. Every day my father would ask me, 'Did you phone Micky?' 'Did you make an arrangement to see him on Saturday or Sunday?' I had sex with Micky. It was logical given that I'd done it before.

Finally, the day arrived when my parents had to meet with Micky's mother and uncle (his father was dead) and decide on the date of our wedding. My parents came back from this meeting humiliated and depressed. The uncle had begun by saying that he'd married off all of his nephews, and married them well. He talked about money and asked about the dowry. My parents had offered an *appanage*. This French term indicates that the parents aren't able to pay all of the dowry in cash and so will make monthly payments of a percentage of the agreed amount. It was, you could say, a dowry in instalments, a kind of mortgage, in this case guaranteed by the factory. But at the time the factory was no guarantee for anything, so Micky's uncle, who had accepted the *appanage* in principle, later backed down.

In the end my parents had fallen into their own trap. I saw Micky one more time and went to bed with him out of pure spite to show him what a bastard he was. In fact he wasn't that bad, but he was so weak that I was able to make him feel extremely guilty after this last occasion. What's more, I realized completely that I didn't love him. I felt a great relief when all of this happened, which didn't stop me from following my parents' orders, although now with a double disadvantage – no dowry and no virginity. I won a fundamental point, however: I could continue with my studies.

MY FIRST HUSBAND

My parents had to go and live in Czechoslovakia, where their factory was. There could no longer continue to run it from a distance in Vienna, because the bank required the owners to occupy it directly I stayed on alone in the enormous apartment, which was later subdivided in order to let part of it. I was seventeen years old and was on my own in Vienna. I could sign my own absence notes for school and do whatever took my fancy. This wasn't completely true, however, because in the end I had all my parents' restrictions inside me. About this time, a school friend invited me to a party where I met Teddy, a decent, silly lad interested in making money. He seemed to be successful because he was a partner in an important firm. It was only later that I realized the poverty his family lived in. Teddy fell in love with me and I with him, as ought to happen for us to get married. I didn't tell him I was no longer a virgin because my mother had cautioned me, 'You don't tell a man that, just the way you don't tell him that you go to the bathroom.' At one point he had a doubt but I made up some story and there was no problem. What's more, the first night 'he couldn't do it' and within a week when things were normal he was so enthusiastic that he didn't question anything. He accepted me without a dowry, of course, and the *appanage* was such a large sum that within a month of our being married Teddy had left the supposed import company he was a partner in. Even so the *appanage* was enough to support us and help the impoverished family.

A few months before I married Teddy I told my academic supervisor, Aline Furtmüller, that I was going to leave school come what may. I had only six months to go to finish. 'Don't waste your studies!' 'But everything is arranged, my parents want us to get married in December.' After thinking for a moment she said, 'What would happen if you got married and kept coming to school?' Although today this is no big thing, at the time it was considered ludicrous. However, I decided to continue my studies. My grandmother paid for a wonderful honeymoon trip for us. In Tunis I rode on a camel and visited a harem, and we went to Rome. On our way home in the train, just before we arrived in Vienna, Teddy said to me, 'It must be fun to be famous, to appear in the newspapers, don't you think?' 'Maybe,' I replied, 'but we don't have much chance.' When we arrived at the station, we saw that we were in all the papers: 'The married student', 'Mrs Pupil', 'What's her husband going to say when she gets a bad mark in Latin?' – nonsense like that.

Journalists came to the school twice, before the headmistress said to me, 'You can finish your studies. You won't have any problem with us, but you mustn't talk to any of the journalists.' The fact that a girl could be married and maybe pass on details of her intimate life to her schoolmates was considered scandalous. This was the root of the problem. I was like a married nun and that was what attracted the scandal.

Teddy was a Catholic. We first got married in a civil ceremony and later on in a church, though this wasn't common in Vienna because one usually married in either a civil or religious ceremony. But it was all the same to me. Besides, our church marriage only meant going to the vestry and promising to baptize our children. Later, when I wanted a divorce, I was told that divorce existed for civil marriages and, while it didn't exist for Catholic marriages, I wasn't a Catholic. In fact, I had renounced my Jewish faith some time before but I never got baptized.

I think it was in part due to my marrying Teddy that I was able to finish my studies successfully and enrol in medical school. Thanks to the private classes I took with an engineering student I passed all the mathematics exams that had always previously caused me problems. All of a sudden, I could understand everything very well. My life was no longer taken up with Peter and getting married; I didn't feel guilty in the eyes of my parents or society. In the final exam I was even able to write the answers to three or four of the mathematics problems in the bathroom so that the other students could copy them. Later, at university, I never failed a single exam.

I separated from Teddy three years after we married. We were divorced on grounds of incompatibility, and the reasons I gave were very funny. I mentioned things like, while he loved opera, I liked the mountains; that, while he hated sports, I skied and swam in the Danube; that, while he was conservative, I was an ultra-leftist. It was a good divorce and it was a good marriage. I suppose that he was always faithful to me, as I was to him. When I got involved with someone else I didn't tell him right away; I told him three or four weeks afterwards and we separated. I felt immensely relieved. I remember thinking: now nobody can expect me to be a virgin or to have a dowry, the last because I knew how to earn my living.

There were five men to every woman in the school of medicine. We were virtually the first women. Anti-Semitism and fascism continued on the rise. In anatomy we had two lecturers, Julius Tandler, a famous Jewish Social Democrat scientist, whose classes all the Jews and leftists attended, and Hochstatter, an Aryan, where all the Nazis went. I don't know if he was reactionary or not. The provocations were also increasing and rumours that gangs of fascists could attack the university were more alarming by the day.

One morning it happened: a fellow student came to the Anatomy Institute, which was on the first floor, and ordered all the women up to the museum and told all the men to get ready to fight. The fascists came in and demolished everything: the lecture rooms, the chairs, the instruments and the books. The students tried to defend themselves with scalpels or whatever, to no avail. On another occasion when I was present during an assault on the university, the male students who looked Jewish were pushed down a long ramp between two lines of fascists, who beat them with canes and their fists. They reached the bottom half-dead, about to expire at the feet of the police, who were looking on passively; the autonomy of the university could not be violated.

Many years after those incidents, I saw the film *Julia*, and read Lillian Hellman's book, *Pentimento*. The book is not about these events because she didn't witness them or perhaps because nobody ever told her about them. But Fred Zimmerman, who is Austrian, must have been there and must have seen them because every one of the details in the film is absolutely correct. No one could have conveyed it better.

In 1932, I had just separated from Teddy when a friend and I decided to spend a term in Kiel working in the laboratory of Hober, the great physiologist. I remember that the research we were given to carry out was all Greek to me. We had to inject a coloured substance into male frogs and then decapitate them. Then over the flame of a burner we converted thin glass tubes into very fine cannulas, to use as catheters which we inserted into the urethras of our poor mutilated frogs to measure the amount of the coloured liquid that was eliminated in their urine. It made me so nauseous to go to the basement and choose the victim from the damp floor covered with frogs (more specifically, male frogs) that my hands were swollen during the whole of my stay in Kiel. 'What's the use of all this?' I asked my colleague in dismay. 'We'll publish it and one day it'll serve, with many similar experiments, as the basis for an important discovery,' Rusty replied optimistically. Actually, our work later appeared in the *Pfluger Physiology Files*. But I doubt, however, that anyone would have used it for anything.

Kiel is on the sea, relatively close to Hamburg in a region which was largely Nazi-fascist. At that time, our acquaintances there, third-generation converted Jews, were already preparing their exodus. Hitler was campaigning in the city when we arrived, and my friend and I went to an enormous, impressive rally at which he spoke. What a great honour to see and hear the Führer! I was taking photographs and at one point a member of the SS came up to me and said with much camaraderie, 'Don't just take them anywhere to be developed; those Jewish pigs are capable of ruining them.' Without realizing it consciously, I learned a lot at that rally. It determined the decisions I took when I returned to Vienna, decisions that separated me from the frogs for ever.

RED VIENNA

In April 1932, while the Nazis had still not taken power in Germany, they'd won nearly all the regional and municipal elections in Austria. They didn't, however, dislodge the Social Democrats (in Vienna) in spite of all the damage done by the huge economic crisis, the crash of 1927 and Seipel's Catholics. The Nazis were capitalizing on the losses of the Christian Socialists and the Heimwehr (a military organization supported by the landowners and the Church, the maximum expression of Austro-fascism, and in opposition to the Schutzbund, the debilitated armed wing of the Social Democrats). Two types of fascism tried to destroy the Left and the democratic Republic formed thanks to Social Democracy: Austro-fascism, which wanted to preserve the independence of the nation and was supported by the remains of the old imperial army, the landowners, the bankers and financiers in Vienna; and Germanizing fascism, which no longer sought the Anschluss with the Germany of the Weimar Republic, but with the Great Germany, which would soon be completely Nazi.

Seipel was the Catholic (Christian Socialist) Chancellor committed to the destruction of the Socialist Party and the democratic government, and to the restoration of the Church, a reactionary Church. When he died, his death didn't mean the end of his policies. His successor and son of the Catholic Church, Engelbert Dollfuss, the 'Wicked Dwarf', pursued exactly the same ends and dedicated the fervent last two years of his life to achieving them. The many obstacles were the Socialists, the overwhelming majority, and the Nazis, an increasing minority, as well as some of his own Catholics, but also the Communists.

A short time ago, an Austrian friend who didn't know I was writing about my life sent me a book, *Die Zerstörung einer Zukunft: Gespräche mit emigrierten Sozialwissenschaftlern*, which really fascinated me because it's a portrait of my generation and its fate. Among the other exiles from the Nazi era who are mentioned is an old acquaintance, Marie Jahoda, a well-known Austrian social psychologist, a few years older than me, who went to the same school, the Schwarzwald Schule. Marie Jahoda says things that I understand completely. She writes:

When we were young Austria was the centre of the world. It had the only mass social democrat party in which the proletariat truly participated in the cultural life. No other country in the world could have competed with Austria when we were young. We skied with the Socialist Party, we trekked in the mountains; our lives unfolded with the Party . . . In my youth, I probably didn't know anyone of my age who was not in the Party. For me it was the only thing a decent person could belong to . . . Between 1918 and 1919, Mrs Schwarzwald, the principal of a high school for girls which had an extraordinary influence on the cultural life of Vienna, began to organize summer camps for the pupils where the monitors and the director were maybe six or seven years older than us; there were Socialists amongst them. We ran these camps ourselves and they formed an important part of our education; it was understood that every day had to begin with an assembly in which the entire camp talked for at least five minutes about the political events of the day before. (Greffrath, 1979)

With Marie Jahoda I share so many things, and so much time! Not the militancy in the Socialist Party, however, despite my admiration for Austrian Social Democracy. (The Social Democrats [Socialists] are in power once more and I'd say they are the most decent party in the Second International.) When I was asked why I chose the Communist Party and not the Socialist Party – which at the time meant culture, politics, human relations, the Schwarzwald Schule, feminism, the unions, so many things – I could answer that I joined because the Communist Party promised revolution.

I grew up in the 'Red Vienna' of the Social Democrat government. My parents, like the majority of progressives, voted for the 'reds', the Social Democrats, in the municipal elections and the 'blacks', the Christian Socialists, in the national elections. Not even the majority of the Social Democrat leaders seriously wanted change. They opted for the status quo even though they promised socialism in the future. They would reach it when, thanks to their achievements and struggle, they could demonstrate through democratic elections that more than half of the Austrian people were with them. It was a tragic mistake, as the military coups in Chile and Bolivia still show today. I doubted that possibility long before having read Lenin's *State and Revolution*.

What was done in Vienna was good, with the workers' universities and the enormous working-class sports clubs. It was good, but it wasn't the revolution, because (as I soon learned from Lenin) a true revolution implies the overthrow of the ruling class.

The Russian Revolution had taken place in October 1917 and Czarist Russia had been transformed into the Soviet Union. It was the revolution Vera Figner had fought for; the revolution attacked by the entire world, including Russia's old allies. I learned of the atrocities of the invading armies from Upton Sinclair's 'Jimmy Higgins'. And this country, the only socialist country – yet the promise and guarantee of a future in which everyone could achieve Communism – was also attacked, opposed by Austrian Social Democracy.

However, I recall a very moving exception which must have occurred around about 1927. We'd had elections in Vienna and were anxiously awaiting the results. A crowd was gathered in a big square in front of a large screen. Loudspeakers had been installed and, while we awaited the results from the different districts, Sergei Eisenstein's *Battleship Potemkin* was shown. The revolutionary scenes in the film were greeted with the same enthusiasm and joy as the election results; at the end everyone, the whole crowd gathered there, sang the Internationale as well as the national anthem.

It was also the Party which freed me from the isolation and confusion of being a young woman no longer rich, but who still lived off an allowance from her parents in a city full of poverty and unemployment and who'd reached the point where she would never have accepted a paid job. Even my bourgeois friends would have reproached me for taking a job, and the bread, from someone who needed it. There was even a law which prohibited a husband and a wife from occupying local government posts. If one partner was lucky enough to be earning, it was unfair for the other to try to do so too. Fortunately, it is difficult to imagine the poverty then when one thinks of Austria today. It was surpassed only by the prevailing unemployment in Germany, unemployment which ultimately brought Hitler to power because he promised jobs and he effectively provided them through arms manufacturing.

Before I went to Germany, I knew about surplus value and man's exploitation of man. I'd learned about them at my Marxist high school. I also knew that my monthly allowance, like the luxury in which my sister was maintained, came from the labour, only partly remunerated, of the workers in our textile factory. In high school I had read *The Weavers*, the dramatically revolutionary work of the great Gerhard Hauptmann, who nevertheless later made a deal with Hitler in an insane, senile fantasy that that was how he would achieve the fame of a Goethe.

Yes, I knew about that before I made the trip to Germany, just like I knew beforehand to whom I'd present myself in the Party. It was the engineering student in whose classes I suddenly understood mathematics. He was the son of the widow of an aristocratic general in the imperial army. He and his mother lived in very poor circumstances. He was jokingly called the 'Red Baron'.

YOUNG COMMUNIST

It was only after the National Socialist rally, when I came back from Kiel and gave up the frogs and physiology, that I began to attend psychiatry lectures. Within a short time, I joined the Communist Party. Joining the Party meant finding myself in a new environment with new values, solidarity as daily practice. It meant that my life had acquired meaning beyond the personal, the individual. It meant having a new, different family with which I could share goals and ideals, setting aside personal ambition. I never had an important Party post. I didn't mind the 'ants' work', as they called it then.

None the less, I won't deny that I had doubts. These first arose when Stalin modified the family laws drawn up under Lenin and declared homosexuality a crime. When I asked my better-informed comrades the reason, they told me it was because homosexuals, being alienated from society, succumb to enemy blackmail more easily and could become spies. It seemed more logical to me that to avoid this tragedy one ought to go back to how it was before and not alienate them further.

Another problem was raised by the purges, the big trials. We all asked ourselves how it was possible such and such a hero of the revolution could have later betrayed it, and even more so when his subsequent confession and repentence confirmed that deep down he'd never lost his loyalty to the Party.

Perhaps the paranoid climate of the time is better understood today as the response to the very real persecution of a whole nation by the entire world. But what I also find hard to understand today is the desperate, often unscrupulous zeal for power, to which neither psychoanalysis nor Marxism offers us a satisfactory answer.

Returning to doubts, but a few years and historical events further on; While the Non-Aggression Pact between Stalin and von Ribbentrop saddened me, it didn't make me doubt the Party, unlike others, such as Arthur Koestler, who left the Party at the time. Already at the time, I understood it as a necessary tactic to save the USSR, the only socialist country, a bulwark for the future, against the growing war-like conspiracy. History proved me right and even today I can't wholly condemn Stalin. It was he, it was the USSR – it was the tenacious and self-sacrificing resistance of Leningrad under siege (in which a third of the total population died) and the heroism of Stalingrad – that saved the world from a Nazi triumph.

And it saved me too, but the Party had already saved my life previously, thanks to the objective understanding we had at the time of the certainty of the Nazis' cruelty and that they really were going to exterminate the Jews and the leftists. This conviction was not shared by many Jews, who believed that, because of their value to the German nation and because the Germans were such cultivated people, they would never be seriously persecuted. I remember the dentist's wife from *The Diary of Anne Frank*, who is caught and exterminated because she doesn't want to give up her fur coat. We in the Party were willing to give up everything and also we knew that fascism meant an inevitable imperialist war.

My later departure for Spain in 1936 could be interpreted as a heroic act but in fact it saved my life or at best it saved me from having to flee two years later as a Jew persecuted by the Nazis. I could leave my country voluntarily and save my self-respect. I think of what our schoolmistress, Furtmüller (to whom I've referred frequently in these pages) taught us. She said, 'There are people who say you shouldn't get involved in politics, that politics is dirty. None the less, if you don't actively participate in politics they'll make politics with you all the same.' And I think of Gramsci when he asked

. . . is it not preferable for one to consciously and critically elaborate one's own conception of the world and, as such, choose from within the appropriate sphere of activity related to this effort of one's own mind, to actively participate in the production of the history of the world, be one's own guide, rather than take passively lying down the stereotype imposed from without on our individuality?

I could say that the Austrian Communist Party has helped me to answer that yes, yes it is preferable to choose and to act.

The Party was declared illegal and went underground six weeks after I joined. The persecution took many different forms; there were times when it was unrelenting, but frequently it could be endured with some ease. It is less the objective conditions, for which we were nearly always well prepared, than the subjective which astonish me today, how we existed in secrecy. Once again I think of Lillian Hellman when she finds her friend in England and is surprised that she can express enthusiasm only for the scientist, John D. Bernal, when her memories of Julia in early adolescence were of an extremely well-educated girl who loved art and literature. Yes, in the Party and above all in the underground, everything not serious (which at that time in Vienna, and in my environment, was a lot) was considered frivolous . . . and so was reading literature, talking about art, listening to music, playing bridge and discussing the unimportant things in life . . .

Being clandestine essentially consisted of following rules about security: that is, absolutely never mentioning anything about the Party in front of people who were not Party comrades, nor knowing the names and surnames of people in the Party. My first encounter with these rules seemed funny to me. The bell rang and a man a few years older than me was ushered into the house. 'So and so sent me,' he explained, 'I am to be your superior.' 'Pleased to meet you, comrade. Would you like a cup of coffee? What's your name?' 'What would you like to call mee?' he replied. 'I don't have a name.' 'Well, you'll be Edward to me,' I said when I'd overcome my confusion. 'Very well, and you? What will we call you in the Party?' 'I don't want to change my name. I think it's enough if you call me Mimi; it's my nickname.' 'OK, whatever you like.' When they arrested me much later, the police asked me if I knew someone called Mimi who had been mentioned frequently during interrogations. But they didn't succeed in finding out that I, Marie Lisbeth, was she. Other than that, my life carried on completely abnormally normal. I went skiing in the mountains from time to time, which I'd always loved, but could no longer do in the same way because I felt it was vaguely reprehensible for a militant. My conversations with my friends always left out a fundamental part of my life and the life of the times, politics. And they were strange in the same way Julia seemed strange to her friend. Although physically I never had to hide in unfamiliar houses or under other names, I often had to conceal my thoughts.

I was assigned to Agitprop (the preparation of agitation and propaganda) in the underground, because of my bourgeois connections and also because my parents' flat where I lived alone was used for secret Central Committee meetings, so I was always very close to the members. Besides, the Secretary General, Koplenik – the 'Old Man' – had married a Jewish girl of bourgeois origin who was my second cousin. A good part of my work consisted of finding places to hold meetings and conferences. The Hauser Palais was a large building in the French-Foucher style and many strangers had moved in as sections had been rented and sub-rented; the *concierge* was more like a policeman and had to be continuously avoided. I can legitimately take credit for having organized the last congress of the Austrian Communist Party held inside the country before the war without exposing any of the sixty provincial delegates to danger. My memories of that week are of the never-ending movement inside my flat and of the blisters on my right hand from cutting bread for so many people.q

At the time, I was never sure if I'd be able to finish my studies, as happened to Vera Figner. I knew that the police were looking for me and had a description of me, so I couldn't turn up at the university. Vera Figner couldn't finish her studies. But I studied à la Viennese, in the different cafés, in great haste so I'd finish as soon as possible. I managed to do it.

At the beginning of March 1933, a few days after the burning of the Reichstag and the day before Hitler won a huge majority in the general elections, a ludicrous situation which would have grave consequences developed in Vienna. The Dollfuss government, in serious economic difficulties, began to pay the railway workers, who were state employees, in three instalments instead of at the beginning of the month as was customary. The workers held a two-hour work stoppage and the government used the opportunity to fire the most active leaders, among whom were some comrades. The problem was taken to the parliament and the government was defeated by one vote. Later, it was discovered that a member of the Socialist Party in confusion had voted with the wrong ballot and the Catholic (Christian Socialist) government used this as an excuse to stir up an argument about the validity of the vote. In the Socialist outrage which followed, the President and two Vice-Presidents resigned. As a result there remained no authority capable of convening the legislative assembly, a situation which Dollfuss naturally took advantage of, as a way out of the crisis provokd by the railway workers. But besides this triumph, the resignation of the members of parliament caused the 'Wicked Dwarf' to be left suddenly in the role of dictator, the sole, self-appointed leader of a country deeply divided politically.

In 1933 three forces remained: the Left, made up of the Social Democrat majority and the tiny Communist Party (of course, they were not formally unified); Austro-fascism, composed of the Christian Socialists and Dollfuss; and the Nazis. All three had their armed movements: the Left's Schutzbund, armed but more and more debilitated by the Christian Socialist governments, beginning with Seipel and continuing under Dollfuss; the Heimwehr, Austro-fascist and totally supported by the government but deteriorating rapidly in favour of the Nazis; the latter, on the rise under the patronage of a triumphant Hitler.

The Dollfuss dictatorship depended in good measure on the differences between Italy and Germany with respect to Austria. Mussolini was firmly opposed to Hitler controlling the Brenner Pass and direct access to Italy. Hitler for his part was in favour of the Anschluss. Dollfuss's plan, very different from both Italian fascism and German Nazism, included the totally anachronistic participation of the Catholic Church in all aspects of Austrian life and, more anachronistic still, a return to Church involvement in all the instruments of government. The most obvious contradiction was that the Church was opposed to large-scale industrialization and finance capital, and these sectors constituted some of Dollfuss's major supporters. No less contradictory was the fact that, in a country with a Socialist majority in the unions (and where there also existed important Christian trade unions), Dollfuss attempted to introduce a model of social groupings which disregarded class barriers. The only possibility was to disband the unions comple- tely and to persuade the opponents within his ranks to accept the necessary participation of the industrialists and the bankers. The complete hopeless- ness of this option was demonstrated in June of 1934.

After a few amorous flurries with the Nazis, Dollfuss ended up convincing himself that attempts at moving closer to a tendency interested only in an Anschluss with Germany, and that had Hitler as its idol, were destined to failure. The Nazis responded to this attitude with a campaign of terror. Dollfuss's response none the less was not directed principally against the Nazis: the government sought the defeat and complete disarming of the Socialist Schutzbund, and it stepped up the searches that ended in the police occupation of the Socialist Party offices in Linz, in February of 1934. The Socialists in Linz decided to fight back without waiting for instructions from the Vienna Central Committee and the uprising spread to other regions. When Vienna heard the news, the Central Committee of the Socialist Party decided, by one vote, on a general strike. (It wasn't so simple: the disastrous economic conditions didn't allow for good prospects.) A part of the Vienna Schutzbund rose up in arms.

We discussed it in the Communist Party. We knew that it would be impossible to win. We knew that the general strike would be a failure. I wasn't there the night the Central Committee decided to participate in the uprising in spite of everything. We couldn't have let down the workers on general strike. The fighting took place in the working-class areas, we fought heroically for four days (I wasn't in any of the battles), but all was lost when the government ordered artillery to be used against the municipal housing projects. Karl Marx Hof, stronghold and symbol of Red Vienna, was badly damaged, and there were many injured among the peaceful inhabitants. They began to execute the prisoners and it was only due to international outrage that the hanging of left-wing combatants was halted. One of those executed was Weisl, a nephew of the headmistress of the Realgymnasium.

Those were very strange days for me; I felt depersonalized, ludicrous. Not so much because of the clandestine work or my bourgeois lifestyle, the medical school, my conversations with Party people, but in my relationship with Gucki. I went to my sister's house on various occasions, perhaps as a security measure, on the nights of this brief civil war of February 1934 and found uniformed fascists dancing, enjoying themselves and drinking toasts to the victory.

The uprising was the perfect pretext for Dollfuss; he blamed the Socialist Party, and, even though not all the Socialists had taken part, he dissolved the Party. He did the same with the Socialist unions. The principal leaders went to prison, underground or into exile. Otto Bauer went to Czechoslovakia; Deutsch, the organizer of the Schutzbund, also managed to escape. But the persecution didn't destroy the opposition. The Socialists continued their work illegally and still counted on the support of the working class against Dollfuss and the Nazis. They made use of the existence of the Christian trade unions and transformed them into centres for Socialist gatherings. The 'unified trade union' (*Einheitsgewerkschaft*), based in the Catholic unions, managed to become a powerful workers' organization with Socialist tendencies until it also disappeared. We Communists continued with our agitation work.

July 1934 arrived and with it the total decomposition of the Dollfuss regime. The Nazis attempted a military coup: groups of them took over a radio station and announced that the Chancellor had resigned and been replaced by one of their sympathizers, Rintelen. They occupied the chancellory and injured Dollfuss, who bled to death without their bringing him either the doctor or the priest he'd requested. Meanwhile, government troops surrounded the building and the Nazis had to give themselves up because they didn't seem to have any support. Some of those who took part were hung, but this was more in response to the horror Dollfuss's assassination caused among the Catholics; the failed coup was not followed by a coherent policy against the Nazis.

The Anschluss had still not come to fruition, one reason being that many saw Austro-fascism as a way out of the crisis and the political discord. The fact was, the government troops had remained totally loyal and moreover the Nazis had no support in Vienna, which was still 'red' in spite of everything. But the main reason surely was that when Mussolini found out about the coup he sent troops to the frontier. Hitler, for his part, had prepared an Austrian legion comprising Austrian Nazi refugees living in Germany, and was ready to cross the frontier and support the coup until he learned of the Italian troop movements. He wasn't sufficiently armed to confront Mussolini – his future ally. He took his legion back to Prussia and abandoned those who took part in the coup.

Dollfuss's successor was perhaps somewhat better than Dollfuss had been. He was a moderate aristocrat, quite advanced on some things. For example, he was not opposed to the 'unified union' being strengthened by the Socialist workers from the dissolved unions. He continued the Dollfuss dictatorship because he had no other alternative, but he was softer. What's more, a short time after he came to power he managed to get the following people out of his government: Commander Fey, the son-of-a-bitch who had been in charge of the February repression and the bombing of the working-class neighbourhoods; Prince Starhemberg, one of the strictest of Seipel and Dollfuss's Catholics (Christian Socialists); and Schuschnigg, a gentleman soldier in the old imperial style, who nevertheless had founded the un-stoppable Austro-fascism. Not only did we Communists continue under-ground but the repression was enveloping the majority of the population.

The members of the Central Committee were so hounded by the police that for security reasons the Central Committee was set up in Prague. My job was to get Koplenik, the Secretary General, to Czechoslovakia. Tall and thin, with a long bony face, he was easily recognizable. We managed to get across the frontier thanks to a cousin of mine who let us use her expensive car and chauffeur. Two of us disguised ourselves as a couple of lovers who had to take an old sick man across the border. He crossed in a blanket which covered his body and part of his face, without once getting out of the car. At the border the chauffeur got out and opened the door for us, and only we, the young couple, got out. That's how we did it. A few months later I took Friedl Furnberg, the second-in-charge in the Party, to Prague by similar means, only this time by train and with a false passport.

For the rest, Agitprop activities were usually somewhat entertaining. Running off propaganda on the rudimentary mimeograph machine at home – agitation work as it really is – the discussions, the Marxist seminars that I attended as both teacher and pupil which included a smattering of jokes, Weil's music from *The Threepenny Opera* and good friendships.

My best friend was Marianne, whose husband worked for the Comintern. Strangely, my first contact with her was not through the Party, but through Manja, the Polish blonde who was the girlfriend of a North American student. One day she asked me if I wanted to earn a few schillings doing some easy, entertaining work. 'Is there such a thing?' I asked puzzled. Yes, there was. Manja got me work as an extra in a film. We became friends and with time she told me that she and her boyfriend were in the Comintern. When he qualified they were going to go to the Balkans to work. At the time, that was certainly not entertaining work, but very committed and dangerous. It was to be a spy, for a just cause. A doctor, and what's more of a nationality so esteemed and above suspicion as North Americans were, was invaluable for this task. I listened with interest and attention but I didn't accept the contact they offered. I had my membership in the Party and that was enough.

Some time later I had another encounter with a member of the Comintern – a pretty horrific encounter, although I didn't think so at the time. Almost all the rank-and-file comrades I'd had anything to do with were in jail. It was then that a comrade whom I didn't know well phoned me to set up a meeting in a café. I went to the appointment, and we sat down to what I thought would be a friendly talk. But that wasn't the case. I saw he was very tense, and frowning. 'A few words, comrade that's all, but remember them. I've noticed that everyone who has worked with you is dead, except you. Think carefully about what that means. The revolution is going through blood and shit and traitors will be shot. Do you understand?' He got up and left me with the bill for our two Viennese coffees. I was stunned, but he didn't scare me. I went to friends on the Central Committee. 'Don't worry,' they told me. 'Nobody is suspicious of you. But the poor man, he just got out of a Bulgarian prison and he's broken from the torture. He simply lost his mind.' Two weeks later, at a meeting of pacifist doctors, they arrested me.

It was because of my fear of torture that I'd never thought seriously of joining the Comintern. But I admired the people who did a lot. The Comintern defended the Third International, watched over the security of the Soviet Union and ensured international solidarity. That's why the USSR wasn't alone.

I knew another Comintern agent, Hans, Marianne's husband. Hans was cultured, well read and very different from the one with whom I'd had the meeting in the café. The three of us chatted together during the meetings of the Central Committee. We often talked about our hopes and plans, of when it would be safe enough seriously to have a relationship and a family; what the socialist world of the future, for which we were ready to work day and night, would be like. Marianne's health was frail. She was in Paris expecting her second child when war was declared. She and Hans were interned in the winter stadium along with thousands of other foreigners of enemy national-ity. Marianne didn't survive the bleakness of this temporary confinement; she became ill and died a few days after having been freed. Hans carried on in the struggle. When the Nazis entered Paris, they found him and shot him. No, it was not a time to start a family. But our pride and glory, and the Comintern's too, was Georgi Dimitrov, a Bulgarian linotypist who was secretary of the German section of the Comintern. I paid homage to his tomb in Sofia nearly forty years later. In his glass coffin, identical to Lenin's in Moscow, I could see his trim figure and intelligent face. It was Dimitrov who, in Germany's darkest hour, after the burning of the Reichstag, managed to inflict the first defeat on the Nazi propaganda machine, the first and last for many years. Those of us in Vienna, along with the rest of the Western world, followed his trial fascinated, glued to the radio, day after day.

We were witnessing a miracle: that one man – due to his intelligence, integrity, and brilliance, and also thanks to his Communist training – could defeat this monstrous machine at the Leipzig trial. Humiliating Goebbels, leaving Goering impotent and demonstrating to the world Nazi hypocrisy and deceit in the face of truth. But it was the last victory until Stalingrad.

MEDICAL STUDENT, ANALYSAND

I qualified as a doctor at the beginning of 1935. In the Red Vienna of the Socialists there was a long tradition of feminist struggle. What's more, the Social Democrats maintained from the outset that women should be the ones to make decisions about their own bodies; this was translated into the fight to legalize abortion and against Article 144, which declared it a crime. This was the banner of the proletarian women of the Socialist Party, and naturally of the Communist Party. At that time, Fritz Jensen – a gynaecologist friend who was a Communist and had been in one of the Austro-fascist concentration camps (which weren't particularly cruel, but were concentration camps all the same) – asked me to help him with the anaesthetic because he had to do a scrape. He explained to me that, in addition to his clinic and his militancy in the Party, he was active in this other cause. He helped out pregnant working-class women who for economic reasons couldn't have another child and women comrades who were underground and couldn't face the birth of a child in their situation. Thanks to his intervention, these women could have an abortion in a clinic under the best conditions, because in Austria a registered doctor could prescribe an abortion by claiming that the pregnancy endangered the life of the mother.

I worked as his anaesthetist for a while. Our fees consisted of lemonade and a ham sandwich. That's how I learned to do anaesthesia, which would be useful later for going to Spain. We were also lovers for a while. It was a happy, light-hearted relationship, without commitment, since our real commitment was to the Party.

My later professional inclinations were decided by Austro-fascism and my interest in psychiatry. In order to be a Social Security doctor and get good clinical training (medicine on the whole was socialized), one had to do various hospital specializations for two years, a type of residency. Since the rise of Austro-fascism, however, no hospital would hire Jewish doctors; it was a discreet anti-Semitism which prevented one from confusing the Christian Socialists with the Nazis, but it was equally efficient. That left only the Jewish hospital, but there was a long waiting list. Furthermore, I'd renounced my religion at the age of seventeen. Through the procedure of declaring myself 'without profession of faith', I'd renounced the rights and obligations Jews have in their community.

I tried to get some medical training as best I could and at the same time I continued to attend the women's section in the psychiatry school. Heinz Hartmann ran the section. He later became very famous in the United States as a theorist in the psychoanalysis of the ego but he could never satisfactorily explain the dynamic of a psychotic in analytical terms. (No one did it better than Enrique Pichon Riviere, later, in Buenos Aires.) At the time I thought that analysis would suit me fine, as much for my own neurosis as my feeling that something more than the mere detailed, phenomenological description of symptoms (that they did then) was necessary in order to understand my psychotic patients. I went to Hartmann and very timidly said that I wanted to do analysis with him. He looked down at me from his handsome six-feet, two-inches and with much disdain said, 'I don't think you could pay my fees.' I was furious. I went to another training analyst, Richard Sterba; much later we became good friends. I started my analysis and a year later, when it was evident that it would be impossible for anyone who wasn't a Catholic to get a post in a hospital, I began to think seriously about analytical training. I didn't know at the time that Sterba was a training analyst nor what this title meant. At a certain point in the analysis he proposed formalizing it as a training analysis provided it was accepted as such in an interview with a professor at the Wiener Vereinigung Institut, Freud's Institute of Psychoanalysis.

In Buenos Aires, around about 1960, Enrique Pichon Riviere did an interesting survey among students of medicine, sociology and psychology to find out what were their unconscious motives for choosing such careers. As a central point he took Melanie Klein's concept of 'reparation'. It turned out that the students who had a vocation for medicine were those who, in their childhood, had suffered as a result of the serious illness of a close family member whom they would've passionately wanted to cure, or were those who had hypochondriac tendencies themselves. That is to say, studying medicine corresponds to an unconscious need to 'repair' a loved one, or oneself. The future sociologists generally came from families that were victims of difficult social situations. And psychologists, through the tool provided them by their science, endeavoured to control their own madness or that of others close to them.

In my day, the career of clinical psychologist didn't exist in Vienna. But I, already nearly a doctor, chose psychoanalysis and psychiatry for the same unconscious reasons. I must've been trying to repair my 'hysterical' mother and sister and also learning how to understand myself. I think I chose well. Psychoanalysis is a valuable tool, not so much for 'curing oneself', but in order to understand oneself, to handle one's own madness better and to stop lying to oneself.

So, I began my training with an interview with Anna Freud herself and enrolled in the Wiener Vereinigung, the psychoanalytic institute, where I spent a little over a year – not, you would say, very successfully. I didn't study much, although maybe not as little as it seems now. When I was accepted at the Wiener Vereinigung, Sterba said to me, 'Now you must read all of Freud's work.' I told him that it was very difficult to buy at the time. 'Don't worry,' he told me, 'go to the exchange library and read it there.' I don't want to appear like an arrogant European, but in Argentina or Mexico it's not easy to find students who have read all of Freud's work; at that time I read the complete works. The most difficult thing for me was the studying involved in the seminars. Nearly all my interest was taken up with politics and in addition I was trying to finish my medical degree at top speed in case I was taken prisoner.

Living with psychoanalysis and the Communist Party was not easy. At times, I would look at my watch during a meeting and get up to go to some unavoidable appointment, a supposed class, etc. The comrades thought that I was giving classes in order to earn some money, but in reality I wasn't leaving to go to a class but to a session. I would have been ashamed to confess how much I paid for my analysis, although Sterba wasn't one of the expensive ones.

Some months later, in February of 1934, when Social Democracy was also banned, something occurred that would put an end to my experience in psychoanalytic training in Vienna. Hitler was already in power in Berlin and the Gestapo captured Edith Jakobson after following one of her patients. In order to protect psychoanalysis and its patients, the staff met with Herr Professor, as everyone referred to Freud, and decided that no analyst could be active in any clandestine party, still less treat persons who were. The Socialist Party, the Communist Party, even the National Socialists, in other words the overwhelming majority of political organizations, were banned. This presented analysts with the alternatives of either interrupting their patient's treatment, which goes against medical ethics – what's more, the vast majority weren't in training analysis, there were patients with serious problems – or avoiding the subject with patients during their sessions and going against the most elementary rules of analysis; or violating the regulations of the institution of analyst-analysand.

My analyst informed me of this dictum of – according to him – Herr Professor (just a few years ago, in Vienna, Bergasse, I learned that the measure had been proposed by Federn) and told me that we would have to stick to it. None the less, I continued to be active, being very discreet about analysis in the Party and vice-versa in analysis. Sterba very soon declared me cured; we agreed that I was fine and that everything had concluded normally. This ending saddened me and wasn't good for me, but at the same time I accepted that while the world was burning was no time to be contemplating one's navel.

I continued to go to the Wiener Vereinigung irregularly and without much enthusiasm, until a personal incident sullied my relationship with the Institute for good. At the time, I was given the task of creating a pacifist organization (of anti-war doctors) backed by the Party. One afternoon, I was arrested along with eleven other doctors who didn't belong to the Party, among them Max, my future husband. We were only held prisoner for two days, as they couldn't prove anything against us, but from then on I was no longer good for Agitprop work because I'd been exposed.

When I returned to the psychiatry lectures, a friend who tried, but always failed, to function as my super-ego, scolded me for having been absent. I, in turn, told her the story of what had just happened to me. Some days later, Bibring, the Director of the Institute, called me in and told me he'd found out that I was carrying on with my activism and that in so doing I was breaking the established rules. He said that my case would be discussed in a meeting of the authorities and that I'd probably be expelled. I was not to comment in any way to anyone on the situation until the authorities had reached their decision. Apparently, my friend had told my prison story in her session and her analyst, without respecting professional confidences, had told the Director.

I was very frightened and depressed. Frightened, for a very concrete reason: in all the meetings of the Wiener Vereinigung, as in the meetings of all clubs, schools, etc., at the time, there were police present. The fact that whether my political activity was legal or not was going to be discussed in front of the police seemed to me a complete aberration. I spent a good part of that morning walking around feeling awful. At one point I went to the maternity clinic where I worked on an experimental, analytical project with Kurt Eissler (now a famous New York analyst). 'What's wrong, Frau Colleague?' Eissler said; we were very formal then. 'You seem to be very depressed.' So I said to myself, to hell with Bibring and his rules about secrecy, and I told him all about the affair. Indignantly, Eissler suggested that I speak to my analyst even though the treatment had finished. Sterba explained to me, 'This is a result of personal grudges and tensions. Bibring has a lot against me. That's why he's set against you, because you are my analysand. Don't worry, I'll fix it.' And he fixed it. He made me an appointment with Federn, who read me a sermon, and that was the end of it. As to the rest, Federn's own son was imprisoned for being a Trotskyist. Later, in 1938, the Nazis sent him to a concentration camp for being a Marxist and a Jew. He was saved by a real miracle and is at present in charge of the Sigmund Freud Museum. It was he who told me a few years ago that the rule against party activism by analysts and analysands had been proposed by his father.

When Federn gave me the lecture I didn't say a thing. Later, talking to Sterba (in May 1936), I told him, 'I don't want them to throw me out but don't worry, I'm not going to cause any more complications. I'll soon be leaving of my own accord.' In July, the Spanish Civil War broke out; in September, I said goodbye to Sterba but not to the Institute. In a way, I was in agreement with the Party's attitude to psychoanalysis – in a certain sense, it was frivolous. 'One cannot be contemplating one's navel while the world's burning,' I repeated to myself once again. And the world had never before burned as it was doing at the time. The little relevance that analysis had for me then was reflected in my lack of enthusiasm for studying and for going to the seminars.

What's more, the relationship between psychoanalysis and politics, as had occurred in Germany with Reich, the Communist Party, the Left, had become impossible in Austria by that time. We were more concerned with rising Nazism, the banned parties, the intrigues of the Catholic politicians; in short, it didn't occur to anyone at the time to discuss Marxism and psychoanalysis. Ever since Social Democracy, there had been Marxist analysts (the great Fenichel, for example); and, of course, my analyst, like many others, knew what Marxism was. But this didn't mean there was any theoretical discussion of these problems. It was only much later that I learned that Fenichel had written 'On psychoanalysis as the embryo of a future dialectic–materialist psychology'. Moreover, certainly the Party, even less the Party of my time, has never had a very understanding attitude towards psychoanalysis, nor psychoanalysis towards the Party.

I never met Freud. It would've been very difficult for a young woman student at the Institute, not very convinced of her psychoanalytical vocation, to have had any dealings with a man so famous and so withdrawn at the time, because of his cancer. When they had his eightieth birthday celebration, I didn't go nor did I want to go. I was too full of resentment towards the Institute and anger towards the people who pretended that nothing was happening, and the psychoanalysts played this dangerous game of denial better than anyone.

In those days the Institute was full of Jewish refugees who came primarily from the Berlin Institute, and everyone from Freud down ignored the Nazi persecution going on in Germany. I still can't understand how they could turn their backs when faced with the evidence, and I understood it less at the time. I fail to understand it thanks to the Austrian Communist Party: unlike the left Social Democrats, it was impossible for us Communists to ignore it. The very German analysts who had been persecuted, when they arrived in Austria, immersed themselves in psychoanalysis once again and seemed to have stopped thinking about what was going on 'outside'.

I remember some influential people I came in contact with during my incomplete training in analysis and psychiatry in Vienna. I attended one of Helene Deutsch's seminars; I saw the first insulin comas with Sackel. Potzl was the head of the psychiatry faculty at the university and had taken on Sackel, who had to leave Berlin because he was Jewish. I began my supervisions with Jeanne Lampl de Groot, a very important figure in the International Psychoanalytical Association, but I had only a few interviews with her before I left.

SPANISH CIVIL WAR

Some months after the Spanish Civil War broke out, the British Labour Party organized a team of doctors and nurses but oddly enough they didn't have any surgeons willing to go. They went to the Austrian Social Democrats in search of volunteers. That was when Max, my companion, who was a surgeon, decided to go to Spain and proposed I go with him. I went to the Party and explained the difficulty for me working in Austria now that I had a police record. 'Fascism has got to be fought in Spain,' they said and gave me permission to go. Thanks to my experience with my friend Fritz, the gynaecologist, I was able to go as an anaesthetist.

My friends and acquaintances could not be told of my departure but I had to say goodbye to my family. My father wasn't in Vienna, so I told my mother and my uncle Emil. My mother roundly refused to give her consent in any form. I persisted (in trying to persuade her) because I didn't want to part from her on bad terms.

'Very well!' she said in the end. 'But we aren't going to send you your money every month the way we've been doing up to now.' I laughed, with a certain sadness, because at that moment I realized that my mother and I hadn't understood each other for a long time: I wouldn't need the money in Spain and anyway she would never have been able to send it. 'I always told your brother,' she said to my uncle, 'that this girl should never have been educated. This is what happens when a woman is educated.'

Max went to London to iron out some administrative problems before going to Spain. (Among them was the ridiculous affair of our uniforms, which had to be a perfect fit, according to the committee for aid to Spain; Max was able to solve the problem, as the woman in charge of making them had more or less the same measurements as me.) We met up in Paris. In the days before I left Vienna I'd felt afraid and had doubts. So I called Fritz and we went for a coffee and I told him about my leaving for Spain.

'Fantastic,' he said. 'I really congratulate you.'

'No, don't congratulate me. In fact, I called you to ask you what I should do. I'm scared, very scared. I'm afraid of dying; besides, my mother . . . There's a big chance of dying in a war and my mother wouldn't be able to stand the pain.'

'You shouldn't be afraid,' Fritz assured me after recovering from his surprise at my confession. 'Think about it a bit: you are going to the war in Spain as a doctor; I don't think they will kill you on the first day. You're going to save the lives of x number of comrades and these comrades have mothers. It might be true that it would drive your mother crazy if you were killed, but aren't their mothers worth as much as yours? If they kill you it will be a great pity but with a little luck you will have saved the lives of many comrades. And it will be one sorrowing mother to many others whose sons were saved. The balance will always be positive.'

I thanked him and left feeling relieved. At that time, I could think like Fritz, and distance myself from my personal fate; but later on as a mother in Argentina I lost this ability to put the 'cause', the collective, above the individual. More recently, towards the end of my stay in Buenos Aires, I recovered it slightly. I believe that this way of thinking and feeling – incomprehensible to the majority of people and the reverse of the English saying, 'charity begins at home' – differentiates the true militant from the apolitical person, even from the sympathizer. And Fritz was a true militant. I'll explain with a brief summary of his later history: We met again in Alicante when the end of the Republic was in sight. 'Yes, I'm afraid everything will soon be lost here,' he said to us. 'But it's in China where they really need us doctors. Do you want to come?' 'I'd go,' Max said to me. 'What do you think, shall we go?' 'Let's pass on the war in China,' I replied, half-joking, half-serious, 'there'll be lots of others to collaborate in. I want to have a child and it would be born with slanted eyes there.'

Fritz went. He took part in the Long March until the end, working as both a surgeon and a journalist and writing beautiful poetry. Then he returned to

Vienna. When he was invited to a Party congress in China after Mao's victory, he travelled in the same plane as the most important functionaries of the Comintern. The plane was sabotaged and exploded in full flight and Fritz met his death in the sky over China.

But let's go back to my leaving Austria. Some of the fear stayed with me: in spite of our brief conversation, on the journey through Paris on the way to Spain, I dreamt the whole time that I was crossing the Pyrenees on a mule; back and forth, back and forth.

We landed in Spain without understanding much of what was happening there. Never before, nor ever again, would I see a city so alive, so full of music and enthusiasm, so exciting as Barcelona at that time. Overflowing with posters, slogans and even decorations made out of long narrow strips of paper on the store windows. Although we knew they were put there to protect the glass from enemy air attacks, they seemed to exist simply to beautify the city and heighten its joy. La Rambla was like a party. The militia were seen everywhere, some still virtually children, in uniform and with rather improvised arms. From time to time you could still see women militia, although it had been decided to withdraw women from the army after the atrocities that many of them suffered when Mallorca fell into enemy hands.

The Labour Party had assigned us to a village on the Aragon front and we spent the first few days with a fever, caused by a typhus vaccination, forcing ourselves to learn our first few words of Spanish. (In our ignorance, we were studying Catalan, believing it to be Spanish.) We soon realized that there was no work in that sector: the surgeons were fighting over any wounded that arrived or any peasant that might have appendicitis.

So we went back to Barcelona and presented ourselves to the Sanitat as volunteer doctors. Something very funny happened to us there. We were wearing our top-quality English uniforms and gas masks when we went to the Generalitat and the Sanitat and we didn't know enough Catalan or Spanish to say we wanted to work, we wanted to go to the front to help, Max as a surgeon and me as an anaesthetist. 'Come back tomorrow, come back tomorrow,' they said. And the following day, 'Come back tomorrow, come back tomorrow.' And the next, 'Come back tomorrow . . .' We didn't understand what was going on: we could see the people saying goodbye at the stations, evidently they were going to the front, and we thought there must be an urgent need for doctors. On the fourth day after the same reply, I turned to Max and said in German that I didn't understand what was going on. The fellow who had received us asked us with surprise in French, 'You're not English?' 'No, of course not, we're Austrian.' 'Sorry, we thought you were English and were trying to take over again.' They took us on.

Two days earlier in a very important-looking building on the main square (I think today it's the National Bank of Catalonia) we had seen the headquarters of the Catalan Communist Party. There were large signs in Spanish and Catalan that said, 'Proletarians of the world, unite!' and 'Join the Communist Party!' which we could, of course, understand. As Max was not a member of the Party, I went up on my own and said, in my best Tarzan (my crude Spanish), that I belonged to the Austrian Communist Party and wanted to join the Catalan party.

'Your card, comrade.'

'I don't have one.'

'That's impossible, you must have your card.'

'In Austria, the Communist Party is illegal; I burned my card a year ago.'

'You burned your card?'

'Yes, I burned it.'

'And you say you want to join the Party?'

'Yes!'

'Come back tomorrow.'

I went back twice and something similar always occurred. Finally they accepted us for the front and I didn't go back any more. Months later – by then a member of the International Brigades, behind the lines at the time, in the hospital in Murcia – I met a trade unionist comrade from the Austrian CP, Gartner, whom I knew well. He'd come to talk to the Austrian comrades because we were under the Austrian Communist Party there. (Max, as a sympathizer was included.) After we had greeted each other he said, 'Do you know that I saved you from something very serious? When I contacted the Party in Barcelona they asked me if I knew a woman of such-and-such physical characteristics, a so-called Marie Glas, alias Mimi. When I told them who you were, they were delighted because they had taken you for a spy who was trying to infiltrate them, since you'd been so insistent about joining. They'd been looking for you afterwards and fortunately for you they didn't find you.'

It was an absurd incident which amused me more than anything because, from the political point of view, I don't remember a happier or more relaxed time than when I was in Spain. Clandestine party work, having two lives, not being able to talk to anyone about what is uppermost on your mind, the danger: none of this exists in a civil war. In the Brigades we had our superior; everything was perfectly clear. There were no arguments about the ends we proposed to reach; we were with the Party we wanted to be with and we had complete trust and confidence in it.

As a woman, I felt completely comfortable. I met Dolores Ibarruri – La Pasionaria – when I went as a delegate from my hospital to a congress of anti-fascist women. Her intelligence and her friendliness really impressed me. Women on the Left took part in the decision-making in the Spain of those days. La Pasionaria was the maximum authority in the Spanish Communist Party and Federica Monseni was the same for the anarchists.

As I've already said, when we went to the front, we understood nothing about Spanish politics, nor the language, nor Catalan. In Grañén, on the Aragon front, we were fascinated by the political climate. We lived in a train/hospital. There were various carriages for the patients and sleeping cars for the staff. There wasn't a lot of work. When the alarm signal was given the train started moving and went into a tunnel until the danger passed. We were in territory controlled by the anarchists and we went to the villages and heard the speeches. The people were happy and enthusiastic. It was a beautiful and unreal experience and is so well reconstructed by Hans Magnus Enzensberger in *Anarchy's Brief Summer*. Money didn't exist: everything was acquired with a little slip of paper and it was presumed that no one would ask for more than they needed. There were no hierarchies either; instead there was enormous solidarity and comradeship.

At a certain point things quietened down on the front and we were of little use, so we went back to Barcelona, a Barcelona that had lost a great deal of its joy. I met an Austrian comrade there who, after hearing our story, said we were crazy. 'Didn't you know that they've formed the International Brigades?'

We hadn't been aware of their existence but, once we found out, our roles as revolutionary tourists and spectators ended. The war started seriously from then on. We were assigned to a medical unit led by Walter Fischer, Ernst's brother. Ernst Fischer was already famous. A relatively short time before, after February 1934, he had moved from the Social Democrat Party, where he had been an important ideologue and functionary, to the Communist Party. Rossana Rossanda says of him, 'his character was full of subtleties, of distinguished courtesy, and he had a profoundly critical spirit'. A long time later, when the USSR occupied Czechoslovakia in 1968, he broke with the Party. I knew him before I left for Spain; I once accompanied him to Tyrol to help him establish contact with a small group of peasants; on another occasion I visited him in Prague to hand over some messages.

I mention Ernst because it's hard for me to get to the point, to get to the Jarama front. We were at the front with his brother Walter. As the leader, he had the rank of lieutenant colonel; my husband Max, as surgeon-in-chief, had the same rank; meanwhile I, 'Dr Langer's assistant', as the English had marked my bag and the other things I'd been given, was simply a lieutenant. And I still haven't come to the point.

We left in trucks, amidst great excitement, for the Madrid front. Decades later, I covered the same route by train but in the other direction, from Madrid to Barcelona, in search of the landscape of the past. That first time we passed through Valencia, we were very moved by the enthusiasm with which the people greeted us; the grace of Spanish peasant women, so different from the heavy Austrian country girls; the generosity with which they filled our trucks with oranges. Later, we left the coast and entered a rocky, barren landscape. Hostile? We stayed overnight, then carried on, a small group of foreigners and the Spanish comrades. Much later I learned that we foreigners formally belonged to the foreign legion, which fascinated me in the romantic sense. We finally arrived at our destination, Colmenar, where we were stationed in the village school which had been converted into an improvised hospital.

It was November. I had imagined Spain to be different: hot, with the sky always blue. But it was cold and a drizzle turned the little streets of the village into mud. Until the work began, everything seemed depressing, but the arrival of the first wounded turned our misgiving into alertness and efficiency. We learned to live for the day without thinking about the past or future. I soon stopped being an anaesthetist, as Max and Walter showed the ambulance drivers how to do it, as well as how to give tetanus vaccinations – we were proud of never having a single case of tetanus. I learned how to stitch wounds, to set fractures and to take out the damned shrapnel which complicated everything, especially the open fractures which inevitably ended up in osteomyelitis and frequently meant amputation, since neither sulphates nor antibiotics existed then. But we found out the effects of these deep wounds only months later, when we were transferred to Murcia and Max was put in charge of the orthopaedic section of this behind-the-lines hospital.

As more and more of the seriously wounded arrived, my function was mainly to assist Max with the laparotomies. The disaster caused by a bullet going through the abdomen of a soldier who'd just eaten his rations was usually terrible. We opened him up and Max checked the intestine foot-by-foot with his experienced fingers to detect where the bullet had made the holes through which chick peas and scraps of meat split out on to the operating table. Meanwhile, we didn't have anything to heat the operating room with; the intestines, exposed to the cold air, inflated and grew larger, so that, once the holes had been sewn up, they nearly didn't fit back in when we had to close the person up. It was the damned cold that caused such a high level of mortality and often made us recall the black joke, 'Operation successful, patient dead.' I learned a lot and not only about surgery. However, I found out that my poor Spanish was sufficient for the seriously injured and the dying, since all they asked for was 'water' or 'mother'.

It seemed just like any other morning. Two or three wounded arrived and we attended to them as usual. But later, more and more arrived and suddenly the entrance hall, the ward, the classrooms of our school/hospital and its corridors were full of comrades on stretchers on the ground, bleeding and groaning, and those who already were or seemed to be dead. 'I brought you an Austrian comrade,' a stretcher bearer said to me in German. I leaned forward and recognized Robert, the young man I had left for Max. There he was, emaciated, unshaven, virtually unable to talk. Max crouched down beside him to examine him, 'Fortunately, it's not the abdomen. A bullet went through his thorax. If it didn't touch the mediastinum it's not serious. We'll look after him next. I'm sorry, but you'll have to do this operation with me first, the patient is already anaesthetized and it is his abdomen.' 'But we're not going to leave him like this?' 'No, of course not. Get them to take him to our bed; he'll be much better off there than on this stretcher.'

We went to do the operation. My hands obeyed automatically but my mind was somewhere else. I thought to myself, 'Uncle Paul was shot in the lung during the war and he recovered. It's not serious.' But my anxiety was mounting and I suddenly found myself praying, for the first time in a very long time and for the last time in my life: 'My God, don't let it happen. Don't make him die, he's an only child, the only one his mother has.' Someone opened the door of our improvised operating room. It was the comrade who had brought Robert; he had an odd look on his face and was gesturing to me. 'My God, don't let it happen, you must save him.' 'Go on,' Max told me in a tired voice. 'That's it. I'll close this one up myself.' I went to my bedroom; Robert was buried in our bed with his face turned towards the wall. I called his name and he didn't answer. I pulled his cheek gently with my hand to turn his head towards me. To this day, I can still feel on my hand the light but unyielding resistance with which a dead body opposes all movement.

The wounded continued to arrive, there was no time to cry. We worked like automatons right through the night and all the following day. They came to bomb the village and the hospital the following night and when the alarm was given: 'Everybody on the ground. Protect yourself against the walls.' The only thing I wanted was for a bomb to finish everything off. But this

87

time the Brigades had saved Madrid: Madrid which was both symbol and myth, Madrid, which we sang to in all the languages of the brigades:

Wir im fernen Vaterland geboren,
Nahmen nichts als Hass im Herzen mit
Doch wir haben die Heimat nicht verloren
Unsere Heimat liegt heute vor Madrid.

('We who were born in a faraway country/left with only hate in our hearts/ but we have not lost our fatherland/our fatherland is in Madrid today.')

Madrid, where one lived under bombs and where one travelled by tram to the front. But we hardly knew it. I only spent one day in Madrid. We were shown the telephone building, very tall and modern, the architectural pride of Madrid in the 1930s. All of its windows were broken and its walls pocked with bullet holes. There were also entire blocks which at a glance appeared normal, until upon looking more carefully you realized they were pure facades of houses which concealed the rubble behind.

Three months after the battle of Jarama, we were transferred behind lines. A very good hospital had been set up in the University of Murcia and Max was put in charge of the orthopaedic section. Our colleagues were doctors and nurses from all over. There were two North American surgeons, a father and son, the chief nurse was Dutch, the hospital director, Bulgarian, and so many other nationalities. We learned practically no Spanish because the language of the brigades was French. There were some phrases, however, that we had to learn and the bitterest one was, 'If you don't get rid of this leg, it'll get rid of you.' That's how Max learned to convince the patients who needed amputation because of the accursed osteomyelitis. It was very painful. What's more, you couldn't even offer them a decent prosthesis. That's how the idea came up for a prosthesis workshop. Max had a lot of technical ability; he often compared his profession to that of a good carpenter. He made a plan for a workshop that was accepted. This was at the end of 1937. Since there weren't any of the necessary machines in Republican Spain, a Spain that was shrinking daily, it was proposed that we travel to France to buy them. We were to wait in Paris, where we would be sent the money. That's how we left Spain.

I never realized that we'd been suffering from hunger there. All things considered, the food at the hospital was the best and, as I was pregnant, I'd even had a right to a special diet. But when we boarded the plane which had arrived from Africa and found the remains of the sandwiches that had been served to the previous passengers on our little tables, we eagerly devoured them, to our own surprise.

FAREWELL TO EUROPE

From Paris, the situation in Spain already appeared virtually desperate. In spite of the openly shameful fascist intervention, the French Popular Front and the British government stuck strictly to the non-intervention pact, the equivalent of a blockade of the Republic. At the same time, the clandestine flow of international combatants continued through the Pyrenees. The money for the workshop did not arrive. The comrade who was our contact finally said, 'Why are you waiting here, just hanging around? Why don't you take a few weeks somewhere nice and when the money arrives I'll let you know.'

We took his advice and got the train for Nice. I was halfway through the seventh month and began to feel contractions during the journey. Was it the movement of the train, guilt from being a tourist while others were dying in combat, thinking of Robert's mother who had lost a son, or the fact that if my child was born all right I would have to be separated from her and hand her over to my parents to return to Spain? I suppose that these premature contractions were the result of all these factors. It must have been this very painful experience which led me much later to try to understand it and to dedicate myself to the study of psychosomatic mechanisms in pregnancy, miscarriage and premature birth.

We arrived in Nice, and found a cheap boarding-house to stay in. I fought against the contractions, walking very little and carefully. I stopped smoking and I talked to the child: I asked it not to be hasty, to have a little patience, and I counted the days to go until it would be all right. I became Max's scientific secretary as well. Together we studied clinical histories and the X-rays of cases of oesteomyelitis that we had brought with us to make the most of the time while we were waiting. Max dictated the outline of a work on traumatology and war orthopaedics to me, though in the end it was never written.

I didn't manage to keep the child for the necessary amount of time. One night, the birth started and I had to go into a clinic. A baby girl was born and I knew that she couldn't live, but the most awful, and somehow irrational and unforeseen, thing for me was that she was born alive only to die slowly over three long days. There was no incubator in the clinic and when I begged the doctor to do something for my child, he offered me an emergency baptism. Max went to the maternity hospital to bring me breast milk for the little thing. She was brought to me crying.

In Nice, I went through the worst time of my life. The money didn't arrive, the baby had died, so many comrades as well, and not only Spain but

all of Europe was falling apart. I remember a little verse from the First
World War that went around in my head obsessively:

> Drüben am Wegesrand sitzen zwei Raben,
> Wer wird der Nächste sein, den wir begraben?

('At the edge of the road sit two ravens,/Who will be the next to have to be
buried?')

Finally, when it was clear that we would not be going back to Spain, we
decided to accept my parents' invitation to go to Sudetendeutschland, the
Germanic part of Czechoslovakia, where my parents had the factory and
their lovely house. They welcomed us warmly. 'I'll fix you up a beautiful
flat,' my mother told me, 'with a blue-tiled bathroom.' 'We hope you'll stay
here even though the situation in Austria is getting back to normal and that
Max will work in the factory. Do you know about Schuschnigg's speech after
his meeting with Hitler in Berchtesgaden? He didn't accept the Führer's
orders and there will be a plebiscite next Sunday. The parties are not illegal
any more. You must go to Vienna to vote.' A few days after the plebiscite,
German troops entered Austria and it disappeared as an independent
country for many years.

It was then that we had no doubt about the fate of Europe. We went to
Prague; the Party discharged us from the Brigades and authorized me to
leave Europe. When we learned that President Lázaro Cardenas had opened
Mexico up to all political and racial refugees, I came out of my depression.
'Let's start over again,' I said to Max. But at the Mexican consulate they
weren't yet ready to put into effect Cardenas's generous offer and we didn't
want to wait. We did the right thing. While we were on the boat to Uruguay,
Hitler occupied Sudetendeutschland and my parents and uncles and aunts
left that small city as the Nazi troops were entering from the other side.

Yes, the situation had been clear to us. That's why, when we were leaving
and my uncle said to Max in a reproachful tone, 'You are an adventurer',
Max answered him, 'I think that by staying on, you are much more of an
adventurer than I am.'

When we got off the boat in Uruguay, we received the Mexican visa that
we had asked for from Europe. By then, we didn't have the money to be able
to use it. So we lived in Uruguay and later for many years in Argentina,
which went well for us. We had our children and organized our lives. All of
this, at least from the professional-political point of view, I will talk about
further on. I became a widow in 1965. I went back to politics and at the end
of 1974 I had to emigrate once more and came to Mexico. It was as if I had
finally fulfilled destiny.

PART TWO
Conversations on Psychoanalysis
with Enrique Guinsberg

I believe that only departing from an examination of the articulations between theory and praxis will it be possible to realize the former and conceptualize the latter.

We believe that the theoretical moment and its exercise need an adequate study, but we also believe that if it is not really part of lived experience it remains an abstraction in the minds of individuals.

We also believe that empiricism or practicism is an aberration and a rejection of thought as a real process.

What we want to continue to affirm is that while praxis (not practice) is not about exercise, while we cannot integrate our thought and our behaviour, while we totally dissociate (not instrumentally) the theory of action and emotions, we will not comprehend either psychoanalysis or Marxism.

I think the ultimate articulation between both is our lives, our relations with others and our political commitment.

The rest will be concealment; ways of hiding the fears produced by the exercise of what we really think in the face of the repression of the system, and lastly, the discovery of the limitations imposed from without, but also, especially, from within.

Armando Bauleo, *Cuestionamos*

Marie at Third Latin American Congress, Chile, 1958

EXPERIENCE

Enrique Guinsberg (EG): As I understand it, the political incident which caused you to leave the Wiener Vereinigung in an unfortunate manner and later your work as a doctor during the Spanish Civil War postponed your psychoanalytic training. Why don't we begin with your re-encounter with psychoanalysis?

Marie Langer (ML): I can't answer without first referring to some personal details. While my husband Max and I were boarding the boat which would take us to Uruguay, my parents were leaving Czechoslovakia with the Nazis at their heels. We were finally reunited with them in Montevideo. (My sister Gucki would arrive later.) My mother went back to work, once more thanks to a war, only this time it was from real necessity. One of my father's business partners who was in London owed them a large sum of money but, seeing that my father had gone into exile, didn't pay back any of it. My mother opened up a boarding-house in Montevideo, on the Rambla, where she worked really hard.

Contrary to what Max and I had been assured by the Uruguayan consul in Czechoslovakia (who of course was not Uruguayan), we couldn't get our medical degrees recognized. We had to leave Montevideo shortly after we arrived because Max was offered an opening in a textile factory thanks to his having learnt some of the basics of technical drawing during the three months we had lived in Czechoslovakia. So we went to Puerto Sauce. I was pregnant again and Tommy, my oldest son, was born there. We lived very modestly there for three and a half years. To earn a few pennies I cooked for two of the employees who were friends of ours and also refugees, until Max was fired from the factory over a misunderstanding.

From our arrival in Montevideo we joined the German-Speakers Section of the Committee in Solidarity with the Spanish Republic. (I admit the name is a bit long for an organization, specially since it wasn't a very large one.) Finally, one fine day while Max was in Buenos Aires looking for a job and I was living at my parents' boarding-house, a comrade – Willy Eckerman, a dockworker from Hamburg with all the intellectual training that German

93

workers had at that time – asked me to give a talk on psychoanalysis and Marxism to raise funds for the organization. 'Whatever you want on Marxism,' I said, 'but I don't remember anything about psychoanalysis.' To which he replied, 'Read this book and give the talk.'

The book was *Psychoanalysis and Marxism*, by Osborne. I read it and gave the talk. Of course, I repeated what Osborne says. I explained thesis, antithesis and synthesis . . . I'd have to look at the book again; I haven't read it since then. But I suppose it also says that behind the manifest, Freud, as well as Marx, discovered the latent – Freud on the individual level and Marx on the social level . . .

A short time later, Max wrote for me to join him (in Buenos Aires) with our son; he'd got a good job in a textile factory, where he became manager before his medical degree was approved. In Buenos Aires, I became aware of the existence of a Hungarian called Bela Szekely, who was famous at that time in psychological circles. When I met him, he invited me to his mental health institute, an organization supported by the Jewish community. He showed me what he was doing and asked me if I would like to dedicate myself to psychoanalysis.

While I was in Uruguay, I'd often thought of going to Buenos Aires to get a job as a secretary, because I can type well, or as a language teacher, although I wouldn't have been very good because, while it's true that I speak English and French as well as Spanish and German, my grammar and spelling leave a lot to be desired. In short, I'd have ventured to be a secretary or a teacher without too much difficulty . . . but an analyst! In Montevideo, friends who knew that I had some analytic training had already urged me to work as an analyst because there wasn't anyone who was doing so there at the time. But I never felt inspired, and then later on we went to live in the provinces, where I had still fewer opportunities.

However, Szekely took great pains to make it clear to me that he was the only serious one; really he wasn't that serious. 'If you want to work creatively,' he told me, 'stay with me, but if you want orthodox analysis and to earn money then go to Dr Garma'. I must tell you why I went into 'orthodox analysis'. In Austria, when I was about to join the Communist Party, they asked me if I wouldn't prefer first to join Red Aid, a less radical organization. 'All or nothing,' I said to myself, and joined the Party. Something very similar happened with analysis. I could have had myself analysed by someone from Wilhelm Stekel's school, but I found out that the 'orthodox' analysts were more rigorous and I went to them.

I didn't have any doubts in Buenos Aires either. I went to the orthodox ones; besides, I couldn't take Szekely seriously. I went to see Angel Garma, the founder of the analytical group, who welcomed me warmly. I gave him my particulars, which were minimal, but in Buenos Aires at that time they were more than sufficient: a completed training analysis, a year and a bit of seminars and three supervision sessions was pretty poor, but what was there in Buenos Aires? There was Garma, who had completed his training and was a member of the Berlin Association; there was Celes Cárcamo, a member of the Paris Association; there was Enrique Pichon Riviere and Arnaldo Rascovsky, who were being analysed with Garma; and, finally, there was Ferrari Hardoy, who later went to the United States. Garma and Cárcamo had more than me, academically speaking; Rascovsky and Pichon Riviere, who were in analysis, knew much more than me, but had much less formal training. So they accepted me.

I had to write to Sterba, my training analyst, so that he could confirm what I had said. While awaiting the reply I read all of Freud for the second time (Szekely helped me with this a lot: he lent me it) and the works of Melanie Klein for the first time (also loaned by Szekely). Pichon Riviere's wife (Arminda Aberastury, 'La Negra') was translating Melanie Klein from English at the time. It was a very difficult task; I helped her by checking the translation with the German. In this way, we could both study and discuss it seriously.

Between the six of us (Garma, Cárcamo, Ferrari Hardoy, Pichon Riviere, A. Rascovsky and me), we founded the Argentinian Psychoanalytical Association (APA). We were provisionally recognized as an analytical group by Ernest Jones while awaiting the confirmation that would be granted by the first International Congress when the war ended. We found premises and teachers and candidates, we began the seminars; among the candidates were Arminda Aberastury, Louis Alvarez de Toledo, Heinrich Racker and Louis Rascovsky. Our first task was a collective reading of Freud co-ordinated by Angel Garma.

EG: What happened to your political practice, which up to then had been the focal point of your life?

ML: Yes, political practice had dominated up till then. I'll tell you something else: the first seminars that I gave in Vienna were about Marxism and on China, a subject I was so imbued with that I was once asked if I'd been there. I didn't give up my political practice when I began my activity in the Argentinian Psychoanalytical Association (APA). At the time, I was in the Victory Committee, an organization which included the 'governments' in exile, dedicated to every type of collaboration with the Allies – we were in the midst of the Second World War. Cora Ratto, a young, very intelligent, bourgeois Argentinian woman who was a Communist, had organized this committee at the time, with the participation of foreign anti-Nazi residents such as the exiles or refugees, as they were called, from various countries. My husband and I belonged to the Free Austria section, although formally we were German expatriates; to Argentinians we were Germans from the Ostmark. The Austrian section was a strange mixture of monarchists, aristocrats, Jews and Communists. Max belonged to the executive committee.

On the other hand, there was my link with the Argentinian Communist Party, especially with the German-speaking group. They considered me a 'sympathizer'. However, my negative experience in the Vereinigung and what I had learnt from clandestinity made me decide never to mention this in front of the members of the APA. That's why I never talked about it.

EG: How were you able to maintain this situation of duplicity: the political on one hand and psychoanalysis on the other?

ML: The only person I could talk to about all this at the time was Enrique Pichon Riviere, who had been very involved in solidarity work with Republican Spain. He liked to tell how they'd collected money from among the bus-drivers of the No. 60 line and were the first to send an ambulance to Spain. I simply did not say anything to the others. This was perhaps what kept me from being completely at one with, or, if you want, a little detached from, the Association. There was a part of my life – not the private, because my husband was really integrated into my activities and all my friends were Argentinians from the APA – that I never, or not until much later, meshed with the rest . . . We'll talk about this later on.

EG: It could be said, then, that there's a period, up to the end of the 1960s, when you leave politics?

ML: Yes, I left politics after the war. I was very afraid when Perón came to power, when I heard one of his speeches for the first time; I thought that it was fascism. For me at the time, it was Hitler's style of speaking. My husband and I seriously considered the possibility of leaving. Later we decided that since we were foreigners we could experience fascism from the inside this time. We stayed, but I had children and I didn't have relatives there to confide in; I was very afraid of committing myself to any political activity whatsoever. My husband was afraid as well, for me and for himself: we couldn't be taken prisoner. What would become of the children? Yes, I would say not in 1942, but once the war was over, there was a break: for a couple of decades I effectively substituted for my political militancy an institutional-analytic 'militancy' – in terms of dedication and loyalty – without ever completely breaking the tie with the Left.

EG: This image of Perón was consistent with your proximity to the

Argentinian Communist Party; the Communist Party had in fact a very similar impression, and kept it practically until 1955, the year of the military coup which overthrew the Peronist government.

ML: I never belonged to the Argentinian Communist Party. As far as I'm concerned, I can tell you that I saw him that way only at the beginning. In fact, at one time I was on the point of joining the women's branch of Peronism. I came to have a lot of admiration for Evita. Little by little, I could see – and everyone was saying so – that in the end Perón gave the working class the same social benefits that had existed under Social Democracy in my country before Austro-fascism: retirement pay, social security, the possibility of an education, of housing and of cheap tourism. All of this was to regain what I'd had in Austria and lacked in Uruguay when we were virtually living in a working-class situation. Perón did all this. It's true, it seemed a shame to me that a General should be doing it and from on top. But in the end the important thing was that it was done. So I made up with Perón and, of course, with Evita.

Evita fascinated me, and with the passing of time she has fascinated me still more. At first she seemed to be an ingenuous girl masquerading as First Lady, but at the same time she behaved like a rebel with a cause in the face of the oligarchy, who despised this commoner of illegitimate origin. Her mother, Doña Juana, had been somebody's 'mistress'. It was fascinating to observe how, little by little, *Senõra* Maria Eva Duarte de Perón was transformed into *compañera* Evita. (trans. note: *compañero/a* is widely used in Latin America and can mean, among other things, comrade, friend, companion and colleague) The ridiculous slogan which the Peronists wrote on all the walls, 'Evita Dignifies', began to acquire meaning – and she particularly 'dignified' women. It was important that they gave the vote to women, also that she, a woman, should hold a political position never previously held by a woman in Latin America. The dignity didn't only lie in this but in her dedication and eagerness to solve all problems, especially those of women and children, from the most important to the most tedious.

It was an era when servants no longer feared their masters and enjoyed full social rights. Also, Evita gave the masses confidence, women in particular, since they'd never before been called upon to listen to their rulers in the way they were through her speeches – at times very contradictory, it's true, since she sometimes described herself as a mere sparrow accompanying an eagle and urged women to love the General, but she also said that women's entry into history was the most important achievement of our century.

However, I admit that my admiration for Evita is much more emotional. Enormous anguish swept over the masses when there was no longer any doubt that Eva was going to die. I'd never seen her in real life, but I went to her lying-in-state. I passed myself off as the wife of a deputy from the provinces not to have to queue for two full days in the rain, as did a huge crowd of Argentinians, and managed to get in right away. She lay in state in the palace of the Consejo Deliberante, where the Ministry of Labour and Social Services, in which Perón began his political career, had its offices. I joined the long line that slowly drew closer; I reached her and, like everyone else, kissed the glass that protected her virginal, waxen face and I didn't feel embarrassed. All around, women were fainting, falling on the ground in fits of weeping or hysterical convulsions. I left feeling sad and with a sensation of irreparable loss.

But in my psychoanalytic *gorilla* (reactionary) environment I was pretty alone with my sadness. The majority of my patients felt relief when Evita died, and overflowing joy when the 'liberating revolution' took place. During Peronism they used to complain 'How awful! Nowadays you can't talk in front of the servants.' I thought about it and commented to my husband, 'One, and so what? Two, the servants are right and fortunately they now have something to fall back on; three, if this is what they call repression, they don't know what repression is.' I could never hate Perón for repression, torture or restriction of freedom; in Europe I'd seen situations much worse and for causes much less noble than the defence of the working class.

EG: This is what you said to your husband. What did you say to your patients?

ML: Sometimes I pulled their legs a bit, interpretatively, in the way an orthodox analyst can: 'It's not so bad'; 'Nothing's wrong'; 'There's nothing going on.'

EG: How did you reconcile your opinions and your relationships with the other analysts and the institution? Did contradictions arise in the role of psychoanalysis in its theoretical and practical aspects? Were there no tensions, as there were towards the end of the 1960s?

ML: Let's take it step by step . . . With respect to the psychology of women, there were no discrepancies, at least not at the beginning. The APA was Kleinian and I adopted the positions of Melanie Klein because I could not locate myself or my patients from the phallocentrism of Freud. That's why I began to work on the psychology of women within the Kleinian theoretical framework, which is neither revolutionary nor feminist, but which gives women their own biological and psychological place.

I can illustrate some of my contradictions with an example. In the first edition of my book *Maternidad y sexo* (Maternity and Sexuality) there's a lot about Marxism and the Soviet Union; in the second, published by Paidós, the editor asked me to shorten the book and to take out the Marxist parts. I censored myself. My contact with Sylvia Berman, which became a very close friendship, originates from this time; Sylvia wrote a review of this edition and in it she criticized my lack of attention to class difference. I replied that I was in complete agreement with her criticism and I regretted I'd not had the opportunity to investigate the consequence of these differences because of the environment I worked in.

Another thing against me was that I was an exile. I arrived in Argentina with a precarious background, practically without any economic means. (Max's salary was enough to pay the rent and to leave us with a few pennies over; my first liking for Perón arose when he brought in a law reducing rents.) Until I could get my qualifications recognized, which took place long after our arrival in Buenos Aires, I had to keep quiet on many occasions. I didn't always hold my tongue, however, and we had many battles in which the phantom of clandestinity appeared in my consulting rooms. I became a nationalized Argentinian after the war and, although citizenship could be taken away from a foreigner for political reasons, I felt I was Argentinian. In 1959 I was able to get my medical degree approved in Mendoza and acquired complete legality. I then also obtained the Presidency of the Association, which by right I should have had much earlier; we founders took turns at being President and it was only later that we handed the opportunity over to the younger ones.

It was only then that I was able to adopt a more combative position within the Association. It was sad. At some point I'd like us to talk about the consequences of exile; I was a second-class citizen. I had to keep quiet about my Marxism; I withheld my criticism of a certain hypomanic lifestyle, wasteful and exhibitionist; I kept quiet about the abuses of transference by APA people . . .

EG: Abuses in what sense?

ML: In absolutely every sense: erotic, economic, politically manipulative – power-struggle politics within the APA, of course, not large-scale politics. For the rest, I held my tongue, within limits: on various occasions we were on the point of breaking away, but without any doubt those of us who had to keep quiet were at a disadvantage. We were the 'moralists', the 'super-egos', to those whom we in turn defined as consumerist and totally politically irrelevant. We were often in conflict with this group, which is the APA of today. Our group at present, if I'd remained in Argentina and in institutionality, would be the APDEBA (Buenos Aires Psychoanalytical Association). These are the people I'd feel closest to, although nowadays I wouldn't join their association either; I believe one thinks and acts with greater freedom outside the psychoanalytic association.

The APDEBA is made up of people who split from the APA two years ago (1978). It was recognized as an Argentinian psychoanalytic association, together with the APA, by the New York Congress. If we look at it from the political point of view, the APDEBA brings together the 'scientifics' (in the Argentina of today, you don't survive without this attitude), the serious ones who don't abuse transference. For these abuses alone I'd have broken with the APA, beyond the political reasons which determined the final break.

EG: Why do you believe that one thinks with greater freedom outside the psychoanalytic association?

ML: I attempted to clarify this in a talk I gave in July 1974 in Mexico during a series of lectures organized by Armando Suárez which were later published. I discuss the feelings of unease and repressed social guilt many of us analysts suffer from and the prevailing climate of tension in the analytic societies. Permit me to quote myself; I describe how

> our associations are structured in pyramidical-shaped groups led by each training analyst/teacher. The cohesion of these groups is a result of the use, and often the abuse, of transference and by the counter-transference established in the forcibly regressive situation of the interminable training analysis. The countersigns of each group originate in the leader's conflict, soon shared by all, between his messianic vocation and his idea of mental health. He, as well as his adepts, must be models of happiness. When this is not achieved, the guilt is projected and the opposing group is blamed for all the calamities. I've recently come to understand that these characteristics make us particularly sensitive when faced with feelings of repressed social guilt and turn our societies, comprised largely of analysed people and which should be models of love and collaboration, into models of discord. (in Suárez, 1978)

Upon reading the really fascinating book by François Roustang, *Dire Mastery*, I found that his explanation of our tragedy in part coincides with and complements mine. While I talk about us, the little analytical leaders, he examines Freud's and Lacan's ties to their followers. He shows how Freud, without realizing it, planned the International Association according to the model of the Catholic Church and the Army, which he later masterfully analyses in *Group Psychology and the Analysis of the Ego* (1921). Roustang cites Freud's proposition that this society has an *Oberhaupt* – a leader – who, after the disappearance of the *Führer*, would be his *Ersatz*, his replacement, and would have the authority to 'persuade and dissuade'. Obviously this structure makes us think of Christ, Peter and the Church. Roustang develops this analogy still further when he speaks of the faith existing in the different groups and the efforts to purify and de-ideologize the sacred texts. This bitingly witty analogy has its concrete consequences in practice. Roustang reminds us that the establishment of transference is fundamental in allowing the evolution of the psychoanalytic process, but with the aim of effectively dissolving it through mutual interpretation. And it is precisely this effective dissolution which cannot be achieved in the course of an institutionalized training analysis, since it cannot do away with idealization.

I totally agree with Roustang. But, what's more, I'm grateful to him for having clarified something that has always intrigued me: we in the APA knew each other well and we knew a lot about each other's intimate lives. All the same I was often referred to, half-jokingly, as the Virgin Mary. And really I had nothing in common with her. But if we take into account the analogy between the psychoanalytic institution and the ecclesiastical institution, then it's not so surprising that I, as the first woman among so many apostles and would-be messiahs, should have acquired this title.

Anyway, by leaving the APA I freed myself from being a figure idealized by one group and ostracized as a moralist and super-egoist by the other. I felt a sense of relief and it loosened up my thinking.

But, to go back to the time when I belonged to the APA and didn't have a valid degree, yes, I kept relatively quiet . . . It was another era. Under Perón's government, a law was brought out that declared psychoanalysis or any other form of psychological therapy illegal if not practised by doctors. At the time, Salomón Chichilnisky, a professor in the Neurology Faculty, a Peronist and friend of the dominant group in the Association, offered to give analysts with foreign degrees or without any degree, primarily the case with the wives of important analysts, a psychiatry auxiliary diploma – obviously without their having to take the course or the corresponding exam – thus according them the right to practise. I found out about the offer in an APA assembly when the executive committee proposed that we vote on the decision that in future only doctors or those who had the auxiliary diploma could practise. At that point, to my consternation, I saw how Matilde Rascovsky sitting beside me supported the proposal. I asked her how she could do so, knowing that neither she nor I, nor many others, had this diploma. She replied shamefacedly that she now had it because Chichilnisky had got hold of four or five, but Racker and I had not been included in the list that was handed over to Chichilnisky in order for him to get them the diplomas. Racker was a philosopher and what's more his degree was foreign, as was my medical degree.

What did I do? Racker didn't want to do the course and he was right, but I did it independently and took the psychiatry auxiliary exam. I spent the whole summer studying tests; I was screwed. I remember during the exam one of the psychiatrists, the traditional institutional kind, said, 'But, Doctor, I don't understand. You're a doctor, aren't you? Why are you taking an exam for a diploma more or less the equivalent of a nurse's?' I replied that it had to do with institutional problems . . . in short, I passed the exam and got the diploma.

I put up a fight, but not always, and perhaps feebly. In 1959, I was able to get my medical degree approved thanks to my professional history and fortunately I didn't have to take any medical exams although, I had to take high school exams (which I really enjoyed because I had to write compositions on *Martín Fierro*, on *Facundo*, etc.). From then on, I felt free.

EG: From 1955, when Perón was overthrown in the so-called 'liberating revolution', until your departure from the APA in 1971, were fifteen very convulsive years in the life of Argentina. Let's recap from memory. In 1955, Lonardi was in power; two months later, Aramburu took over; Perón's pact with Frondizi brought him to power in 1958. The military injected a bit of colour into their old divisions, and split into the Azules (Blues) and the Colorados (Reds), checkmating Frondizi who, robbed of all support by his toings and froings, fell from power. The victorious Colorados put Guido in as provisional President, called elections; and, with the abstention of the Peronist majority, Illía took over. Brief years of democratic illusion, marred by the absence of Peronism, but positive in practice. Then later the Onganía *coup d'état* (1966). In 1959, the Cuban Revolution took place, influencing the Argentinian scene. The Córdoba uprising rocked society, and Onganía handed over power to Levingston while Lanusse readied himself to take over. This is, in short, essentially the chronology of the period as I remember it. What happened to you during this period? How did you, finally Argentinian and a qualified professional, act?

ML: Once again I must refer to the personal. My husband, a left-wing sympathizer, although never a member of a Party, had little by little distanced himself from politics. I don't know if I used this as a restraint or a pretext not to get involved in things that could cause me anxiety, but the fact is that my return to politics began exactly with the death of my husband in 1965.

A little before Onganía's military coup in 1966, the Vietnam war was in full swing. My eldest daughter, who was studying at the National College of Buenos Aires, a very politicized school, brought home a classmate who told me they were organizing a big event in the Philosophy and Letters Faculty in memory of the Spanish Civil War. The survivors of the International Brigades who were in Argentina would be taking part. He asked me if I'd come along and speak. I asked him how it had occurred to them to organize such an event precisely at that point, after so many years. He explained the real reason; it was felt that they should organize brigades for Vietnam and that this event, sponsored by various of the left parties, would be the beginning of a mobilization. I asked him to let me think about it, and I really did think about it. I thought that it was a turning point; I thought I would be going back to practically where I'd left off. I thought about it all night. The following day, I accepted.

But a little later a complication arose: the event coincided with the Pan-American Psychoanalytical Congress in Montevideo, which I had to attend as secretary of the APA. How could I be in two places at the same time? Onganía solved the problem: the *coup d'état* and the occupation of the university shattered everything, including the Dean of Architecture's nose, and the event could not take place. But that decision marked the beginning of my return to politics. Very soon afterwards, I joined the Committee in Solidarity with Vietnam and began a period when I finally spoke openly about what I did.

EG: If you had to give a quick professional account of this period from 1942–1965, what would you say?

ML: I'd say that at the time I had to learn about psychoanalysis, since I was a psychoanalyst. I'd say that I felt we were creating something important at the time. I'd also say that in the first instance I devoted myself to analysis partly for economic reasons, for the family; later, after the first year was up and this was taken care of, I felt secure in my choice of profession. By then, I'd read enough psychoanalysis, I'd thought and re-thought about it a lot. I attempted to give a suitable form to my manner of being a psychoanalyst; hence all those institutional battles, for it to be worthwhile to be one . . .

EG: You felt that you were creating something important. Certainly the APA has been important. Now then, I ask myself and I ask you too, how did it happen that out of the five people you've mentioned as the founders of the APA – two of them patients at the time – there came about such a prodigious development in psychoanalysis in Argentina, a development which has no parallel anywhere else in the world?

ML: Before the end of the war, there was a Congress on Psychosomatic Medicine in Brazil. Arnaldo Rascovsky, who was very competent at publicizing and persuading, suggested we all go and take part in the congress. In Rio, we met some of our Brazilian colleagues who would later come to

Buenos Aires to be analysed. This marked the beginning of the importance of the APA in Latin America as a training and teaching institution.

I could say that today I consider them 'enemies', people from the other side; as for Arnaldo Rascovsky and Angel Garma, I also recognize their great dedication and capacity for organization, and for psychoanalysis as they understand it. I don't agree with them on the theoretical level: Garma's propositions seem very exaggerated to me; Rascovsky's theories are very often totally conceited and even reactionary. His theory of the foetal psyche, for example, leads to a ludicrous fatalism: if your future mental health is already decided in the womb, what sense does it make to attempt to change the patient and, in the final instance, man in general?

Regarding the expansion of the Association, Matilde Rascovsky's family, the Wencelblats, brought the first upper-middle-class patients, generally Jewish and willing to pay well; the first upper-middle-class Catholic patients were brought by Cárcamo. And the possibility of extending into Latin America was brought about by Enrique Pichon Riviere, by a complete coincidence. Enrique treated the manager of the Paco Muñoz business, an important men's clothing store, who suffered from severe agoraphobia, couldn't leave his home and had become resigned to running the business by telephone from his bed. Pichon managed to cure him of his symptoms; Don Paco, the owner of the store, thrilled by the curing of his manager, who, what's more, was also his favourite son, offered the money for the Casa Muñoz Scholarship and for the *Revista de Psicoanálisis*, the official organ of the APA. Don Paco Muñoz was our Maecenas (sponsor).

As for the training, first came the Brazilians to be analysed (Walderedo Oliviera, Danilo and Marialcira Perestrello); later the Mexican colleagues arrived (José Luis González, Santiago and Ruth Ramírez, Avelino González, Pete and Estela Remus, Gustavo Quevedo); and afterwards other Latin Americans followed. The majority of the foreigners were Don Paco scholar-ship holders; it was intended to be an honorary scholarship, with the commitment to pay one's debt to analysis at a later date.

The second wave of patients, who went to the beginners, were from the petty bourgeoisie, many of them young Zionists – the state of Israel was coming into being around 1947–48 – looking for an answer in analysis to their doubts about going to Israel; in fact, they were looking for us to convince them that they shouldn't go. And they didn't go. We believed that it would be better for these young people to stay in Argentina and finish their studies. We weren't Zionists and our position must have influenced this outcome. But we'll come back to talking about this 'objectivity'.

EG: Why did they go to psychoanalysis and not to any other kind of therapy?

ML: Simply because it didn't exist. You know that the Communists had their therapy, reflexology, but it wasn't good for much. Pavlov's experiments, primarily carried out with dogs, are very important: they explain the primitive, conditioned reflexes, but his theories cannot be used to help to solve the conflicting complexes of man. That's why today, at least in Argentina, even the members of the Communist Party go into analysis.

Enrique Pichon always told me that the reflexologists could say what they wanted about us and be opposed to us, but when someone from the Communist Party really needed treatment they went to psychoanalysis. In these instances Enrique treated them free of charge, with a certain sense of triumph.

To return to the spread of psychoanalysis in Argentina, another facilitating factor was, without doubt, the importance of the middle class. The European influence in a country where the immigrants are of this origin is enormous, in quantity as much as in lifestyle, specifically in the intellectual arena.

A measure thought up by Garma helped the spread of analysis enormously, due to the fact that it wasn't economically too élitist. In other associations, in order for the candidate to be able to begin to charge for his work he had to treat two cases free for at least two years and, of course, to pay for the supervisions. However, in Buenos Aires, Garma managed to establish – and really implement – that the candidates who were already doctors could give analytical treatment and charge for it from the beginning in their private practices. For the Argentinians – Don Paco's scholarship was only for foreigners – this meant the possibility of paying for their training analysis and being able to support themselves. That's to say, a candidate did not have to belong to a wealthy family to get into the APA. On this point, I sing the praises of my 'adversaries'.

At the end of 1956, the Ibero-American Congress of Medical Psychology took place in the Buenos Aires Faculty of Medicine. Rascovsky and Garma were the organizers. The presence of Garma and Hans Selye (the formulator of the theory of 'stress') brought a large number of students to the sessions. Rascovsky, neither backward nor slow when it came to promoting and publicizing, took advantage of the interest awakened to convince the Medical Students' Centre (CEM) to hold courses in psychoanalysis (to be given by Garma, Arminda Aberastury and Rascovsky himself), and thus obtained the Centre's patronage.

A generation of university activists entered the world of psychoanalysis;

therapy groups were organized along with the courses and on more than one occasion the students were to see their militancy endangered under interpretations about masochism. Many would go into psychoanalytic private practice, frequently more as a result of excessive sublimation than true vocation.

In 1957, a degree course in psychology was created at the University of Buenos Aires. Prestigious APA analysts were called upon and carried out good teaching work, always finding it convenient, however, to make it clear that the practice of psychoanalysis belonged exclusively to the APA. The psychoanalysis boom in Buenos Aires was a fact, although, even when an attempt is made to make an ideology out of psychoanalysis, many people will retain their social preoccupations or return to them. Only a community practice will be sufficiently strong to rescue psychoanalysis from its cyst-like position in the system.

EG: At the time, what were the most important developments in psychoanalysis in Argentina and which did you participate in?

ML: The research into psychosomatic problems proposed by Garma and Rascovsky was very important. My introduction to the theme, which I would later develop in *Maternidad y sexo* (Maternity and Sexuality), began when Arnaldo sent me a close relative of his saying she was fine except that she was sterile and she couldn't pay me much. I asked him what he intended me to do with her, since I'm not a gynaecologist; he replied that her illness was psychogenic. I took her on and within nine months she was pregnant.

The early research in psychosomatic medicine is characteristic of the APA; the Kleinians became concerned with these problems much later; the Lacanians are still not concerned with them.

What Enrique Pichon Riviere was trying to do with his social psychology is much more difficult to define; what's more, given Enrique's ambivalence towards the APA, and its towards him, he always worked outside the institution. We owe the understanding of psychosis to Enrique. In the early years, he gave classes for brief periods. I remember in Las Mercedes Hospice the classroom was at the end of the morgue and one had to hold one's nose to get to it; beyond the classroom were the bathrooms, where we always thought a 'nut' would get in and turn on the shower. His classes were wonderful; I've already said that Heinz Hartmann, head of the school of psychiatry in Vienna, never explained psychosis as well as Enrique did. Later, for a short time Enrique was head of the adolescents' ward in a hospital; he developed operative groups for the first time and transformed the interned patients into nurses; he began with group therapy, etc.

I'd say that one of the greatest contributions to this period is Pichon

Riviere's. Enrique offers us an analytic criterion for psychosis, even though it has been very eclectic: at the beginning, it included an enthusiasm for electric shock, later for psycho-pharmaceuticals . . .

EG: Does your interest in groups stem from this period?

ML: No, from later on. Enrique had begun with these groups of adolescents in the hospitals. When Emilio Rodrigué came back from England he brought his experiences with groups along the lines of Melanie Klein, Bion and Ezriel. At the beginning, Emilio was with the APA, but later he had a problem which coincided with a wave of bad feeling between different subgroups. At that time (1955), I felt very confined in the Association, and was looking for new methods and a more 'social' application of psychoanalysis; that's why I asked Emilio if he'd let me be his observer to learn how to work with groups. Other analysts had already experimented with groups before: Resnick, Usandivaras and Morgan; along with them we founded the Association of Group Psychology and Psychotherapy precisely at the time the Mexican colleagues were in Buenos Aires doing their training.

Predictably, we had many difficulties with the APA. For the first time the situation arose in which I was the only training analyst involved in an enterprise with another generation approximately twelve years younger than I was. We had to back down somewhat in front of the APA and accept some of their members as honoraries and founders of the group association, even though they didn't have the slightest idea of what it was about. We continued with our objectives and our group psychotherapy courses in which the Mexican colleagues took part.

A lot of things have happened since then. I've thought, talked and written a lot about these events and similar ones. Rather than answer you in the chaotic form of spontaneous dialogue, I'd like to refer you to the text that appeared in *Razón, locura y sociedad* (Reason, Madness and Society).

While a psychoanalytical association is small and struggles for its survival, the fight is directed outwards, against the non-analysed world which puts up resistance to analytical knowledge; but, in the measure in which a group of this kind is recognized, and the APA was very quickly recognized and grew very rapidly, the struggle turns inward on itself and consequently the tension increases. That's why Angel Garma proposed, as a rescue action in 1957, to dedicate a symposium to the thorny matter of the relations between analysts, a subject which was taken to the Latin American Psychoanalysis Congress held in Chile the same year.

The symposium was an attempt to re-establish the lost unity in our association; of course, it failed because the exclusively analytical resources that were employed in the discussion, and the attempt to understand the problem solely at a libidinal level, were not enough to clarify and define the institutional differences and complications. The lack of unity finally led to the split, in which the ideological was finally made explicit: in 1971 large groups of psychoanalysts, Plataforma and Documento, parted company with the APA. (in Suárez, 1978)

EG: I want to make a comment, slightly off the topic and in jest, on the work which you presented in this symposium in 1957 on relationships among analysts. I read it recently and I think that this dissociation which is very characteristic of you appears in it. On the one hand, you indicate a trifle ironically how people attempt to transform psychoanalysis as a scientific theory into a world view and you also note the consequences of hybrid therapies (what's more frightful). On the other hand, however, you put forward positions very difficult to understand for those who are familiar with your thinking today. For example, you speak of 'sharing a common ideology, emerging out of psychoanalytic theory'; you also say that the function of analysts is to achieve 'in the first instance their patients' happiness and ultimately that of the world'.

ML: Did you take this seriously? It's totally ironic, the last part, I mean. In general I think you are right. As a result of our conversations, I also recently re-read this paper and was left completely puzzled. Thanks to its clever title, 'Ideología y idealización' ('Ideology and idealization'), I had imagined something better. What's important here, and I think in the reading of the whole of this number of the *Revista* dedicated to the symposium, seems to be that it can help us realize the alienated world one lives in when one belongs to a psychoanalytic association (Langer, 1959).

Now then, what do I mean in the paper when I refer to the ideology shared by psychoanalysts? We share, I believe, the capacity for self-analysis and something like an internal demand not to lie to ourselves, as far as possible. We can be very cynical, but the majority of us lie to ourselves very little. This, of course, does not presuppose a conception of the world. And, of course, today in no way would I contend that what is shared is enough to create an ideology. In fact, our split took place not because of what we shared but precisely because of what we didn't share, that's to say, for ideological and political reasons, and I'm now referring to a 'true' ideology.

The ideological differences had always existed, only they were pretty much denied. But, denied or not, they formed the basis for the formation of the different subgroups: those of us who at a certain point left (the Association), because we knew we could act beyond the politicking of the APA with genuine freedom, coincided in our uneasiness and our troubled social consciences. It's true, none the less, that some of those we thought were with us for sure stayed on in the Association; I'm thinking of Enrique Pichon Riviere and José Bleger. On the evening all of us in the Plataforma group signed our resignations from the APA and the International Psychoanalytical Association, we waited for them with cider to toast the historic event. We waited until half-past two in the morning. And when we finally had the toast, without accepting that they were not going to resign with us, it was a very sad toast. We should have predicted their absence and not have reproached Pichon Riviere, who for a long time had only showed up in the APA like an apparition maybe once every two years. Enrique was too involved in his own thing, in a very creative way. He was too much of an individualist and also too proud and physically exhausted to be involved himself in Plataforma.

EG: And José Bleger? He was the Marxist theorist of the Association. Why didn't he leave with you?

ML: José Bleger was a very special person. He was called the 'Red Rabbi', and was the grandson of two rabbis, on both sides of his family. He was very badly treated by the Communist Party for his attempts to link Marxism and psychoanalysis at a time when the Communists loathed psychoanalysis. With the years he became a Zionist. He loathed Stalin and Hitler and saw the Peronists as their possible followers. There weren't many left-wing Peronists in Plataforma, but enough for him not to join. What's more, he held that we were going to lose our psychoanalysis by abandoning the institution. The analytic instrument could only be protected within it.

EG: The break with the APA took place at a time of great social upheaval: the uprisings in Córdoba and Rosario, the appearance of guerrilla movements, the spread of a militant and class-conscious trade unionism . . . I wonder if all these factors didn't contribute to awakening a combativity, negated but not eliminated.

ML: You're right, of course, but before talking about this I'd like to mention something that to me seems to be fundamental. Among those who left the APA, there were only five teaching analysts, of whom I was the oldest; when we founded the institution I was the youngest. Certainly, counter-transference factors influenced my departure: as parents learn from their children, we also learn from our analysands. Long before the split, a whole generation of young people from psychiatry, who had previously been very confrontational towards us and even towards Marxism, had already joined the APA. The Communists had abandoned reflexology in disillusionment. Up till then, the Communist Party and other left groups prohibited their militants from going into psychoanalytic therapy. However, there came a time when many young people went into training analysis, as much from the hospital practice area (the majority specifically from the psychopathology unit at the Lanus Hospital run by Mauricio Goldenberg) as from left-wing groups. This generation of 'children' taught us five training analysts a lot. Personally, they helped me to put an end to my dis-association and to bring my political convictions and psychoanalytic focus together in my practice.

EG: And the social causes of the split?

ML: Speaking as a Marxist, we'd never have said that the entry of all these young people into the field of psychoanalysis and the APA happened in and of itself. These new candidates already had enough political consciousness not to be afraid that psychoanalysis might change them and alter their convictions. These political beliefs already existed in the social environment in Argentina and many other parts of the world at the time. Here I'd prefer to quote myself once again, only because I believe that the quote is more coherent than my on-the-spot improvisation. My article in the first *Cuestionamos* says,

> How and when did change occur? I don't know. It was anticipated in isolated publications, in timid discussions inside and outside the institution. But the political activity of each individual developed irregularly and in secret. It was a long process which evolved latently in many places and in many analysts, nurtured by the scale of violence and inequality in the world, aided by the thaw in the Soviet Union and stimulated by the appearance of a new Left. We owe a lot to the North American intellectuals who found a new strategy for attacking the system and its war. We're indebted to May of 1968 in Paris. The key date for change for us Argentinians is also the year 1968, but in Rosario, Córdoba and Buenos Aires. The Institute of Psychoanalysis supported the general strike at the time and declared itself against the violent repression of the workers and students – Jorge Mom, as president of the Association, made our protest public. From then on, a significant number of analysts took up the social question openly, in a new way. Many of us had already arrived at the conclusion that psychoanalysis, Marxism and revolution were not exclusive and we lost our phobia of the world outside our institution. (Langer, 1971)

You, Enrique, as someone who's never belonged to a psychoanalytic association, don't know that it really is a question of a phobia. Following Freud's concept of the resistance that psychoanalysis provokes in people who have not been analysed, psychoanalysts always move in a throng: they spend the holidays together, they amuse themselves together, they also fight amongst themselves and are opposed to interdisciplinary work, since nobody would understand our language. They often asked me how my marriage could have lasted, since Max had never been analysed. They jokingly nominated him 'head of the resistance'.

But we're in another epoch. Yes, we began to overcome our ideological agoraphobia.

EG: The story of the rupture with the APA is well known. Various publications refer to it and analyse it; it can be read about in the two volumes of *Cuestionamos* (Langer, 1971, 1973) and in your contributions to *Razón, locura y sociedad* (Suárez, 1978). However, for me there are at least two situations that up to now I know nothing about. Why did two groups with similar positions, Plataforma and Documento, come out of the split? And why, a short time after leaving the APA, did both dissolve?

ML: I'd have to tell you a little of the history . . . For obvious reasons, I know Plataforma better than Documento; however, I can say that, in spite of the 'internationality' of Plataforma, the two movements carried the same weight and had the same importance in Argentina. Everything began – everything for Plataforma, I mean – during the World Congress of the International Psychoanalytical Association, which took place in Rome in 1969 and where I arrived late because I came from Moscow and East Berlin with my youngest daughter. The Congress was charged with all the climate of 1968; for us, the Argentinians, it wasn't only what we knew about 1968 and the world; we brought with us the Córdoba uprising along with our confusion over the assassination of Vandor, a trade union leader who was willing to make a deal with the military, which had taken place just a month beforehand, in open defiance of the military government.

One of the themes in the Congress raised all our expectations. The workshop on youth violence, led by Mitscherlich, a German psychoanalyst who had stayed on in Germany during Nazism, refusing to collaborate, attempted to comprehend youth protest. The workshop, and the Congress itself for that matter, was a disaster; to try once again to explain the extremely complex social, economic and political reality of 1968 with the sole means of psychoanalysis was totally disappointing. Once again, the threadbare rhetoric of an 'Oedipal generation gap' served only to irritate many of the participants.

Plataforma, in fact, appeared as a graphic symbol. In the lobby of the Rome Hilton there were enormous blackboards and banners announcing the Congress. Suddenly among them appeared a banner in which the last 's' in psychoanalysis was represented by '$', a normal 's' with two lines drawn through it. And below the banner a blackboard announced the place, themes and timetable of the Para-congress, cordially inviting all those taking part in the Congress. And if the official Congress took place in the Cavalieri Hilton, the most expensive and luxurious hotel in Rome, the Para-congress was to take place in a working-class beer parlour nearby. The initiative for the Para-congress came from a group of young candidates who belonged to the Viennese, Swiss and Italian societies, but they also had already been in contact with Armando Bauleo and Hernán Kesselmann from Argentina. It was led by Berthold Rothschild, a very intelligent young man, who translated with impressive ease from one language to another.

The Para-congress aroused a lot of curiosity, particularly among the North Americans, but also among the Argentinians. Everybody came and went between the two very disparate congresses. What's more, it was a pleasure to watch the organizers who – in contrast to the 'officials', correctly dressed older people – were young, attractive people in hippie clothing. They were carrying on the climate of 1968 in Paris.

There were two subjects to discuss in the Para-congress in two different rooms: the training of a psychoanalyst and the ideologization of psychoanalysis. Towards the end, an international committee was formed that drew up a series of complaints to place before the International Association, which, for its part, continued with its deliberations in the Hilton. These complaints referred to the problems of psychoanalytic training, its totally excessive cost, the training texts and their ideological content, the prerequisites for enrolment, etc. They formed a virtual platform, hence the name. It was then agreed to establish Plataforma groups in the different countries; they were established in Switzerland, Italy, Austria and Argentina. That's how Plataforma was founded, with the hope of altering the history of psychoanalysis, its ideology and its goals.

EG: Plataforma Internacional was then, at least at the beginning, a 'challenge' to the International Psychoanalytical Association. What did the 'challengers' achieve in the face of the institution?

ML: You know the case of Argentina well: faced with the APA we managed to get out, which is a lot in itself. In Zurich nearly everything was achieved. Plataforma took over the running of the Institute from the Association, in other words all the problems of training and courses. The authorities replied in a typically Swiss fashion: 'You're completely right. It's time that you took all this thankless work off our hands and took charge of your own training. From now on, the Institute is in your hands.' It was wise. But also possible because among the 'oldies', who obviously weren't, there were several (subsequently they became very close friends of mine) who sympathized with Plataforma. Unfortunately, the running of the Institute by Plataforma did not last very long. The original group fell apart. All the same, the Institute was run by a committee of candidates for many years until the International Psychoanalytical Association pressured the Zurich Society into taking over again. In rebellion the Institute then moved to 'Tellstrasse' and at present provides training for an ever-increasing number of pupils; it doesn't suffer from the vices of traditional institutions, as there is freedom of access, there are no sacred monsters, etc. In other words, the experience was worth it.

EG: I knew about the Para-congress, but not about Zurich. Obviously it's also worthwhile to mention this experience, but let's go back to Plataforma in Argentina.

ML: Armando Bauleo and Hernán Kesselmann, as representatives of Plataforma Internacional, called for an APA assembly. It was all very disconcerting. We'd never before talked about such strange things – like internationalism, revolution, a proposal for a congress in Havana, etc. – in our wonderful *petit hôtel*, prettier than the Hauser Palais of my childhood. Yes, we all ended up confused; nothing was clarified. But, from then on, Plataforma rapidly gained followers within the APA, although the process towards the definite break would last for more than two years; in other words, it included the next congress, my last congress, held in Vienna and dedicated specifically to the history of psychoanalysis. And while the bad feeling increased in APA between those who would later belong to Documento or to Plataforma, our membership and 'militancy' in the Argentinian Federation of Psychiatrists (FAP) grew.

EG: And the break?

ML: I realize now that we began talking about the split with the APA leaving aside the two years that we needed, with the help of the FAP, to overcome our phobia of the 'outside'. So first I'll tell you what happened with the FAP.

EG: Yes, it'd be interesting to know how the link between a psychoanalytic association and another of psychiatrists came about, taking into account that the majority of the latter were from the old school, anti-analytic and very attached to their hospitals.

ML: The Argentinian Federation of Psychiatrists was a professional organization, very dormant, and traditional in its professional methods even halfway through the 1960s; its proximity to the Communists didn't help it much to wake up. The history of the new FAP, which I knew, began around 1964 when Mauricio Goldenberg, chief psychiatrist in the psychopathology unit at the Lanus, was, quite rightly, seeking the Chair of the Psychiatry School. Mauricio had a very good relationship with the APA and, in fact, helped his psychiatry students to join the association and become psychoanalysts or take psychoanalytic training. Around this time, one of these students came to the executive committee of the APA to ask us if a large number of the members of the APA would join the Argentinian Federation of Psychiatrists in order to support Mauricio's candidacy; we joined the FAP *en masse*. Mauricio Goldenberg didn't get the Chair because Onganía's military coup took place at that point and the university was closed down. But we continued to belong to the FAP, paying the minimum and not taking part in anything.

In 1969, when Emilio Rodrigué had finished his term as president of the APA, a Communist psychiatrist went to him to propose that he take over the Presidency of the Federation in the capital region, in other words, Buenos Aires. It was an attempt to rejuvenate and revitalize the FAP with Emilio's creativity and charisma. The proposal amused him, but he was doubtful about accepting it: he'd never had anything to do with the FAP, he was a psychoanalyst and he was convinced that nobody would vote for him. But it turned out that in the assembly the seventeen members present, already worked on by the CP, voted unanimously for him. That's how Emilio Rodrigué came to be President of FAP Capital and with a sporting spirit started right away to get things moving.

When I found out about it, I reproached Emilio for not having invited me to participate in the FAP; with extraordinary foresight – Emilio generally didn't have much sense of reality, but in this case he predicted the virtually unpredictable – he told me he hadn't wanted to expose me to a dangerous situation. I didn't see any danger whatsoever, but rather a worthwhile project and joined the executive committee, at first simply as a collaborator. We were all together, future members of Plataforma and Documento with Communist psychiatrists and others belonging to small left-wing groups and psychoanalysts 'for freedom'. Emilio, in his first presidency, was really great. And I re-encountered politics, the solidarity of the party of my youth, the companionship of the beginnings of the APA and the desire to do things with others, with shared goals and without personal ambition. Of course, this climate didn't last very long. Viewed from the present, we were naive, fascinated by a children's game. But the fact that we, who for many years had been virtually armchair intellectuals, could do something, could achieve something with such and such a congress or with such and such a declaration filled us with enthusiasm. And also that young psychiatrists began to join the FAP in large numbers. Our meetings were no longer of seventeen people, they were full.

EG: What happened afterwards?

ML: I want to mention briefly two events that took place in the two years between the Rome Congress and the split: the trip to the USSR and the Vienna Congress. The latter was announced amidst great tension. The candidates were going to participate for the first time as a result of the Rome Congress. They wrote a paper, Plataforma-style, criticizing the authoritarianism of the training. They chose a delegate who was rejected by the APA. I had not intended to participate in this Congress, but when I discovered that they were specifically asking for papers on the history of psychoanalysis (because this was the first time, since the Nazi invasion, that Anna Freud had agreed to return to Vienna and hold the Congress there) I decided to go. Now that I was no longer afraid of speaking about my political past or my convictions, and saw how the APA was apparently giving in to the demands of the young people – while in fact they were being manipulative and becoming more and more politically hardened – I was going to go to present 'Psicoanálisis y/o revolución' ('Psychoanalysis and/or revolution'), which appears in *Cuestionamos* and tells about my experience with the Wiener Vereinigung in 1936. It warns against the political blindness of the International Psychoanalytical Association and denounces its ideology. The paper was accepted and I attended the Congress . . .

But beforehand, I went to Moscow and Leningrad once again. I had gone as a tourist two years before, but this time the situation was different. The Communist Party *compañeros* from the FAP had invited a few analysts on the trip in order for us to become acquainted with the Soviet mental health system.

This was the manifest reason; the latent was the hope of getting us to join the Party. It didn't come to fruition, but in any case it wasn't such a ridiculous expectation as that of some of our people: to be able to convince Soviet psychiatrists that psychoanalysis could be Marxist and revolutionary. The result was a dialogue among the deaf, fortunately interrupted by some valuable experiences: we visited the really splendid child-care centres in Moscow, its psychiatric hospital with an excellent social therapy unit. But not even our interpreter understood correctly what we meant when we asked about psychotherapy – less so in Leningrad, in the Bekhterev Institute, where they didn't work very differently from us in our health centres. We attended a lovely class given by the great Luria and another by the great Leontiev – brilliant, old, courteous professors whom we could speak to in German. We met and had a discussion with old Bassin, who tried, amid many misunderstandings, to introduce the notion of the unconscious into Soviet psychology. I could have had his book (*The Problem of the Unconscious*) translated and published in Spanish and personally written the prologue. However, when a totally erroneous critique of psychoanalysis by him and his team appeared in a French magazine under the title 'Ce que nous pensons de la psychanalyse' ('What we think about psychoanalysis'), Armando Bauleo and I angrily replied in an article: 'Quel che pensiamo di quel che voi pensate della psicoanálisi' ('What we think about what you think about psychoanalysis'). This is like the Tower of Babel; I don't know why our reply appeared in an Italian magazine. On our visit we also initiated friendships with Spanish-speaking students from the picturesque and anarchic Lumumba University, where students from all races, backgrounds and colours are educated. They explained to us that, in spite of the erotic sterility of their films, the Russians were in no way puritans, although in the opinion of the young women the Latins were much better lovers.

The trip was interesting but without any doubt we 'revolutionary psychoanalysts' were strange creatures to the Russians. Our interpreter expressed it best when, unable once more to impose a modicum of discipline on our bus, she screamed at us in annoyance, 'You say you're Marxists, but I'm telling you you're ANARCHISTS!' She said it with a mixture of humour and disdain. Then Bulgaria: Sofia, with its lively, light-hearted socialism, psychiatric hospitals and child-care centres once more, Dimitrov's tomb and, finally, the countryside with extensive fields of sunflowers stretching to the horizon, the white beaches of the Black Sea. And then I arrived in Vienna, in *my* Vienna, to read *my* paper at the International Psychoanalytical Congress.

This time we were not in a luxury hotel. More than that: we were in the imperial castle, in the Hofburg.

EG: Is this the same Congress that Erica Jong describes in *Fear of Flying*?

ML: Yes, and she does it very well. But, of course, I, like the other 'rebels', was involved in something else.

EG: In something markedly ideological.

ML: I was involved in the FAP, in Plataforma, which was coming into being in Buenos Aires; in the traditional family versus the splendid child-care centres of the Soviet Union; in the APA. Well, I'd say – today I realize it – I was also involved in the Congress.

I must have known it would be my last. And it was nice that it took place in Vienna, that it was precisely there that I should present a paper affirming the right of the analyst to also concern oneself with the social. Because it was precisely there that they had attempted to throw me out of the profession, and I had gone on later without them, seriously and successfully, in another country.

I'll tell you: I was sitting in the Café Rathaus, virtually on the Ring, near Hofburg, drinking a *cuba libre* (trans. note: rum and Coca-Cola) and remembering the many congresses I'd attended. The first, Paris 1957, where I met Melanie Klein and where her group welcomed me as one of them. Edinburgh, 1961: the previous Congress had rejected the request of the Uruguayan psychoanalysts to be admitted as a study group recognized by the IPA, the step previous to becoming an Association. They were going to do so once again. Something had to be done, but what? And me, hardly anyone there knew me since I was a Latin American, in other words, a 'native' with feathers in my hair, as we would say in Argentina. I asked if I could go into where the sacred monsters, the IPA executive, were in counsel. After a prudent lapse, I was allowed to enter. And I addressed them directly, not in English but in German. 'Miss Anna Freud,' I said, 'of course you don't remember me, but many years ago you interviewed me before I entered the Vereinigung. You, Dr Lampl de Groot, naturally will also have forgotten me, but you taught me my first clinical steps; with you I supervised my first patient. The Nazis, the war, took me to Argentina but I am Viennese.' (I'm one of you, you can trust in me, was the implicit message.) And then I spoke to them about the Uruguayan group, which was good and serious; what's more, this was completely true. That's how I got them admitted. And I felt Latin American and capable of making them acknowledge us and set aside their prejudices.

From that point on, it was easy for me to move around in the congresses. Yes, I was also involved in the politicking to get important posts in the upper echelons of the IPA for the APA and Latin America. But, truthfully, I don't believe I had personal ambitions in the IPA. It was during one of the Scandinavian congresses – the lovely trips that the congress made possible, always in Europe in mid-summer so that the Americans could travel during their holidays, writing off their summer holiday expenses against their taxes, since they were academic trips – maybe in Stockholm or Copenhagen, that an Argentinian friend, an important member of the APA and the IPA, came to my hotel room all excited: 'If you want, you can be elected Vice-President of the IPA. Isn't that wonderful? The post that Melanie Klein never got.' I said to him: 'What would I want it for? If I've eaten enough I'm not going to take the cake somebody else wants.' His wife, who was present in the conversation, said to me, 'You're wise.'

There in the café, I also thought about my friends in the IPA. My analyst, Richard Sterba, who had become a friend after we met again at the Paris Congress. No, I wasn't going to lose him, although he would disagree with my paper. The Kleinians? Yes, I would lose them, because for them the spreading and convincing of the truth of Kleinian theory *was* militancy, and you couldn't be a militant on two fronts at the same time.

I was in the middle of all this when an older, pleasant gentleman approached me and struck up a conversation, obviously with the intention of picking me up. I didn't take it seriously; throughout my long life I've never accepted a pick-up, it must be a prejudice from the turn of the century. But I went on with the conversation, thinking, 'How nice, in Vienna I'm still fanciable in spite of my sixty-one years.' Suddenly, I heard giggles from the table beside me. Sitting there, inseparable at the time, were my friends and the representatives of Plataforma, Armando Bauleo and Hernán Kesselmann, both ex-analysands of mine. No, I thought, no childish scenes. It's bad for the kids, even when they should already be grown-up. I said goodbye to my gentleman and left with them for the Congress.

I read my paper in front of a large, expectant audience. As always on these occasions, I was slightly detached – this time, with reason, because if I raised my eyes from my papers and looked up, I encountered the fat Empress Marie Theresa of Hapsburg (and Lorena, I think), surrounded by little angels as if it were the Ascension of the Virgin. Yes, it was disconcerting to talk about psychoanalysis in the Hofburg, and even more so about Marxism and revolution.

I finished reading. At first there was silence. Then a criticism, not at all aggressive, sad rather, from my Kleinian friend Hanna Segal. Friend? We never saw each other again. Then, a supportive intervention from a thin, dark analyst with an intelligent face. Yes, I lost friends, but not all of them, and I gained others; Donald Meltzer invited me to go for a coffee afterwards to criticize the Association and show me his support. The analyst with the intelligent face was Paul Parin, from Zurich, the analyst of Berthold Rothschild and other founders of Plataforma; he and his wife Goldie became true friends. I learnt that in a split you don't only lose, you also gain.

EG: And Plataforma? Was there a parallel Congress?

ML: They met in Vienna on the premises of a Protestant church for the second and last time. Paris 1968 was over.

EG: Would you say that your paper, written with so much enthusiasm, didn't have many repercussions?

ML: It did, but not during the Congress. As the return of Anna Freud and psychoanalysis was a true historical event, there were journalists at all of the meetings. There were various papers presented with a social focus, among them one by Mitscherlich and another by my old rival from the APA, Arnaldo Rascovsky. In his paper, he upheld his theory of filicide, which scandalized the journalists. They referred to Mitscherlich to confirm that psychoanalysts did not seriously believe that wars were caused by the filicidal tendencies of generals. ('Don't you see,' Arnaldo used to say, 'the generals are all old men and they give orders to kill the youth on both sides.') And they quoted my paper as an example that even an analyst could view the world in a more realistic way. I had press and radio interviews on my article, and fortunately *Kursbuch*, the famous radical magazine, published it in German, since the *International Journal*, which automatically published all the papers presented at the International Congress, sent me a polite letter sincerely regretting that for lack of space . . . But this incident made me think – above all because the theoretical link between Marxism and psycho-analysis was not very strong, but did interest many colleagues – that we needed a space for publication. That's how *Cuestionamos* came about and two years later, *Cuestionamos* 2, and I suppose that we would have continued with this publication if it had not been for the majority of us being scattered throughout the world.

EG: To sum up, your departure from the IPA and international congresses was sad, victorious or . . . ?

ML: It was gay. Vienna treated us very well. The analysts' banquet and the ball took place in the town hall, where so many years before I'd taken part in a political rally for the first time. There were many speeches in honour of Freud, of Anna, and all of us. To make amends to Freud the Austrian, the orchestra played the national anthem and the Strauss waltzes; and to make amends to Freud the Jew, the Jewish wedding dance (the *scher*) was played and danced. I had never heard it before. It is a kind of lively ronda, which I danced with a Latin American colleague and with Donald Meltzer and his new wife. That's how the Congress ended for me.

EG: We are now in August 1971. And the split is close at hand. And the question of how Documento is born and what distinguishes it from Plataforma.

ML: The origins of Documento are very similar to those of Plataforma, but it was a strictly APA movement, in other words, Argentinian. In fact, the name also corresponds to a series of demands put to the APA by a group of analysts, united around a document. Therein they requested the vote for all associates, the right for all diploma holders to become teachers automatic-ally, etc. We (Documento and Plataforma) had many demands in common and there were people who oscillated from one group to another, such as in joint meetings or meetings with delegates from another group. Now, why were we not all together in one group? I think that Documento brought together all those I used to refer to jokingly as 'the young officers' corps of the APA'. The majority were associate members, in other words without a vote, intelligent people who had a good career ahead of them. The majority had political experience, since they came from student politics and had belonged, very actively, to the CEM, the Medical Students' Centre. Many of them expected to be able to change the APA from within. Meanwhile Plataforma, very much at a disadvantage in terms of the hierarchical level of its members – perhaps the most pushy and ambitious were candidates in their final course or recently qualified analysts – aimed for a split from the beginning and to be able to offer alternative training outside the APA.

Later on it was demonstrated, through the internal political struggles in the Argentinian Federation of Psychiatrists, that in effect those from Documento had much more practical experience in the manipulating of assemblies, contact with different left-wing party groups, etc. From them I learnt the magic words 'point of order', with which you could interrupt any annoying discussion, impede any voting that appeared inopportune, etc. But, I admit that very soon the use of the famous 'point of order' and other tricks became common knowledge.

Plataforma had a longer history. In the two years between the two congresses it had been very active in the FAP and was in theory, or in rhetoric, more radical. But I think that the objection to forming one group with Documento didn't end there; Plataforma didn't want to share the glory of the split from the APA with anyone. We were going to change the history of psychoanalysis. For the first time a split was not occurring as a result of personal differences and ambition – disguised as scientific differences – but for political reasons, not due to politicking, but for real political issues and the desire to link psychoanalysis to the outside world. We felt ourselves to be the vanguard and relegated those in Documento to the role of followers. Contributing to this was the fact that, when we left the Association, Documento, virtually devoid of any members with the right to vote, could no longer continue with the project of changing the APA from within and also split off, although a few days later. We in Plataforma had maintained our right of seniority in the psychoanalytic revolution.

EG: I remember this caused a huge commotion in the APA as well as among mental health workers.

ML: At first, the APA wanted us to stay on, especially the teachers. Afterwards, when we'd already left, many maintained that we had succumbed to a late adolescence, particularly with respect to Emilio Rodrigué and myself. Later still, and today, it's as if we never belonged to the APA. But it's true that for APDEBA I continue to exist – at least, I think so – and that some good friendships were preserved.

EG: Did the accusation of 'late adolescence' anger you?

ML: I'd say not. I love adolescence. I agree with Serge Leclaire who maintains that in analysis we should achieve 'the killing of the child' within the analysand, but it is of the magically narcissistic and omnipotent child. I agree, but I think that we should preserve that which is vital and positive in the adolescent. While as adolescents we are conscious of what we lack, we also retain our capacity to be enthusiastic, to take risks for things and to change. I think that in the APA we had 'lacked' a lot, dressing ourselves up in solemnity and mutilating our concern for the outside world and our desires to change it. When we became aware of this lack, we left like adolescents.

EG: We are at the point when the two groups have broken with the Institution. What were the next steps?

ML: In FAP Capital, we had already organized various post-graduate courses, at first with psychiatric subjects such as psychopharmaceuticals, geriatrics, etc. But the number of enrolments was minimal. Nevertheless, when a well-known psychoanalyst gave a course or a conference, the classroom would fill up with young doctors and psychologists. One way of increasing the number of members of the FAP was, then, to teach psychoanalysis. And the psychologists?

We APA psychoanalysts had always been idealized and envied because of our systematic training – and, it is true, we had that – but also loathed for our élitism. And now we were available; upon our leaving, many 'pre-candidates' refused to join the APA for ideological reasons and left in order to follow us. We felt that we owed them an alternative training, given that they had refused out of solidarity with our positions. In addition, among those who sought us out, there were many psychologists who had always been prohibited from entering the APA. At first, there was an attempt to channel all these people into the FAP courses. But there wasn't enough room and the FAP was, all things considered, a medical federation. We also very soon understood that the demand for training, for doctors as well as the psychologists, was totally legitimate from the professional point of view. We had to give them a working tool which the university had never given them in an adequate form. What's more, among us ex-APA from both groups there were many who wanted to teach. And, finally, those of us who were really politicized realized that to create a serious, common training institute could be an agglutinating factor which would increase our political strength. It would also increase everyone's political interest and willingness or disposition to join a true professional struggle.

In meetings with the large and powerful Association of Psychologists and the recently founded Association of Educational Psychologists, it was decided to create the Mental Health Workers Co-ordinator (TSM), and under that, the Teaching and Research Centre (CDI). It was in this new organization that the two groups were dissolved, although certain differences and tensions continued for a long time, but many friendships also sprang up among those who at one time had been unable to unite.

The Co-ordinator, which had defined political goals, automatically resolved the problem of the psychologists, who up until then had suffered from class discrimination on the part of the doctors, as happens in nearly all countries and has recurred in Argentina. Up to that point, the psychologists' organization had no political goals because they were totally caught up in the struggle for recognition and for the right to practise psychotherapy, including psychoanalysis, without any success. The paradox was obvious and insoluble. For example, many psychoanalysts – Bleger and Liberman, to mention the two best known – were professors in the School of Psychology. In other words, on the one hand they were teaching psychoanalysis to future psychologists; and on the other, the Psychoanalytical Association prohibited them from practising because they could not receive training – because they weren't doctors – by the Association itself, the only institution authorized to give the training. At the same time they had no legal right to therapeutic practice.

The younger generation graduating from the Association lived and supported themselves thanks to analysing the psychologists, whom they supervised and offered study groups, although formally they maintained that these psychologists whom they had trained had no right to call themselves psychoanalysts. We forget that Freud himself maintains, in a famous work on *The Question of Lay Analysis* (1926), that the university education of the psychologist lends itself much more to his later becoming a psychoanalyst than does the study of medicine. By making the conditions equal for belonging to the Mental Health Workers Co-ordinator and by having the possibility of alternative training through the Teaching and Research Centre, the psychologists automatically stopped being discriminated against and became the same as everybody else, mental health workers and *compañeros* in the professional and political struggle. Achievements that were unthinkable a few years before can be attributed to the Co-ordinator: the putting of an end to the discrimination against psychologists and to the confrontation between psychiatrists and psychoanalysts and also to the confrontation that existed between Communist psychologists or psychiatrists and psychoanalysts.

EG: The experience of the Teaching and Research Centre is surely unique in its attempt to wipe out the differences among the mental health specialists and in offering the same training opportunities to everyone.

ML: Some time ago, Ignacio Maldonado and I wrote an article, not published, in which we talk about the Centre: I think in it we adequately cover what you are asking me about. What's more, I can tell you in passing that Ignacio Maldonado belonged to Documento, so you can see that at the time of the Centre, our differences no longer existed. As we said in the article, the main achievement of the Mental Health Workers Co-ordinator

> was the founding of the Teaching and Research Centre. There, professional and political demands were brought together with the theoretical and technical training of mental health workers, paying minimal attention to the training of the so-called 'auxiliaries'. The greatest effort was directed towards programming serious, basic training for mental health workers as a whole. As we considered psychoanalysis the soundest psychological theory which could guide our practice, we moved towards an epistemological effort to separate the strongest nuclei of psychoanalytic theory from those that had important ideological connotations or that were mere rationalizations of the only esteemed practice: individual, protracted psychoanalysis.

For my part, I'd still add: individual, protracted psychoanalysis, and private and costly.

EG: What was the teaching like at the Centre?

ML: As a pilot plan, there were three areas of training. The first consisted of historical and dialectic materialism; in this area the teachers were paid, since philosophers, especially if they are Marxists, are always poor. The second was given free by psychoanalysts, since all of us continued with our private practices; it consisted of epistemology, psychoanalytical theory, the classification of diseases and psychopathology. The third area, where attendance was recommended but which was never very well attended all the same, was the most problematical, since it attempted – through concrete experience in treatments carried out in institutions – to unite theory with practice in order to achieve a new praxis; in fact, it was what we could call a critique of praxis.

To quote our article (Langer and Maldonado, 1983) once again:

> Through its brief existence, the Teaching and Research Centre and the Co-ordinator left us as an important legacy some valuable verifications:
>
> (1) the possibility of breaking down the stratification and fragmentation of the different groups of mental health workers upon integrating them into a single professional movement;
>
> (2) the proof that serious high-level training can be provided and

acquired outside the official psychoanalytic institutions, for a minimal economic contribution which serves for the upkeep of the premises, inasmuch as the worker was affiliated;

(3) the advance, in this manner, of a few concrete steps in the much-debated terrain of the interrelationship between Marxism and psychoanalysis, granting practice the privilege merited it by Marx, Gramsci and Mao.

EG: All this process took place between 1971 and 1974. I think that it would be worthwhile to locate it in the context of the most important political events of this era. And not only in Argentina, but also in the Southern Cone.

ML: Yes, you're completely right. Without that, one can't understand what happened, or our optimism or confidence. Let me think: the Rosario Congress, when we took over FAP Nacional, was in August 1970. A comrade from the Communist Party was elected President. I presented a paper in which I pointed out that the ideological 'objectivity' of the psycho-analyst was fictitious. In fact, his 'being objective' implied opting for the status quo.

In 1972 we were under the Lanusse dictatorship, which was beginning to weaken and give way, especially under pressure from the Peronist masses (the JP or the Peronist Youth, which in fact reunited the left wing of Peronism), accompanied by the Peronist guerrillas (the Montoneros) and by the PRT (the Revolutionary Workers Party), whose 'armed wing' was the ERP (Revolutionary People's Army). The Revolutionary Communist Party, anti-Soviet and pro-China, had its influence above all among the intellectuals, although in Córdoba it came to have a lot of importance among the workers also.

All these groups had their representatives in the discussions in the FAP assemblies. It was in one of these that I lost the election to the post of academic secretary of FAP Capital – you see, not everything has gone well for me in life – to somewhat later acquire the job of participating in the organizing of the Teaching and Research Centre.

But I'd like to tell you about a very special trip I made. We had to go to Mendoza, to a scientific symposium given by FAP Regional on the subject of alcoholism, a hackneyed subject. The funny thing was that, since Mendoza is in an Andean region dedicated to the cultivation of grapes, the closing dinner took place in a warehouse where they showed us vats full of wine, whose fumes intoxicated us even without drinking any. But for us Mendoza was simply a stopping-off place on the way to Chile. We wanted to get to know the mental health work that was being carried out under the government of the *compañero* president, as they called Salvador Allende.

We were received by the principal mental health planners. They showed us their plans. Alcoholism was talked about there also, but something serious was being done to combat it, too. It had been declared 'mental health enemy number one', for many reasons: because of the havoc it produced within families, the amount of beds taken up in the general hospitals by those ill with cirrhosis and other consequences of chronic alcoholism, the number of people suffering from *delirium tremens* in the clinics, and also for the work-hours that were lost. The number one enemy was fought in the neighbourhoods, in the parishes, in meetings using behaviourist techniques, in community work, in alcoholics' groups, but also, and this attracted our attention, in groups of alcoholics' wives. This was because it was discovered that, if the women were not helped to become aware of their attitude, they often created problems in the reintegration of their rehabilitated husbands in the home: tired of their husbands' bad temperedness, their *macho* violence, and relieved once they had learned to do without them, the women had taken over the reins of the home themselves.

As I've listed, there were many reasons why alcoholism was being fought, but the most important was that it was considered counter-revolutionary, just like *machismo*. And what was sought through all the therapeutic techniques in use was 'a change of values'. This was the slogan of those who worked in mental health. They were trying to show the population that the man who could drink a lot and hold it from an early age wasn't a 'real *macho*', nor was it any longer a compliment to be a *macho*, but that companionship between the sexes was what was sought after. When Pinochet took power, one of his first measures was to raise the price of meat and lower the price of alcohol. His advisers must have also known that alcoholism, intimate companion of *machismo*, contributes to counter-revolution.

We had a lovely, long interview with Salvador Allende. Even the North American consul was kept waiting while he spoke with us. He explained the history of the Chilean process to us, he told us how the country had been sick and that's why they had elected him, because he was a doctor. He described the difficulties and dangers that threatened 'the Chilean path to socialism'. He told us that he was going to respect the Constitution, on principle, but also because any other way he was going to lose. And finally he assured us that he was not going to abandon his post, come what may, that they would only be able to take him out of La Moneda palace feet first. He was calm, warm; at times he joked, but he knew his fate perfectly well. I'm an old woman and I've met a lot of people, but never anyone with so much dignity and strength of character.

Upon my return I became part of the organizing committee of the Teaching and Research Centre. It was a lovely job and we all got on well. I became friends with a psychologist, Lina, who knew a lot about politics. She was in her third party militancy. 'The third is the winner,' she used to say to me; 'this time I'll have chosen well, this time we'll make it.' Of course, she was wrong that time as well. I went to the Graphics Union with her; they lent us their premises, since the members of the Co-ordinator and the CDI no longer fitted into our tiny office at the FAP. That's how I met Raimundo Ongaro, the secretary of the graphical workers. What a man! He was jovial, enthusiastic and hot-headed, with lots of charisma. Later on, as president of FAP Nacional, I had to sign a declaration protesting some arbitrariness on the part of the government. Ongaro sent for me, in fact for something else, but he received me with words no feminist could imagine more complimentary. 'Congratulations *compañera*,' he said, 'you have to have ovaries to sign a declaration like this on your own.' And afterwards, when I'd thanked him for his subtlety, he launched into a long speech condemning *machismo* and the marginalization of women. 'They don't even allow you to be Catholic priests,' he said indignantly and then, seeing my puzzlement, added, 'Well, maybe that's not so important to you.'

The union of graphical workers, from the porter to Ongaro, were all *compañeros*. It was lovely to be there, at home. But precisely because they were the most militant trade union and had so many problems and court cases, we had to move to the FOETRA (Federation of Telephone Workers and Employees of the Argentinian Republic) headquarters. Finally, we got our own premises.

Shall we continue with history? On 22 August 1972, the Trelew massacre. Sixteen prisoners were shot, all of them young men. Three survived because they were protected by the bodies of their companions. And our despair, indignation and impotency. The Christian funeral of the victims, in which the tanks of our Christian army intervened.

1973: There were to be elections! The old Peronist Cámpora presented himself as a candidate. The Federation of Psychiatrists had requested permission some time earlier to visit the prisons where the political prisoners were being subjected to inhumane conditions, to 'the top security ruling'. They hadn't replied. Then, after the electoral victory of Peronism, the invitation arrived. At the same time, the special ruling was lifted. A colleague and I went to the Villa Devoto prison. Bars, bolts, keys and guards. Never-ending corridors and more bars. The prison psychiatrist received us amicably. We could talk to whomever we wanted. I'd like to squeeze in just one thing about this visit, although I could mention more: our conversation with the mothers, that's to say, young girls who had been taken prisoner when they were pregnant. They told us about the obstetricians' discomfort and doubts when faced with their questions: 'And the electric prods they tortured me with on the genitals, could they have damaged the little one I'm expecting?' The obstetricians didn't know how to answer; they didn't have any experience in this. Two of the women came with their babies in their arms. One was very pale and sickly looking; the other seemed fine and healthy in spite of everything. They told us how they were bringing up these children. According to the prison rules they had the right to be with their children until their second birthday. What's more, the mothers and their children shared the same wing. They wanted to create 'the new man'. They wanted to give their children an upbringing that would socialize all their relations. That's why, although every child was brought up to know who its mother was, all the other women acted as aunts and took turns in giving the child attention and even breastfeeding at times. 'When you get out, tell me more about this experiment and how these children turned out,' I asked them, extremely interested. 'When we get out, we'll have other things to do,' they replied.

They were released on 25 May, the day Cámpora took over the government. Do you remember? The crowds gathered in front of the prison shouting 'Freedom, freedom' for hours, while the prisoners answered back, sang, and waved improvised banners. And finally, like a miracle, as if the biblical walls of Jericho had fallen as a result of the shouts of those besieging it, the huge door opened and two by two they all came out. I've never seen anything like it. But the majority of these children I've just mentioned are now orphans and scattered throughout the world.

1973: Ezeiza, the arrival of Perón. Virtually the entire FAP committee went. Only those who had an old grudge against Peronism were missing. It was an impressive sight. It reminded me of *War and Peace*: endless columns of people with their banners arriving from all sides. They say that there were a million, or three million? It was a long way to the stand in front of which the plane carrying the General, as though he were Father Christmas, was due to land. In the stand, there were the Peronist Youth and the Peronist right wing. The most militant trade unions were going to arrive from the south. We were coming from the north, chanting and marching. 'We're never going to make it to the stand,' I commented to a friend. 'If you want we can go on ahead and we'll make it.' We separated from the rest and walked ahead of the columns going in the same direction. But there were many other people already turning back. 'Do you know why they're going back? Perón can't have arrived yet.' And then we reached the stand. We sat in the middle of the people who were shouting 'Argentina! Argentina!' Over the loudspeaker they were giving orders, yelling at those who'd climbed the trees to get down for security reasons. I didn't understand. I was sitting on the ground beside my friend. 'You know,' I said to her, 'I never imagined my old age would be like this.' 'Like this? How?' she asked me. 'Like this, so happy.' At that point, the shooting began. And while they were shouting, 'Everybody down!', while they killed the old and the young, yes, especially the young, hundreds – it was never known exactly how many – Arnaldo Rascovsky, on television, was hailing the promised arrival of the General and afterwards talking about filicide, his pet subject, without realizing the irony of fate.

1973: Cámpora resigns; Lastiri is president. The Perón–Isabelita formula and behind them both 'the wizard', López Rega.

1973: The assassination of Allende. Torres, the Bolivian President, had already fallen much earlier. And the CDI was full of Bolivian and Chilean refugees who had nowhere to sleep. The death of Perón. A short time after Ezeiza I realized that everything was lost. But one kept on all the same. And the University was 'ours'. I joined the faculty of medical psychology at the UNBA (University of Buenos Aires) at the beginning of 1974. I had already returned to hospital work before that.

Since we had become active in the FAP, many of us had begun to work in hospital services or health centres. In 1970 I had joined the psychopathology unit at the Avellaneda Hospital. I was really enthused by my re-encounter with psychiatry. However, the possibility of treating psychotic patients didn't last long since, after a few months of my being there, the two in-patient wards we had were closed, for a lack of staff and a lack of money. To use a friend's expression, 'the redistribution of poverty' was always our problem in the Argentinian psychiatric hospitals.

We continued to work in the out-patient clinic doing research and teaching. Group psychotherapy with a psychoanalytic focus provided the possibility of training future therapists, since we worked in co-therapy, one or two experienced analysts and various young psychologists. This model allowed the psychologists gradually to acquire the confidence and comprehension necessary for interpretative intervention. I'll go into this experience in more detail later. Ever since the CDI existed, young people in training had had the opportunity of learning theory complementary to their hospital practice.

In January 1974, when I joined the Faculty of Medical Psychology as an associate professor, I cut down my activity at the Avellaneda Hospital by half. Medical psychology – so broad, complex, undefined and ideologized – was, nevertheless, familiar to me since I'd worked a lot on psychosomatic medicine and on the problem of the doctor–patient relationship.

I was pleased to be in the School of Medicine and I felt 'at home'. What's more, it was a very special time, since everyone who worked there, from the director to the students, shared the same goals and enthusiasm. The faculty of medical psychology was an important one and it had many functions. It had a clinic, where people from the vicinity came with their 'nervous' problems, in other words psychopathological problems. It supervised the interns who were thinking of specializing in medical psychology; it was responsible for inter-consultation with the other medical specialties, since it was located in the university hospital, the San Martín; and it was linked to a new specialty, to which those involved tried to impart a new ideology, the Faculty of Industrial Medicine – industrial medicine not in the interest of the bosses, but of the workers and the unions. In their pre-clinical years, the students were taught the basics of psychology, which they would need at their disposal when they were faced with the patient. There was a Department of Post-Graduate Training for the psychologists and doctors who worked in the clinic; this was my responsibility. Along with my assistant, Alberto Siniego, an excellent head of practical projects, I drew up a lovely programme in which psychoanalysts, psychologists and psychiatrists all participated.

Yes, we worked hard and with enthusiasm. The number of patients constantly increased, as did the young psychologists and doctors who offered their assistance. They weren't paid, we didn't manage to get them positions; but they came just the same with the commitment to give eighteen hours a week: six for treating the patients, six in therapy supervision and six in seminars.

EG: But this all came to an end. How?

ML: It was the beginning of October 1974, when my 'boss' called me to say: 'Please, for the time being at least, don't come to the hospital any more. Nor should you go to the places you usually frequent. I don't want anything to happen to you.' A short time later the clinic was closed down.

EG: But you didn't leave the country as a result of this advice? What else happened? I know it was because of a threat. But do you think the 'Triple A' (trans. note: the Argentinian Anti-communist Alliance, a right-wing paramilitary organization which carried out hundreds of political killings in Argentina at this time) threatened you because of the FAP, the School or Plataforma?

ML: I suppose it was a bit of everything. That's true, I haven't told you anything about the FAP.

EG: You were elected President in the Córdoba Congress in 1972. Because of the importance of FAP at the time, I think it would be important to talk about your presidency.

ML: There were the routine, bureaucratic tasks, and there were others, sometimes gratifying, sometimes very distasteful. I'll tell you a bit about the lot.

A very gratifying experience resulted from the request of a psychologist in Rosario for us to visit his institution because he was having a lot of difficulties with the authorities and was afraid of losing it and needed our support. Well now, our support in those days often turned out to be rather counter-productive, but the colleagues knew that as well as we did; all the same, they usually asked for it when faced with abuses and we gave it just the same, of course.

EG: What did this psychologist want?

ML: He had taken over a reformatory for adolescents some time before. As a result of complaints from the neighbours that he gave the boys too much freedom – they'd been locked up behind barbed wire and maltreated in various ways until he'd taken over – he had been notified that he would soon have to leave his post.

To me a visit to a reformatory meant, more or less, to be confronted with a horror film. I was relieved that there would be a few of us from the committee; I'd have been afraid on my own, not of the adolescents, but of the Dantesque scenes I imagined. Well, we went to Rosario, a large city about 300 kilometres from Buenos Aires. And we went to the reformatory, which from the outside looked exactly like I'd imagined. Even, I'd say, from the inside: a barren, cold, sparsely furnished environment. But the psychologist and the boys were very different from what I'd imagined. They were, simply, free. The younger ones went to school to finish their studies, the older ones were apprentices in mechanics' workshops, electrical workshops, etc. They were badly dressed – there was no money – but they were well fed. And they loved their director, the psychologist. He was a shy man, but zealous; nervous, but totally idealistic and very willing. He had concentrated all his libido in helping these boys get on. He didn't have a lot of training, but he made up for it perfectly with his intuition and warmth.

We had lunch together at long tables. One or two of us were seated at each table with the boys so that we could talk to them completely freely. And they told us with delight how the arrival of the director, some time ago, had changed their lives. I remember one boy in particular that I chatted to while we ate; he was worried because he would soon be eighteen and would have to leave the institution because he'd be 'free' then. 'I don't want to go yet,' he told me. 'I want to finish my apprenticeship in the workshop and help out here. I hope they'll allow me to.' They sentimentally referred to the psychologist as 'Papa'. Within a short time the 'reformatory' was shut down because 'it went against the image of the state in its lack of order and cleanliness'.

Let me tell you another episode: after the assassination of Salvador Allende, when the streets of Buenos Aires resounded for days with the cries of the demonstrators, 'The People United Will Never Be Defeated', and they had been defeated all the same, for the time being, in the midst of the news of horror and death. Among those detained in the stadium in Santiago were various psychiatrists and psychologists. My job, rather quixotic, as President of the FAP at the time, was to send telegrams to Pinochet and the other members of his government demanding guarantees of the physical and psychological well-being of those detained, and their immediate release.

Sending these telegrams was not easy. I had to go to the post office with my personal papers and others that proved my position as FAP President and speak personally to the head of the post office in order for him to authorize the sending of such a telegram. Only then could I hand over the text to an employee I already knew. He was fat, dark and placid, and every time he would look at me with a mixture of curiosity and irony upon receiving and reading the text of my telegram, and laconically say, 'They'll shoot them just the same.'

In the Federation of Psychiatrists my routine task, like that of the other members of the committee, was to meet every few months with the Federal Council. This meeting always had to take place, in rotation, in the city of one of the regions that formed the Council. That's how I travelled throughout the country from north to south and east to west, without realizing it was my farewell to Argentina, my adopted country of so many years.

I've already told you about the trip to Mendoza. In Paraná, the pretty colonial city on the river as broad as my Danube, we held the Council meeting in conjunction with the Southern Cone Psychiatric Symposium. It was a very good Congress, marred only by the closing speech, given by a fascist whom the health authority had deliberately sent us for that very purpose.

I travelled with a colleague by car for many long hours, throughout the whole of the rich province of Buenos Aires, the humid pampas, towards the south, towards Bahía Blanca, to take part in academic and administrative meetings. I went to the west, to the Cordillera, to Tucumán, the city in which the independence of Argentina was declared, the city they call the garden of the Republic, and to neighbouring Salta, where we were warmly welcomed by a representative of the regional Federation along with the San Luis representative, who 'disappeared' a short time after my leaving Argentina and was never heard of again. My last trip was to Mar del Plata. Various members of the committee and myself went to choose one of the union hotels – Mar del Plata is the Argentinian Acapulco – for the upcoming congress where I was going to end my term in office. We chose one with a beautiful view of the sea, but already with the doubt: could there be a congress? There was one, but I had already left. Upon returning from Mar del Plata I found out that I was on the list of the 'Triple A'. I left, but for a long time I felt guilty and ashamed that I hadn't stayed until the end of my term. However, when a colleague reproached me by letter, I replied: 'Maybe I left ahead of time, but without any doubt I'd have had to go in the long run anyway.' And I was right.

EG: And you came to Mexico, which you were unable to do in 1938.

ML: It was the end of 1974, the era of Isabelita and López Rega and the 'Triple A'. After the assassination of Sylvio Frondizi and Ortega Peña, a climate of terror reigned in Buenos Aires, especially among the intellectuals. One Monday morning, a patient mentioned to me very nervously that he'd found out I was at the top of a list of the 'Triple A', which had condemned various mental health workers to death. I didn't take it seriously; I interpreted it, I don't remember how, and we went on working. The next analysand, a young psychiatrist, as soon as he saw me said, 'What a relief to see you're all right! In the hospital they told me you'd been shot and were badly injured.' And that's how it escalated. Somebody telephoned and on hearing my voice, said, 'Oh, how good to hear you. I thought that already . . . !' An analyst from the APA that I had been very friendly with at one point, but who I hardly ever saw then, phoned me to tell me that I could go to him if I ever needed anything.

In a family get-together my children convinced me that, whatever the situation was, it would be best for me to get away for a while.

I chose Mexico, for personal as much as professional reasons. One of my daughters, who a short time before had married Jaime del Palacio, a co-author of this book, was living in Mexico. In addition, I'd been in Mexico City a few months before at the invitation of Armando Suárez, the founder of the Mexican Psychoanalytical Circle, to take part in a round-table on Mexican television on anti-psychiatry, and in a series of conferences in the School of Political Science at the National University on *Razón, locura y sociedad*. I had met many Mexican colleagues who years before had been to Buenos Aires to be trained as psychoanalysts, and on this last trip I'd established new ties with the members of the Circle . . . You could add to all this that I'd been on the point of coming to Mexico when we left Europe and had been in the country as a tourist fifteen years before; Mexico had fascinated me, as it does many foreigners. Precisely during the family reunion in which my sons and daughters-in-law insisted I should leave Argentina, my daughter called me from Mexico very concerned about what was going on in Buenos Aires and invited me to come. 'Speak to Armando Suárez,' I said to her, 'and explain the situation to him. If he has work for me then I'll come.' He had and I came.

EG: How has your work progressed since your arrival in Mexico?

ML: When I left Buenos Aires, I was an associate professor of medical psychology at the School of Medicine. With a very large group of people we'd carried out a very valuable experiment, an experiment which the new authorities cut off at the roots. This saddened me a lot, above all because we left a good number of patients without treatment. In Mexico, I found myself in the university once again; I'm a post-graduate professor in clinical psychology and my area includes the supervision of treatments within a psychoanalytic referential framework being carried out in institutions, free of charge or for a nominal fee. For many years, I had a similar job in the Youth Integration Centres. Probably in January 1981 a university clinic will be opened under the supervision of the Department of Psychology in the UNAM (National Autonomous University of Mexico); as a result I'll have the opportunity of participating in the training of clinical psychologists.

I'm very grateful to Mexico for allowing me the possibility of continuing my work along the lines which have always interested me, in other words, to be able, as do many psychoanalysts and psychotherapists with analytic training here, to put the discoveries and therapeutic possibilities Freud offers us within the reach of the non-wealthy classes. In addition, I help in and am an honorary member of – it both embarrasses me and gives me pleasure to show off – the Mexican Association of Group Psychotherapy (AMPAG), an institution I hold in great esteem since it has known how to avoid most of the major pitfalls of psychoanalytic societies.

The problems of women interest me more and more, to such an extent that I want to include some notes on the subject in this book . . . This is my work in Mexico.

THEORY

EG: Through your recent works, interviews and seminars you demonstrate that you reject neither psychoanalysis nor Marxism, but maintain your critical position. You insist on the scientific validity of psychoanalysis and have tried to discern its ideological component. What do you see as the scientifically valid in psychoanalysis and what as the ideological?

ML: That's not easy to answer. I would say that the problem centres on Freud's attitude to women, for the simple reason that he focuses on it from the phallocentric point of view, as (Gregory) Zilboorg defines it – more precisely, from his epoch, from the height of capitalism and from within the nuclear family. This implies that Freud focuses on the problem of women, as with the Oedipus complex and the family, from an atemporal, non-dialectical standpoint. It is true that all human societies are founded on the prohibition of incest but also that the consequences of this norm differ in each and are linked to the relations of production. Juliet Mitchell, in *Psychoanalysis and Feminism* (1976), says some very intelligent things in this respect in affirming that Freud, in studying the Oedipus complex in women, gives the best description possible of the intense psychological state of the nuclear family in that period of capitalism.

However, when Freud applies his concepts to the remote past, as in *Totem and Taboo* (1912), for example, I think – and I'm not the only one, many anthropologists have also said so – those concepts are untenable as historical elaboration. At one point, Freud argues, men, brothers, the primitive horde killed the father and afterwards renounced the women. But these women don't exist for Freud in any form other than as objects. And from this point he takes an enormous leap straight to present-day patriarchal society or to Viennese society at the beginning of this century. I think that this is unsustainable, as when he uses the neurosis of Little Hans to explain *Totem and Taboo*. Or, to put it another way, in *Totem and Taboo* Freud establishes an analogy between 'primitive man', who ambivalently worships the totem, and a bourgeois child, Little Hans, who in his Oedipal struggle suffers from a phobia of an animal as symbolically representative of the father as is the totemic animal.

Precisely this analogy between certain emotions and mechanisms leads psychoanalysis to adopt a universalization that omits the enormous differences between historical conditions and the relations of production in prehistoric times and in our present society. 'Man doesn't change and hasn't changed since the time of the primitive horde' would be the logical conclusion, and this same static concept has made psychoanalysis static and conservative. Moreover, Horst Kurnitzky, in *Die Triebstruktur des Geldes: Ein Beitrag zur Theorie der Weiblichkeit* (1974), made an interesting observation: in the Freudian hypothesis of the primitive horde, 'the role of the mother is totally disregarded – which makes us suspect that what we find here is a process of repression, fundamental to the formation of psychoanalytical theory, which can be interpreted as the repression of the return of the repressed (in other words, the existence and power of the primitive mother).'

EG: Let's go back to the original question. What would be the scientifically valid?

ML: The main theoretical concepts of Freud, such as the unconscious, infantile sexuality, repression and latent motivation. An Althusserian would say: the unconscious as a formal-abstract object of investigation. Also valid are the theoretical-technical concepts of transference and counter-transference, although Freud referred very little to the latter.

We enter into the ideological sphere when we turn to his historical-philosophical works, such as *Totem and Taboo*, which delves into the past, or *Civilization and its Discontents* (1930), which analyses the present and the future but where Freud's discourse deliberately omits the relations of production, the social context in other words. In the latter work, he derives our 'discontent' from the repression which our libidinous and aggressive impulses suffer – a repression imposed upon us by society. However, he does not acknowledge the discontent caused us, members of the dominant class, by the denial of guilt feelings about the exploitation of our fellow creatures – exploitation which contradicts what we are taught as children, in religion or ethics.

But perhaps where the ideological appears with most clarity is in relation to the much-debated concept of *reality*. When Freud says that the ego should submit itself to reality along with submission to the id and the super-ego, today many of us ask ourselves – for example, the Swiss analyst Paul Parin – which reality and what concept of reality he is referring to. A concrete reality exists, which is, for example, that the two of us are sitting here across this table, upon which we have put a tape recorder, but Freud is not referring to this reality and neither are we. Then I'd say – using Parin's concept, although I became aware of it only recently – that if we don't have another relevant, scientific body of knowledge as an instrument (in other words, Marxism) in order to analyse reality, then we cannot increase the patient's ego capacity to recognize it, because Reality – with a capital R – does not exist.

EG: This is why Freud has often been criticized for the paradox that when he, who knew how to see beyond the appearances of things – the meaning of latent motivation, the unconscious – speaks of reality, it is limited to its manifest aspect.

ML: Clearly that's right. You asked me before about psychoanalysis and Marxism, and I would say that one thing completely in common to both is that once you have really understood Marxism – and I don't pretend to be an expert, or anything like that – if you've grasped the concept of surplus value and, as a result, the exploitation of man by man, you will never be able to forget it. In the same way, if you have understood the concept of the unconscious, even though it may only be through the analysis of a dream or a slip of the tongue, you can never forget that either.

Going back to Freud's assumption that analysis should help whoever is analysed to increase their judgement of reality and, as a result, be able to deal more adequately with it, we are faced with an inevitably ideologized problematic, because what does it mean to have a better grasp of reality, and which reality are we talking about? Paul Parin holds that for the analyst to be able to comprehend reality – the social context and the ability to help the patient recognize it – he needs a scientific (in other words, Marxist) focus.

In the works of Freud, which are sometimes referred to as sociological, there are very mixed concepts, some revolutionary and others even reactionary. And I would say that Freud almost took pride in not concerning himself seriously with politics.

EG: Freud was also limited by the conceptual framework of his era, influenced by the evolutionist concepts of Hegel and Darwin and by the physics of the time, which gave great weight to the dynamic, to the interaction of forces, etc. These ideas allowed Freud to understand many things not understood up to then, but one could ask oneself to what extent they also constrained or restricted him.

ML: Inevitably, Freud, like everyone else, is the product of his epoch, and employs the scientific instruments it offers. But I don't think he was constrained by having based himself on the physics of his time. Freud was a doctor and used the clinical method; through his discoveries – often intuitive, made with the live material of his analysands, and later verified with other patients – he was searching for an adequate scientific structure that could not be attacked. As the human and social sciences, especially psychology, were poorly developed at the time and had little status, Freud latched on to the trusted sciences, to physics and biology (there are colleagues who did the same until a short while ago). For example, if Freud talks about the importance hormones will have in the future with respect to sexuality, he says so as a result of a more fitting intuition than when, basing himself on physics, he introduces what he calls the 'economic' into psychoanalysis. And it is precisely the former which he has been most criticized for – although I know little Lacan and I'm not going to get embroiled in this subject, the Lacanians dispute him and totally discount all these aspects – but for Freud they are a framework to support his true discoveries. Or, if you want, a metaphor, what he himself called a working hypothesis.

EG: Or, 'metapsychology'. But to return to what we were talking about before, one of the critical observations you make is with reference to his concept of reality which later serves as the basis for the analysis of the ego. What other observations and criticisms would you make of the Freudian approach?

ML: Once again, the ideological, and it has to do with the epoch in which Freud lived. In *The Future of an Illusion* (1927) there is a beautiful phrase: 'a civilization which leaves so large a number of its participants unsatisfied and drives them into revolt neither has nor deserves the prospect of a lasting existence.' And that is very true as we saw in Nicaragua under Somoza and in El Salvador today. But when Freud talks about the 'discontent in a civilization', this phrase is forgotten, and also he disagrees with the Soviet Union, more to save analysis from fascist persecution in Austria and from the German Nazi threat than for any scientific criteria.

EG: In short, you would say, and I think it stands out in all his works, that Freud is an exponent of the bourgeoisie of his time, a fact which does not in any way detract from the great recuperability of the principal Freudian concepts.

ML: Of course, and I would mention your article, 'Freud y Marx, delincuentes ideológicos' ('Freud and Marx, ideological delinquents'), in which you say that there is confusion among psychoanalysts who consider themselves and Freud to be revolutionary (Guinsberg, 1979). It is a half-truth, as you very well point out: Freud was revolutionary in a certain area, in the field of psychology, but in no way was he revolutionary, nor did he seriously pretend to be, at a political level.

EG: And how would you define him at that level, or better still, at the ideological-political level?

ML: As conservative. That's why he was not aware of how the world changed, or how women changed throughout his long life which coincided precisely with a very important stage in the transformation of women, primarily middle-class women. And if middle-class Viennese women can change, others can too. Freud did not perceive those changes, or he did not know what to make of them. With respect to the problem of women, he sticks to what he wrote on feminine virtues in his letters to his fiancée.

Freud is conservative; now, why he is, is another question. As a boy he was very poor: it was enormously difficult for him to reach, at forty, a moderate well-being that enabled him to support his family and continue his research, and the last thing he wanted was that revolutions and social changes should disturb his field of work. When Alexander the Great stands over Diogenes in his barrel and asks him what he desires, Diogenes replies for him not to block the sun. Freud was in need of the sun, which was his cause, and had to get rid of everything that could perturb it. And how was he able to do that? By demonstrating 'analytically' that they were delusions, fantasies, human errors.

EG: Yes, the criticism that has always been made of Freud, and not only from a somewhat rigid, static and dogmatic concept of Marxism, is that he never understood man as a product of history, although, paradoxically, he provides the best explanation of the psyche as a product of history.

ML: Even though, of course, he sees man as a social being. In *Group Psychology and the Analysis of the Ego* he points out that 'in individual psychic life "the Other" always appears effectively as model, object, assistant or adversary; and, as such, individual psychology is, at the same time and from the start, social psychology in a broad, but fully justified sense' (Freud, 1921).

All Freud's discoveries arise out of a bipersonal situation, in which the establishment of transference, that is, the analyst–analysand link, is fundamental. A third is always present in this relationship, in the discourse of the analysand. As in early infancy, the father is soon included in the previously bipersonal situation with the mother, and upon resolving the Oedipal complex, the individual introjects society, through the establishment of the super-ego. In other words, Freud does not by any means omit the social at the level of relations, but he does at the historical level in explaining the Oedipal triangle based upon the model appropriate to the primitive horde.

EG: Could it be said that he makes a psychic X-ray of man in which he includes the social as has never been done before, but only to confirm his psychological findings, and without clearly understanding the deeper meaning of the social?

ML: Yes, and, as a result, omitting the temporal or historical changes that are produced. And that's where Marx comes in together with what is so much debated today, that is, the family as reproducer of society's ideology. For Freud there is no doubt that the family reproduces ideology, but he does not want to change that ideology, nor does he see it as substantially changeable. He explains how a male child, upon introjecting the paternal prohibition of incest, also introjects society, but he does not explain to us how, in turn, he acts upon it.

EG: As far as I know, Freud never deals with ideology.

ML: He never explicitly speaks of ideology, a term which has been interpreted in as many different ways as there are philosophical currents. But he refers to it implicitly in its broadest sense, when he says that it is very difficult to change man because our super-egos do not in fact correspond to our fathers, but to our forefathers. Paul Schilder is the first, and virtually the last, to talk about ideology, using the term explicitly and in the sense of conscious and unconscious structure, whose roots arise in our infancy and families. Those who seek to link Marxism with psychoanalysis often locate this link in the analysis of ideology.

EG: It is precisely with reference to the ideological in Freud that some from within the analytic field criticize the key and deeply debated concept of the death or destructive instinct, which Freud raises in 1920 in *Beyond the Pleasure Principle.*

ML: It's a very complex question. Freud postulates the existence of the death instinct, but many traditional analysts, like Fenichel, for example, don't agree with him; the majority don't agree with him. Melanie Klein later develops the concept further. Now, what position can one take with respect to it? Personally, I am very pragmatic. Later, when we discuss Melanie Klein, I will approach the problem in the same way: I don't know if we achieve any clarity in defining what was previously called sadism or aggression as the death instinct.

Of course, we observe aggression clinically as inherent in the human being and as being directed outwards, against the world, as well as inwards, against one's own self – its internal objects, Melanie Klein would say. But to call this aggression Thanatos does not resolve anything for us or, more correctly, it does not in practice change the problem.

The concept of Thanatos – the search of the living, organic for a return to the inanimate, the Nirvana principle, etc. – has been the object of controversy for many analysts. And the Lacanians, critical of 'Freudian instinctivism', disagree with the concept and try to amend it.

EG: Lacan establishes that Freud, due to his biologistic tendencies, could not comprehend anything that did not originate from instinct. And he frequently uses the term instinct, although Freud never used it. Freud uses *Trieb* (drive) in German. Lacan points out how 'the genius in Freud yields in fact to the prejudices of the biologist who insists that all tendencies are related to instinct' (Lacan, 1980); and how, thus, Freud could not understand the aggression a child expresses towards absence or deprivation as anything other than instinct.

ML: Yes, and to that one must add – because Freud is human, not a god – that he discovered the death instinct when he was diagnosed as having cancer and following the enormous disappointment that the First World War was for him. Then it is understandable why he took up this line of research.

EG: It is interesting to point out how such a controversial theorist as Erich Fromm explains this. He points out that it is no coincidence that a conservative person – an exponent of the liberal development when at its peak – who suddenly sees his world and his dreams destroyed by a war which causes death and destruction of unprecedented levels, without understanding its social cause, internalizes it in man and views it as a product of innate biological factors.

ML: He's completely correct. I don't know if you know Freud and Einstein's correspondence between the two wars, in which Freud also talks about the almost inevitability of the wars due to Thanatos. And I say *almost* because in an optimistic line in a letter he says, 'Our mythological theory of instincts makes it easy for us to find a formula for *indirect* methods of combating war. If willingness to engage in war is an effect of the destructive instinct, the most obvious plan will be to bring Eros, its antagonist, into play against it (Freud, 1933).' Personally, I don't believe that it is easy, nor that the problem rests there. We should not attempt to make psychoanalysis explain everything. Evidently, faced with a problem like war, the notion of the existence of Thanatos is not sufficient to explain its causes, or to avoid them. Nor does demonstrating the sadism of a torturer explain the existence of torture and repression.

Freud knew that the instinctive explanation does not suffice to understand the world. That's why he maintains that psychoanalysis is not a *Weltanschauung*. But, at the same time, in his writings he deliberately leaves aside that which cannot be explained psychoanalytically because, understandably, this is the focus that interests him, and also the focus from which an interlocutor, in this case Einstein, expects his reply.

EG: From what you are saying, it's clear that you don't share the Freudian understanding of the death instinct, or the 'psychologizing' that is carried out in attempting to understand everything through Thanatos. But what is it that you retrieve (from the death instinct)?

ML: The aggression. I think those who believe that man is intrinsically 'good' are mistaken. If you observe little children, you can see aggression and their pleasure in it very objectively; you can also observe that from when they are very small they say *mine, mine* a lot. It is not that they have already been corrupted by the capitalism of their parents, but that the pleasure of possession and aggression arise very spontaneously in them. Perhaps we are being utopian if we think how this would be if the family were different, if the mother–child relationship developed differently from the start. But that's utopia, nearly.

EG: To continue evaluating Freud's work, one of the criticisms that has been made of him – primarily by non-psychoanalysts – is that, being right about the fundamental importance of the first years of life, he concentrates entirely on these years and invalidates other factors which clearly take place later. A Marxist, for example, would mention work.

ML: He doesn't ignore it. Describing neurosis he says that a present-day trauma causes the adult to return to the point of infantile fixation, the result of a stage of deprivation or frustration, or also over-gratification. For Freud there exists a dialectic interrelation, although he does not use this term, between infancy and adulthood. But he doesn't concern himself with the child much beyond four or five years of age, that is, the Oedipal stage. Latency and adolescence don't usually interest him; Erikson is the first to devote himself to the adolescent stage.

EG: In this attempt to evaluate the work of Freud we haven't discussed his ideas on women, a subject you have done so much work on.

ML: As you'll recall, Freud himself says that he does not understand women, that he does not know what women want. I suppose women want the same as men, that is, a certain amount of fulfilment and happiness. But for Freud, women are a mystery. And, because of his phallocentric perspective and conceptualization of the female genitals as a wound (evidence of castration and nothing else), for a long time he did not concern himself with the role of women, the mother, other than as an Oedipal object. Much later, almost at the end of his life, he discovered the importance of the pre-Oedipal mother in the evolution of the child. In his essay on 'Female sexuality' (1931), he describes her as having a weaker super-ego than men do and an innate rejection of culture, as being more jealous than men and with less capacity for sublimation.

All these negative characteristics are supposedly the result of women never having completely abandoned their Oedipal dependence, because they are not, like the male child, under the threat of castration, since they have been castrated from the start and, as such, are destined to penis envy. I don't doubt that Freud could observe all these characteristics in his first female patients. But, except in some early writings in which he refers to the greater sexual repression that the female child suffers in her education, he does not ask himself if it is really the result of her biology or of the scant opportunities for the female child and women at the beginning of the century.

Let's look at the characteristics attributed to women in more detail. In our patriarchal society, it is men who are usually more jealous. It is the women – and especially the woman of before, due to her emotional and economic dependence – who often has to tolerate the infidelities of the man, while he will never forgive hers. If we say that the woman's super-ego is weaker, we find ourselves in the contradiction that melancholy – an illness specifically provoked by the cruelty of the super-ego according to Freud – is much more frequent in women than in men. Woman's anti-cultural attitude is understood as valid while she has no access to culture.

And if we talk about her lesser capacity for sublimation, we reach the same conclusion: if she is not offered the education that provides access to adequate sublimation, then she cannot develop that capacity. Precisely throughout the life of Freud, this woman that he describes – the 'lady', the patient of the turn of the century – undergoes an enormous change, demonstrating her capacity for sublimation, for independence and for the cultural, political and militant activity which Freud denies (as possible for) her. And it is as if Freud does not see it.

EG: Why doesn't he see it, and why does he maintain his inalterable opinions when the opposite was totally evident?

ML: His theory sustains them, because the idea of woman as a castrated being is fundamental to his theoretical construction. It is Melanie Klein who manages to integrate another theory of women's development into the Freudian conceptual framework. But Melanie Klein was taboo.

In practice, Freud accepted women in his immediate circle of collaborators. He respected their intellectual achievements and did not in any way deny their intellectual capacity. But he says that this capacity is a result of their masculine characteristics, since all human beings are bisexual. He attributes, as does Weininger, everything of worth to the masculine side of the human being and everything conservative, earthly and primitive to the feminine. Upon reading a lot of the literature of the time related to this, I realized that Freud was not alone (in believing this).

It's true that he accepted women colleagues and respected their discoveries; however, Roustang says something very distasteful and ridiculing with respect to this:

> When one considers on the one hand the mystical–clinical elaborations of Lou Andreas-Salomé, which Freud hardly criticizes and recommends for publication, and on the other the reductionist interpretations of Anna Freud, which contradict psychoanalysis in the most decisive way imaginable, we are convinced that the trust Freud vested in these women resembled their admiration for, and acquiescence to, him. They did not explicitly question either the person or the work of Freud; and as a result they could turn psychoanalysis into a Russian novel or a student notebook. (Roustang, 1982)

Until the end, Freud interpreted the evolution of the female child up to the 'phallic phase' as identical to that of the male child and, consequently, the vulva as sign of castration. Some years ago – while studying (with another colleague and a Marxist philosopher) Marx and Freud's ideas on fetishism, a subject which is often of interest as a possible link between both – something occurred to me which appears to be an aphorism but does, I believe, contain some truth. Just as the fetishism of goods conceals and negates the fact that the value is produced by the worker's labour, phallic fetishism denies that behind the vulva, which it reduces to a mere hole or wound, the vagina opens up leading to the reproductive organs of the woman. Thus, worker and woman are deprived of the right over their products and their legitimate power.

EG: This discrepancy in Freud is one of the things which links you to Melanie Klein and her theoretical line, which was dominant in the Argentinian school until at least the end of the 1960s. She was considered the continuator of Freud's work. Today, in 1980, what do you think of that school?

ML: Melanie Klein does not share Freud's phallic fetishism. And the discussion on the libidinal evolution of woman leads us directly to her. But since you mentioned her influence on the APA, I'll begin with the history of the APA and Klein. From the beginning Arminda Aberastury, practically the founder of child psychoanalysis in Argentina, based her opinions totally on Kleinian theory. At one point, she had an intense correspondence with Melanie Klein, whom she knew personally. The Kleinian group also accepted me when, in 1957, at my first International Psychoanalytical Congress, I presented a paper with a Kleinian focus. I got to know Melanie Klein and the Kleinians, who were a very marginalized group in the

International Association; they flattered us and showed their appreciation of us a lot.

Now, why did I adopt the theory of Melanie Klein? For its criteria on the psychosexual evolution of the female child and the psychology of women. Despite all the respect that I had for Freud – which at the time was much more reverential than what I'm capable of feeling at present, because I don't believe in the advantages of being reverential any more – his theory on women was, to me, partly incomprehensible and partly humiliating. But, in addition, and this is most important, it was of no use to me clinically. Freud describes the female child as a castrated male child. But a castrated male child would not have the female child's capacity for reproduction. Melanie Klein takes this innate capacity into account and examines the specifically feminine, in other words, the fantasies and anxieties of the little girl pertaining to her still latent biological-reproductive capacity.

Studying the prehistory of humanity, we understand that it is precisely this capacity and not her 'castration', her lack of a penis, which condemns woman to the secondary role that she performs throughout the long history of humanity. It is true that Melanie Klein also considers the woman as atemporal, but she does not deprive her of her biological functions; rather, she explains how, behind the defence of penis envy, the woman conceals and protects her female capacity for reproduction.

Further on, or perhaps at some future date, in another work dedicated specifically to this subject, I would like to sum up certain theories on prehistory and the reasons which led men to appropriate women, together with some of my own reflections. But for the moment, we are discussing Melanie Klein and how her ideas allowed me to understand clinically the problems of women and the disorders of their female functions.

In Buenos Aires, working as an analyst and observing my women patients and myself, in a long self-analysis, I simply saw that our problem was not as Freud defined it, that there was a serious error. Melanie Klein was of great help to me in my understanding my women patients, and myself, more profoundly. During this period I began to write on women. At first I published separate articles on cases of psychogenic sterility, on problems of menstruation, frigidity, etc. Later, I put all these articles together and reworked them around the common thread that linked these disorders and produced my book, *Maternidad y sexo*.

I have already said that one of the characteristics of the Argentinian school was its interest in psychosomatic medicine. We were effectively the vanguard in this field. I also previously mentioned that a colleague sent me a sterile woman patient, and that she was cured in the symbolic period of nine months. She had obviously suffered from psychogenic sterility, since a considerable time before she had given up on gynaecological treatment. I could examine the mechanism of her sterility and we could overcome it analytically. Another patient, who was sent to me not because of sterility but rather because of serious melancholia – a case also published in *Maternidad y sexo* – was a woman who no longer contemplated getting pregnant after thirteen years of sterile marriage. When the melancholia abated, that is the persecution of the super-ego, to her surprise and mine, she suddenly became pregnant. How do I comprehend this? If I only follow the concept of penis envy, I can't. So, what do Melanie Klein and her school say in this respect? She says that what Freud saw as manifest – but which he also took as latent, like the unmovable biological rock (as he formulates it in 'Analysis terminable and interminable', 1937) – what he saw as penis envy is in fact a defence, that is, a secondary mechanism.

When I say that in this society women do not stand a chance, I am not speaking from the culturalist or feminist point of view, but strictly from the level of the unconscious and earliest experiences. For Melanie Klein the female child, from when she is very tiny – and here you have to accept the idea of unconscious fantasy, one of the basic concepts of Melanie Klein which I still totally believe – fears and attacks the stomach and breasts of her mother; it is in envy and jealousy because she believes that the breasts are full of milk and the stomach full of male children and penises. The penises in fact mean the penis which daddy inserts each time he has sex.

To sum up, the female child attacks in envy, and as a result fears the mother's revenge or 'retaliation', the old psychological concept taken from the Bible of 'an eye for an eye, a tooth for a tooth'. She fears being internally destroyed by her. Melanie Klein defines this as the female castration complex, a situation which we can see in sterile women, in the fear of emptying, in the hypochondriacal preoccupation of many women with menstruation, and other anxieties and disorders which I have observed. For a time I was in charge of the psychosomatic medicine unit in the gynaecological section of the Fernández Hospital in Buenos Aires, where I was able to verify these fears repeatedly. I was also able to verify that in analysis – or even in short-term, well-carried-out psychotherapy – psychogenic sterilities, habitual miscarriages and other dysfunctions of this nature were resolved. *Maternidad y sexo* focuses on this problem.

When the sterile or infertile woman is able to identify with her mother – and here we come into contact with another very important concept of Melanie Klein's, *reparation*, when she can 'repair' her and internally reconcile herself with her – she will be able to overcome her disorder and have a child.

EG: This is all from the psychological perspective of the woman. But what does she tell us about the male child?

ML: Her contributions on this subject are also interesting. For example, her interpretation of the roots of male homosexuality.

EG: But, more generally, which of her concepts would you mention as psychological theory?

ML: The paranoid-schizoid and depressive positions, of course. But I think that to enter into the details of her theoretical production would take us too far off the track.

EG: Still, I would like to know what you think of her theory of the death instinct, which is fundamental to her thinking. Whether or not Klein is accepted depends basically on whether or not the death instinct is accepted.

ML: It's not quite like that. How does she arrive at the concept of the importance of Thanatos? She arrives at it from the empirical path of analysing young male children and seeing an enormous degree of aggression and sadism; she takes this to be the expression of the death instinct. Later on, she insists on the importance of adult envy, pointing out the predomin- ance of this feeling in transference material, attributing its roots to early infancy, seeing envy also as an expression of the death instinct. Well, we talked about it in Freud: I don't think it changes anything fundamentally if we call these destructive manifestations the death instinct or aggression, turned outwards or inwards.

But from this primitive aggression, Melanie Klein deduces other import- ant aspects: she describes the paranoid-schizoid position as fundamental to the first months of life, followed by the depressive position. But I don't think that this is the place, nor am I the person, to delve into all of this. It will have to be left to the epistemologists.

EG: Some neurologists consider that at that age the child is not mature enough to experience the feelings and fantasies inherent in these two positions. Does that refute Klein?

ML: I've had children and I have watched them, keeping in mind the Kleinian concepts on early infancy, and there are certain actions – kinds of crying, sudden fear, bodily expressions – that appear to confirm what are described as anxieties belonging to the paranoid-schizoid position. Beyond this, Melanie Klein tells us that these positions arise early on at first, but that we oscillate between them throughout the rest of our lives. I was able to confirm this clinically, in both men and women.

EG: In other words, you continue to accept the key concepts of the Kleinian school.

ML: Clinically, of course.

EG: In your judgement, what is the reason why the Kleinian boom in Argentina has lost part of its tremendous upsurge?

ML: I don't like your using the word 'boom', it's pejorative. But it is true that, after the death of Melanie Klein, the work of her followers (with a few exceptions – Meltzer, Bion) was no longer so influential. At the international level, it was only after her death that serious attempts were made, by those who had not been followers before, to integrate many of the Kleinian concepts into the orthodox body of theory. This took place primarily in France and the United States. Recently the Lacanians have become interested in her theories. The 1980 Caracas Congress on Kleinian and Lacanian developments proved this.

Since the beginning of the 1970s, the group of us who left the APA in 1971 shifted our concern from a theoretical interest in the 'Kleinian' to a preoccupation with the social and the political: how to integrate the reality in which we lived into our clinical work and how to articulate or complement psychoanalytic and Marxist concepts. This also brought us to a greater study of Freud, on the one hand to 'de-ideologize' certain texts, and on the other to look for convergence and complementation either in theory or in practice.

I would say that I, at least, have rather abandoned the Kleinian method at the level of absolute transferential analysis, the five or six sessions a week, the great neglect of external reality. In fact the neglect is not so great in Melanie Klein herself, as she demonstrates in the Dicky case, but it is among her followers. I don't do that any more, and I never really did it in full.

EG: There is some criticism of Melanie Klein from within the same field. Some say that the Kleinian interpretation can be reduced to four or five concepts, where it is always said that this is envy, that's reparation, etc. One of these critics, Ralph Greenson, in *Technique and Practice of Psychoanalysis*, says 'the interpretations are strangely similar from patient to patient: one gets the impression that the individual history of the patient has had little influence on the personal development and on the neurosis' (Greenson, 1981).

ML: If it's done that way then it's bad analysis and a bad interpretation of Klein. It's the same as the 'orthodox' analysts saying that such-and-such-a-thing is penis envy, or a castration complex, or an incestuous Oedipal bond. You can analyse badly or well with any theory. Perhaps there is a certain stereotype at this level in child analysis, where, I suppose, a richer dialogue is much more difficult, although I don't have any personal experience of this.

But I was going to get on to something else, to the ideological aspect. A ten-year analysis with five or six sessions a week, everything interpreted in transference – if you're not dealing with a seriously ill person – brings us to a very conservative and idealistic position, in the Marxist sense. It has also been said that Melanie Klein's concept of reparation is original sin in disguise, a return to repressed religious feelings. Nevertheless, others have interpreted the interest in the social as a need for reparation, that is, in a positive sense.

In practice, the Kleinian concepts continue to be very useful – for example, her idea of envy. In *Envy and Gratitude* (1957), one of her later books, written with complete clarity, she demonstrates how, particularly in the analysis of colleagues, envy is transformed into an obstacle, since it impedes the analysand's being able to accept and take advantage of the interpretations. The analysand attacks them and in so doing impedes the progress of the analysis, so that the analyst cannot achieve success and so that the analysand does not have to envy him his curative and reparative capacity. As a former teaching analyst, that's to say, an analyst of future analysts for twenty-nine long years, who later primarily analysed or re-analysed colleagues, I completely confirm that observation. To Melanie Klein, however, this envy is a re-living in the 'here and now' of the envy the nursing baby experienced faced with the generosity of the maternal breast and is a direct expression of Thanatos. That's where I give up. I don't know if that's really the way it is. I don't think it's verifiable. But that does not prevent me from utilizing the patient's envy in my interpretations as a fundamental factor in resistance, enabling the analysis to progress along with the analysand's understanding.

EG: The most common criticism of Melanie Klein is that she increasingly reduces the formative period and, as a result, interprets it almost exclusively in relation to the breast, neglecting multiple social factors which come into play through the mother . . .

ML: Melanie Klein always insists on the dialectic interplay between external and internal reality with respect to the mother–child relationship. But it's true that she concentrates on the oral and early Oedipal phase. She says little about the anal phase, although her concept that in his unconscious fantasies the child attacks the mother with urine and faeces is important, especially in infantile analysis. She says little about the genital, and extremely little about coitus in adult sexual relations. While reviewing her contributions in this respect it has really attracted my attention that she does not mention pleasure. She describes how sexual relations can calm deep anxieties, can serve to repair, can be used maniacally to humiliate the other, etc., but she does not concern herself with the pleasure that provokes orgasm.

EG: How do you explain this absence?

ML: I don't know. I didn't know Melanie Klein well: I know that she was a pretty, coquettish woman who led a very open life; and she surely must have felt pleasure and not just calmed her basic anxieties in making love. But it's true that in her theoretical focus, she always places more emphasis on the two positions, the paranoid-schizoid and the depressive, linked to the two basic anxieties which Pichon Riviere later re-examined. But perhaps I ought to clarify that she does not use the terms with which she denotes these positions in a psychiatric sense. What's more, she was not a depressive; she enjoyed life, she reached a very old age fully lucid, she was flirtatious, very much a woman.

EG: We have already spoken of how Freud's illness and the deaths of his loved ones played a role in his formulation of the concept of the death instinct. Do you think that in Melanie Klein some similar factor came into play which explains her emphasis on aggression, on consecutive anxieties, on the omission of pleasure in her writings?

ML: I don't know. Melanie Klein begins to get deeply into the concept of Thanatos in the era between the two wars. But to attribute this to the inter-war climate would, I believe, be a complete oversimplification. But her most important work, *Love, Guilt and Reparation* (1975), was written as a result of the death of her son in a climbing accident. She commented to those close to her that she was able to write the book and come out of her deep depression by analysing her dreams and creating theoretically; this helped her a lot in working through her bereavement.

EG: You once said to me that the Kleinian concepts helped you to understand better how certain political militants are able to withstand torture.

ML: Militancy, like any other impassioned activity, is nurtured on feelings which arise from the paranoid-schizoid and depressive positions. Or, in simple terms, along with the desire and the goal of repairing social injustices and achieving a more just society – reparation, depressive position – there exists a schism somewhat unavoidably dualistic, yet effective, whereby *compañeros* are idealized and enemies are loathed. With respect to the latter, you could speak in a certain sense of feelings arising from the paranoid-schizoid position. But in borderline situations, as in torture, I suppose one can only resist it by carrying those feelings to the extreme. And the dreadful reality is obviously conducive to the enemy-torturer being experienced as the embodiment of evil, and the cause as the salvation of humanity. Those who carry out repression also know that the strength of the tortured is derived from this conviction; that's why there is usually a 'bad' torturer and a 'good' interrogator. If the prisoner begins to believe in the interrogator's 'good faith', he becomes confused, breaks down and confesses.

EG: You would say then that Kleinian concepts, so focused upon the internal world and apparently so little connected to social reality, can, nevertheless, also be used to interpret socio-political phenomena.

ML: Without any doubt. Let's go back to the psychology of women. In contrast to the culturalists, and also many analysts like Margarete Mitscherlich, for example, Melanie Klein, in her analysis of the female child's early years, never refers to the fact that penis envy could be the result of the concessions given her brother. She limits herself, from a bio-psychological level, strictly to restoring to her the identity which Freud, considering her to be a castrated male child, has taken from her.

In the 1960s feminists strongly attacked psychoanalysis instead of employing it as a useful tool in their struggle. If we take into account Freud's concepts about women, the attack was inevitable, as well as the ridicule, because, after Freud, embryology showed that his idea that the clitoris is a rudimentary penis was erroneous. It turned out to be the contrary: the penis is an enlarged clitoris. This could lack any importance, beyond academic knowledge, if it were not that Freud deduced from his hypothesis that women, in order to overcome their improper masculine features and achieve full femininity, would have to give up the pleasurable excitability of this organ and the clitoral orgasm, because the clitoris was a supposedly masculine organ. And that's where another psychoanalytic theory on feminine sexuality came apart. Masters and Johnson (1980) showed that, physiologically speaking, there was no difference between a clitoral and vaginal orgasm, and that full orgasm could be released from any erogenous zone and even from fantasies. I think that what we are dealing with here is the same confusion which arose in Reich's discussion on orgasm; we'll examine that later. The important thing, or, if you like, what defines the 'normality' – and I am using this somewhat moralistic and ambiguous word with a certain distaste – of the orgasm results from the interaction of fantasies and the simultaneous sexual act.

Helene Deutsch, a faithful follower of Freud who developed the master's concept of female masochism to such an extreme that she describes birth as a masochistic orgasm, was also the object of violent attacks.

Melanie Klein and Lacan have proffered an end to this sterile debate, Lacan by claiming the acceptance of symbolic castration for both sexes.

Juliet Mitchell, a Lacanian, a feminist and Marxist, wrote an important book on the theme, as did Melanie Klein, proposing a bio-psychological theory which differentiated between both sexes without depreciating either. In explaining the bio-psychological specificity of woman, Mitchell opens the way to her psycho-social analysis. In this way, she makes it possible to define woman's psychology as super-structure between the biological and the social (Mitchell, 1976).

EG: We've spoken at length about Melanie Klein. And you've already mentioned Lacan. It has always been said that economic penetration in Argentina has usually been English and North American, but that cultural penetration has always been French – Sartre at one point, structuralism later, and today Lacan personifies the 'boom' in the field of psychology. Two partially connected issues arise – Lacanian theory itself on one hand, the current Lacanian institutional movement on the other.

ML: I read a book by Roustang about the Lacanian movement a little while ago. He was, I believe, expelled from one of the many *écoles freudiennes* for what he wrote in it. He describes how exactly the same phenomenon occurs with Lacan as took place with Freud in another era: the total idealization of the leader, the complete submission of the students, and then a difficulty in reasoning, crazy fantasizing, etc. Nevertheless, at one time the Lacanians were regarded as leftists, I suppose because they began working in the psychiatric hospitals; that is, they partly abandoned their consulting rooms.

EG: In his polemical and valuable work, *Psychoanalyse und gesellschaftliche Macht* (Psychoanalysis, the Psychoanalytical Order and Power), Robert Castel points to how at present in the developed countries, particularly in France, psychoanalysis is used in the psychiatric establishments in order to supplement the shortcomings of psychiatry, modernizing the forms of repression and social control (Castel, 1976).

ML: That may be so. But there is another problem beyond analysis in private consulting rooms or in hospitals: Maud Manoni, in a casual encounter, once commented to me that the present-day Lacanians analyse the patient's words a lot, but that the patient has disappeared beneath the discourse, which has become more and more philosophical, and incomprehensible, if you don't devote all of your time to learning to decipher it. I haven't studied Lacan, because I haven't wanted to dedicate hours and hours of every day to understanding the Great Master.

EG: The Lacanians say that Lacan's discourse is complicated because it is also the discourse of the unconscious. I think that, apart from that, it is in fact the way French intellectuals write, from the most eminent left theorist to the most minor French philosopher. But, what's more, there is another

aspect one can mention, seeing that in Argentina, where the military authorities persecute one kind of psychoanalysis while permitting another, depending on its 'subversive threat', the Lacanian movement has really grown
without any difficulty.

ML: They persecute analysis which is mixed with Marxism, an explosive
mix in their opinion. But the institutionalized psychoanalysis of the International Psychoanalytical Association has no problems. What you say about the
Lacanian upsurge in Argentina is true. But why persecute it if it's not
connected to any reality, since the only important thing is the word, and the
analysis of the word in order to discover the language of the unconscious,
and nothing else?

EG: In spite of this, what do you think of Lacan's contribution to
psychoanalysis?

ML: He certainly contributes valuable elements. More than that I cannot
say. I am not familiar with his work in general and I haven't gone deeply into
the little that I have read.

EG: To end this very general evaluation of Freud and some of his
followers, there is one thing, which I also once wrote about, that bothers me.
Freud, with considerable modesty, points out on several occasions that his
theory is nothing more than the framework of a still-unfinished psychological edifice open to contributions from other theories, whether they be
analytical or not. I suppose that you also agree that psychoanalysis is the
most important contribution to psychology, but not the only one, and that it
doesn't have to be treated as dogma, disregarding other contributions.

ML: Clearly, it should not be exclusive. Both psychological and interdiscip-
linary contributions should be accepted. I've already told you how I admire
Parin's proposition of focusing on the patient's concept of 'reality' from the
Marxist perspective.

EG: I understand that this was your thinking before you knew Parin. You
end your paper 'Psychoanalysis and/or social revolution', presented to the
International Congress in Vienna in 1971, with the words: 'This time we will
not renounce either Marx or Freud.' How do you concretely, in your theory
and practice, mesh these two theories, which many believe are in opposition?

ML: It has become spontaneous rather than simple. When I wrote that
paper, when I compiled *Cuestionamos* and wrote the prologue, it seemed that
a change was taking place in Argentina, whereby it would be easy and
feasible to mesh both theories in practice. In a prologue I wrote for the
translation of the book by Bassin – the Russian who wrote about the
unconscious – I mention what I was thinking at the time. Walking through
Moscow, I had asked a friend: 'You say you want to make revolution. But

once you have, won't you get rid of us psychoanalysts, as has always happened in socialist countries?' And he replied: 'No, of course not, because you analysts are on our side.'

Going back to your question: I don't know how. I know that we live in the West and that we are rather *sui generis*, psychoanalysts who work in a certain way which takes the social into account, whereby we don't interpret political militancy as masochism and in which we are very conscious that any science – but more so, the human ones – is on one side or the other, ideologically speaking, and that objectivity does not exist in psychoanalysis. I don't know if I'm getting off the subject . . .

EG: In an unpublished work, you and Ignacio Maldonado say something connected to this. In reaction, I imagine, to excessive intellectualization on the part of the 'Left', you quote Mao, emphasizing the importance of practice. I totally agree with this point of view, but it seems to me you describe the relationship between Marxism and psychoanalysis as though they acted in different spheres. What do you see as the synthesis, the unity, the articulation?

ML: I don't know if I understand you correctly, but I do know that in order to understand and comprehend a person completely, we need both focuses.

EG: The problem is how they are linked in an individual. Caruso mentions Sartre's criticism of psychoanalysis because it comprehends the adult as a child and neglects the importance of work, while Marxism generally views the adult as worker, forgetting that he was once a child. On the other hand, some French and German analysts put forth an interesting but unpublished idea: they say that psychoanalysis is the comprehension of the process of transformation to subject, wherein the transition from the biological to the social is produced. I say the concept is somewhat unfinished because the behaviourists would say the same thing.

ML: From the biological to the social, yes, although in a different way.

EG: They would not take the unconscious into account. But, do you think that the articulation between psychoanalysis and Marxism is produced therein? In other words, in how the social acts upon the instinctual?

ML: I already said so, in part, when I mentioned Parin's concept. What's more, I think that's how we have thought of it generally: psychoanalysis is a field, the field of the psychology of the individual, and at the same time, since the individual does not exist in isolation, it is also a means of focusing on the individual within society. Marxism is much more encompassing; it is the science of society.

That's one perspective. The other, Sartre proposes: while for the Marxists man begins to exist when he receives his first salary, Freud concerns himself with man's evolution from birth until long before this period. Now, where are the points of contact? On the one hand in the family, which is enclosed within society, and trains and constrains the members the society needs. This is why the family is a very important link, and psychoanalytic theory allows us to perceive how society enters the individual through the family: the super-ego, the ego ideal and the identifications of the Oedipal stage. I've already mentioned what Freud says in the final years of his life, when he goes beyond his original premise that the super-ego is the internationalization of the father image: 'the child's super-ego is not in fact formed according to the model of the parents themselves but rather the parental super-ego, receiving the same content, becoming the substratum of tradition and all permanent values which have been transmitted by such a path throughout generations . . .'

In practice, we concern ourselves a lot with familial ties, which are tainted by social origin and the ideology of the dominant class, etc. On the other hand, I repeat that one of the goals of psychoanalysis should be to help the individual augment his judgement of reality, and also to question that reality, and increase his capacity to change it.

EG: The first person to adopt this political focus was Wilhelm Reich. Beyond the polemic his work provoked, he was a pioneer, for his theoretical attempt to link psychoanalysis and Marxism, as much as for his practice.

ML: Before giving you my opinion of Reich, I would like to quote what Castel says in this respect:

> It is not only that Reich was the first to deal with the political problem in all its amplitude in psychoanalysis. Nor is it merely due to his being the first really to alter the social impact of psychoanalytical practice to make the analytical relation an instrument at the service of the most emotionally frustrated and at the same time politically exploited class. It appears to me that the relation that exists in Reich between the theoretical transformations and practices that psychoanalysis inflicts on him, and the kind of practice manifest in Sexpol, has not been sufficiently emphasized. It is a surprisingly modern idea to liberate the political potential of areas explicitly given to apoliticism, as are sexuality and the family. (Castel, 1976)

Castel later points out the double downfall of Reich, his rupture with the German Communist Party in 1932 and with the Psychoanalytic International in 1934, as proof of the impossibility of such an enterprise in principle, not only because of the way in which Reich carried it out. I think that Castel, familiar with the French debates, particularly the Lacanians, remains trapped in his condemnation of psychoanalysis and of any attempt at a different ideological application; he is trapped by two demands of classical psychoanalysis, untenable in practice: the placing of social reality 'in parentheses' during treatment and the supposed 'objectivity' of the psychoanalyst. Both are unsustainable. Social reality filters into the analytic process through the discourse of the patient, and also through the interpretations, whether or not the analyst likes it, and his 'objectivity' does not exist, because nobody can be really objective; that's an invention. That this invention should have been postulated by Freud and upheld as valid and feasible by many analysts until now is, in and of itself, a manifestation of conservative ideology.

EG: I completely agree with you about the myth of neutrality; we'll come back to it later. As for Reich's work, I consider it highly respectable, although I don't agree with a large number of his theoretical and practical concepts. But he was not only a pioneer in the linking of psychoanalysis and Marxism; fundamentally he opened up unknown paths and was consistent in realizing practice without limiting himself to the comfort of theory. With regard to Sexpol, you lived during that period.

ML: Sexpol was very important, although in the long run, it was before its time. It originated in Vienna, organized by the Viennese Psychoanalytical Society with the help of the Social Democrat municipality. The Communists also co-operated in the creation of family centres, dedicated to family planning and sex education. And this was at the end of the 1920s! Reich devoted himself to his work with a lot of zeal. Later, in Berlin, when he tried to create a movement within the Communist youth based on the demand for sexual freedom, at the same time as Nazism was on a dizzying ascent and Communism was experiencing very violent and direct confrontations, he obviously clashed with the Party and, finally, he broke with it. In practice he was mistaken in doing that.

But in his analysis of the German family and the consequences of the sexual repression of women, he shows himself to be a pioneer of great brilliance. Today it is almost a platitude to say that the family, as an ideological tool, reproduces the subjects the state needs. At that time nobody except Reich would have said that. But a sexually repressed and frustrated mother is easily converted into being conservative, submissive to men, and dominating and repressive with children. These are the mothers who reproduced the subjects prone to obedience, and to a more or less sublimated homosexuality, which led them to submission to, and admiration for, a Führer.

PRAXIS

EG: You have always dedicated yourself to clinical work. I think it's important that we begin by examining your current evaluation of psychoanalysis, of therapy within a psychoanalytic framework, and of psychotherapy in general.

ML: That's a lot of subjects at once. I still work clinically with patients; in supervisions and with post-graduate students of clinical psychology. I can talk about individual psychoanalysis, psychoanalytic group psychotherapy and short-term therapies within a psychoanalytic framework. I lack experience with the others.

EG: But you know what they are about and the ideological criticisms that are made of psychotherapy in general.

ML: Yes, they are often accused of manipulating the patient and of being conformist; but psychoanalysis is also frequently accused of the same. To a certain degree all psychotherapies are inevitably manipulative. Freud also admits that psychoanalysis is not totally free from a certain suggestion. Whether they conform to the system, that is, to state ideology, depends on the therapist, on the patient–therapist interaction, the institutional framework in which they develop (private practice is also an institution), and the social situation in general. For example, if at a certain point in Argentina, so many of us mental health workers adopted a critical and non-conformist position, it was because the country was very politicized. Whether the era was really pre-revolutionary, as we then believed, is something else. The political climate was anyway.

EG: I would be interested in knowing which factors you would use to define a therapy, or more directly, an analysis since that's your field, as conformist or as critical.

ML: I think there are two defining factors which overlap: the conscious or unconscious goal the analyst has for each of his patients and his idea of mental health. As far as I know, the first person to concern himself with the subject was Heinrich Racker, although not from the political point of view.

In his book on technique he describes how a subgroup of the APA has a mental health ideal, shared by the majority of the analysts in the International Association, that consists of earning a lot and even more, having indiscriminate sexual freedom and foolproof potency, and being able to show off increasingly bigger cars, etc. Racker defines this model of mental health as 'hypomanic', although this adjective borrowed from psychopathology may appear contradictory when used with the noun 'mental health'. But it is a model adapted to the ideology of the consumer society, an expression of the height capitalist development has reached in the countries of the First World.

For Freud, the goal of a well-carried-out psychoanalysis was to reach the point where the patient could work and love better. Freud treated patients from the middle and upper classes and the criteria of 'work better' could be conformist or not, depending to which class the patient belonged, the type of work, etc.

EG: Or depending on whom one worked for.

ML: Yes, depending on one's relationship to the means of production. To say that a worker is healthy because he works better on an assembly line would be totally absurd. ButFreud was not referring to the worker.

EG: This is another example that shows how Freud always refers to a general, abstract man, leaving aside or failing to comprehend existing class differences.

ML: It's not that he doesn't comprehend them, but that they were of no interest to him in his research. He does not talk about an abstract man, but about his patients, who virtually without exception belonged to the middle or upper classes. But, in his early studies on hysteria he was enthused to find a peasant girl who showed clear hysterical symptoms; upon proving that they arose from repressed incestuous desires, he points out how she suffered from the same conflict from which his more sophisticated patients usually became ill. But they were the ones that interested him.

It would be worthwhile sometime to discuss how the concept of mental health varies, a concept which not only has an ideological, political and social basis, but even a sexist one in different societies and classes.

For example, in 'La mujer y la locura' ('Women and madness', 1980), Franca Basaglia shows that society only begins to concern itself with the mental health of the working-class housewife when she is no longer able to carry out her simple role. More is demanded of the an, involved in the work of production, but he also receives help sooner.

EG: Definitely, ideological aspects are present in all health criteria as an expression of the forms of production, and therapies tend towards them in their objectives and goals, whether explicitly or not.

ML: Yes, explicitly or implicitly. In some cases, the concept of healing appears to be freeof ideologization: if, for example, an adult cannot cross the street alone or if he suffers from impotency or frigidity, many consider him cured when he can go out alone or feel sexual pleasure. His symptom is cured. But on the one hand, for Freud, the disappearance of the symptom – and remember that he compared the symptom to the tip of the iceberg – was not the same as real healing. And on the other, the psychological changes that occur while the disappearance of the symptom is taking place depend on the ideology of the analyst-analysand couple.

Furthermore, since Freud began treating neuroses the kind of patients who turn to psychoanalysis have changed considerably, at least in middle-class, private practice. A large number of the cases that present themselves today are usually defined as 'character neurosis'. In these cases the mental health goal depends a lot on the ideology – an I use the term in a very broad sense – of the therapist, and may or may not be conformist.

How does this work in practice? I think that with two examples it will be made clear. During a supervision, an analyst in training commented to me that he was treating the case of an engineer with impotence problems who was very bright, but very success-oriented. I asked him if he meant to say 'successful' (*exitoso*), but he insisted on the word 'success-oriented' (*exitista*). I immediately asked the analyst if he was a Marxist and he replied that he was. What am I trying to get at? This same patient, seen by another analyst, would be described as 'successful' and his professional sphere as 'a conflict-free zone', to use a term from the North American school. For the Marxist colleage his patient's need for success indicates the existence of a patho-logical character feature. Considering it as such, the analyst will obviously focus the treatment differently since his goal will be that the patient manage to diminish or eliminate this need.

A while later, this analyst presented the following material about the patient in the supervision: the patient had mentioned to him that he wanted to lay off an old foreman, the father of five children, because he no longer found it convenient to pay him extra wages. According to Argentinian law, a worker's wages are increased with the birth of every child. The analyst and I began to go over the material related to this problem to see how to approach it. We both arrived at the conclusion that one should be on one's guard to detect and interpret the feelings of unconscious guilt that the patient would experience in the face of this decision. And in fact, the patient did not feel comfortable with the sacking. His discontent could be interpreted on two levels: on the infantile level, he wanted revenge on a father who produced so many sons/brothers; on the other level, more current and adult, the patient repressed his feelings of social guilt.

EG: To us, a certain social responsibility forms part of the individual's mental health. But, I suppose that the mental health criteria of the analyst himself vary in the course of his development. It caught my attention how different criteria appear in two of your publicationsfrom distinct periods. In *Psicoterapía del grupo* (Group Psychotherapy), which you published together with Leon Grinberg and Emilio Rodrigué, you often refer to 'attaining health' or 'a complete cure' (Grinberg, Langer and Rodrigué, 1971), while in your contribution to *Razón, locura y sociedad* (Reason, Madness and Society) you say, with self-criticism and irony, that 'we aimed to save the world through psychoanalysis. And we did not realize – some of us consciously concealed it, others repressed it – that as members of the dominant class we were only saving our analysands, who belonged to the same class and were participating in the exploitation' (Suárez, 1978).

ML: Clearly they were different periods. In 1971, in the prologue to he third edition of *Psicoterapia del grupo*, I pointed out that we three co-authors were no longer in agreement with respect to many criteria. That book was written in 1956 as a result of the great enthusiasm we felt when we began to work analytically with groups; also, we wanted to show that Kleinian theory was applicable to the group technique. For Melanie Klein, mental health corresponds to the entry into the depressive position, with the increase in reparation tendencies and the maximum decreasing of the characteristics of the schizoid-paranoid position.

Freud, as well as Melanie Klein, spoke of healing as going no further than the analytic practice permits. Both consciously left social and political concepts aside. That's why, adhering strictly to Melanie Klein, it was easier for us to talk about healing then than it is for me today. However, it's not that today I try to turn my analysands into militants, but I do agree with Parin in that the recognition of social reality and its mechanisms forms part of the goal of an analysis.

EG: Beyond that, what achievements would you mention as defining a successful analysis?

ML: Analysis helps one in many respects. I am very grateful to it, and upon analysing one of my dreams I marvel anew at Freud's discovery and the way in which you can discover your thoughts and feelings, secret even from yourself, by associating some condensed dream element. Now, we cannot define what would be a successful analysis in absolute terms. And there will be times when we virtually don't achieve 'success'. Freud says so in his final works, in which he refers to this subject. I'll give you some quotes from 'Analysis terminable and interminable'.

In speaking to us of Thanatos and how it is combined wth Eros in different disturbances, he notes that 'For the moment, we have to give way to the superiority of the forces against which we see our efforts annulled. Even to exercise a psychic influence on simple masochism is a task virtually beyond our possibilities' (Freud, 1937). With respect to the terminating of a character analysis, he tells us: 'It is not easy here to foresee a natural termination, even when exaggerated expectations are avoided and an excessively difficult task is not posed in the psychoanalysis' (Freud, 1937). These considerations confirm for us the importance of the subjective criteria of the analyst in this kind of treatment.

EG: You turn to Freud, but I would like you to talk about your personal experience and criteria.

ML: First, permit me another quote, sinceit will be useful when we talk about the 'the neutrality of the analyst', an unavoidable subject today. According to Freud: 'Among the factors which influence the progress of the psychoanalytical treatment and augment difficulties of the same type as resistance, not only the nature of the patient's ego must be taken into account but also the analyst's individuality.'

If you want my personal opinion, I'll give you the informal answer I gave a journalist years ago in Argentina. It somewhat aphoristically approaches the indications and aims of an analysis. Faced with the question, 'When and for what does psychoanalysis work?', I answered:

When one is anxious, frequently and a lot; when one is afraid, afraid to go out in the street alone or to stay at home alone; or, when one is healthy and strong but afraid of dying slowly from cancer or suddenly from a heart attack. There are many 'whens', for example when a pattern is repeated in one's life: your best friend goes off with your woman, when you draw a blank in an exam you've prepared for, or when in an exam you did not prepare for you can't understand why they've failed you again. Many more whens . . . also when as an adult one has an ulcer or as a child asthma, nightmares and a lot of fear.

And why psychoanalysis? Because it works. It works for understanding yourself and others better. It works for virtually never lying to yourself again. It serves for bringing up happier children. And, according to Freud, it serves for loving better, working better and enjoying more. But, watch out, it does not serve for changing the world. That has to be done by other means. And then? If we apply it well, without a doubt, it will continue to be of service.

EG: That's fine, but I have two questions/objections. First, it's bvious that psychoanalysis doesn't serve for changing the world.

ML: I'm responding here to the fanatical psychoanalysts who hold that psychoanalysis is 'subversive' in itself, and that it would be enough to 'liberate the unconscious' in order to change society.

EG: The second question/objection is with respect to 'working better'. To me, this depends for whom one is working. And to me 'no longer lying to yourself' is related to the concept of the false consciousness.

ML: Of course, in the case of a working-class patient, I would say that he should acquire class consciousness along with the consciousness of his psychic conflict. A mental health goal would not be to work harder and better for the boss but rather in his own interests, in his union, for example. A woman, beyond her class background – here what was said about the worker is valid – should achieve consciousness of her submission to men, her excessive dependence on love: an expression of her lack of self-esteem. An important goal of her analysis would be the acquiring of dignity.

In general terms, to the healing concept I would add what Freud stipulated in talking about the need to transform an utoplastic attitude into an alloplastic one – or, in the language of Pichon Riviere, the achieving of an active adaptation to the world. This implies a dialectic interplay within oneself that manages to adapt reality to one's needs, as well as knowing how to adapt oneself to reality. This goes along with Marx's concept that we are in the world in order to change it.

EG: In defining consciousness of one's position in society as part of the goal of a good analysis, you refer to the worker and to women, but what happens with a male, upper- or middle-class patient?

ML: It can be useful for the middle-class or upper-class male to become aware of the discontent caused him by participating so directly in exploitation. You may say I am very moralistic and that I bring my value judgements into my work. Further on, when we talk about neutrality, I want to go into this more deeply. For the moment, I will only say that, of course, Freud also had a scale of values, that up to 'Analysis terminable and interminable' he claims that the analyst should have 'some kind of superiority, so that in certain analytical situations he can act as a model for the patient, and in others as a teacher', and that Erikson dedicated himself specifically to the subject of ethics in psychoanalysis.

At any rate, clinical practice has proved to me the emptiness and insatiable insecurity a 'success-oriented' person suffers from; in other words, his self-esteem depends on external, material achievements which must be repeated constantly. A good analysis ought to be able to fill this vacuum, which arises in the very early stages and is later encouraged by capitalist society, and open up other paths of satisfaction to the individual.

EG: To continue with the subject of mental health, but looking at another aspect: Freud, in 1905 in 'My views on the part played by sexuality in the aetiology of the neuroses', defines a person's normality in terms of his achieving genitality. Later on, he realizes the impossibility of total genitality, pointing out the existence of a determined amount of energy retained from previous stages. Do you think that this is the only criterion to take into account when examining health and so-called 'illness'?

ML: Your question is obviously rhetorical. If it weren't you wouldn't take such an early text of Freud's and comment that he himself later abandoned or at least qualified this criterion. It was Wilhelm Reich, not Freud, who upheld it. To me, total genitality as an indicator of health is a myth. I will give you an example in which exactly the opposite of this health aspiration was produced by genitality. A young woman patient of some thirty-odd years, the mother of two children, had broken off her analysis. But she called me in great excitement one day to say that she wanted to come and see me. She told me happily that she had separated from her husband, who was certainly rather loathsome, had begun a relationship with a younger man, and had experienced the first orgasm of her life. A few days later she entered a schizophrenic episode from which she never recovered. We cannot comprehend this tragedy if we don't know something about her personal history. Elsa, to give the patient a name, lost her mother. She had been a servant, but the father accused her of being a prostitute. A very paranoid man and an admirer of Hitler, he used to tell his daughter an anecdote. He explained that the Jews ere very powerful because of the astute upbringing they received as children. He told her the case of the Jewish father who lifted his little four-year-old son on to a table and invited the child to jump. The child trustingly leapt off the table only to crash on to the floor as the father had withdrawn his arms on purpose. 'Daddy,' asked the child, crying from the pain and confusion, 'why'd you do that to me?' 'So that you'll never trust anybody in this life,' was the 'pedagogical' answer of the father.

That's how Elsa was brought up, educated by a German governess who soon became daddy's lover. As an adult she married a man similar to her father. Yes, she was frigid with him, which is not surprising since she must have been afraid that if she felt pleasure she might be as much of a 'whore' as her mother and die as young as she had. Analysis helped her, but only partially. She managed to become independent from her husband, she managed to separate from him and to fall in love at last. But when she gave herself up to her lover and experienced an orgasm, the loss of control must have been the equivalent of leaping off the table and crashing on to the floor. Feeling herself to be up a dead-end street, she took refuge in psychosis. 'My child,' she said to her little girl, 'I'm leaving you because I'm going to live on the moon.'

I mention this case, fortunately the only one of its kind in my experience, in order to clarify that we cannot take orgastic capacity as an indicator of health, out of context. For Elsa, frigidity had obviously signified a last protection against psychosis. In taking orgastic capacity as *the criterion* of health, Wilhelm Reich erred in being mechanistic and in not taking into account the person as a whole. What's more, he gives way to another misunderstanding: orgastic capacity and genitality are not identical, since orgasm can be the result o pre-genital processes as well as 'genital' excitation.

EG: It is precisely with respect to genitality that Michael Schneider in *Neurosis and Civilization* (1973) asks up to what point in present-day developed capitalist society genitality can be spoken of, or if instead one is talking about what he calls an attempt at manic genitality.

ML: I reject that extrapolation. Something similar has often been said. He talks about manic genitality because we live in a consumer society; others, in referring to the period of the height of capitalism, explain that society was found to be in a phase of accumulaion for the construction of capitalism. Following this line of thought some utopians among psychoanalysts believed that when the establishment of a socialist or Communist society was achieved we would have arrived at genitality. Frankly, I don't believe that these constructions are valid . . . maybe if we use them metaphorically.

EG: I meant it in a different sense. Obviously it's absurd to extrapolate analytic categories to social levels. But it is another thing to recognize that every social system produces individual tendencies in order to create the human being necessary for its preservation and reproduction. The case of Protestantism, to which you refer, has been very debated and it is beyond question that this being, characteristic of the period, whom Freud defines as anal retentive, acquisitive, orderly, the model of obsessive neurosis, was not a product of coincidence but of a structural necessity.

ML: I admit that our pesent-day, middle-class ideal is often maniacal.

EG: Schneider talks about a manic character, apparently genital. I quote him to emphasize that one cannot talk about 'normality' or 'mental health' solely from a libidinal development perspective, without taking into consideration the way the concrete historical moment acts upon this development.

ML: Yes, the social context which is manifested through ideology. In this sense the ideological can be compared to the enviable, to the goals of the dominant classes. These mould the criteria of health and illness.

EG: What you said beforeabout the obsessive nature of the period of the upsurge of capitalism and, I would also add, the hysteria of the Victorian era are not whims or coincidences.

ML: The Althusserians would say that it is the necessary man, the subjected-subject, moulded to fulfil the demands of that society. I think that we have to be cautious in the use of these categories.

EG: Since we are talking about society's influence on the individual, before you pointed out that in Argentina at the beginning of the 1970s a different psychoanalytic practice was possible because the political circumstances made it possible. Some maintain, however, and I don't agree with them, that there were no major differences between orthodox psychoanalysis and those who schematically could call themselves left-wing, since both used the couch, charged fees, had similar settings, etc. They took these factors as indicators that there were no essential changes. For this reason it would be important to point out the theoretical and practical differences in the very distinct positions.

ML: So far we have talked about a very important distinction which is the effect of the analyst's political ideology, the different criteria of mental health and consequently the differing goals of the psychoanalyst. Classically it is always said that the neutral analyst will simply help his analysand to liberate his capacities. Later, he will take his own path alone. But it is precisely this concept of neutrality that was called into question by us 'left-wing analysts'. It is a much-discussed subject but, as faras I know, almost never in writing, so it would be worthwhile to talk about it.

It was in Rome in 1969 at the International Psychoanalytical Congress and the Para-congress on ideology and psychoanalysis, where Plataforma appeared, that this was discussed for the first time. I mentioned before how it was discussed that the same event (participation in the anti-Vietnam War movement) could be interpreted in a different manner by conservative or progressive analysts.

From the recognition of the effect of the analyst's ideology on the treatment to the questioning of the analyst's neutrality is only a step.

EG: But an important step that many analysts have not yet taken.

ML: Yes, and even using the metaphor of 'step' has its history. It began with Freud's postulation that the analyst should be a mere screen, in order to allow the patient to project his images and fantasies on to him. Freud also uses another metaphor, that of the surgeon who must operate cool-headedly in order to guarantee the success of the operation. However, as later studies on counter-transference have shown us, this cool-headedness and total objectivity do not exist nor are they desirable. If you take into account that Freud taught us that in analysis the analyst's unconscious forms a bond with his analysand's and he tells us, as I quoted before, that all aspects of the analyst's personality impact upon the analytic process – and his ideology necessarily forms part of this – then his role as screen or cool-headed surgeon becomes improbable.

Nevertheless, the 'classical' analysts believe in good faith in their neutrality. I'll give you an example which is related to sexist, not political, ideology: some twenty years ago, when I was not yet preoccupied with this subject, I had a young French woman in group analysis. As a result of the war, she had had to emigrate from her country – along with her parents – before she could finish her high school studies, and she came to Argentina. At first she had neither the opportunity nor the language in order to be able to finish her studies; later she got married and had two children. But, with the passing of time, her adolescent desire to study medicine returned. She made an attempt to study and to finish high school, but she wasn't able to. Every time she embarked on this project she became anxious and depressed. She wanted to be analysed for this, as well as for a sexual problem she had with her husband. She joined the group and worked very well. With time she finished high school and passed the entrance exam to medical school, which was very difficult. It was at this point that she showed an interest in doing individual analysis. As the idea seemed reasonable to the grup, I recommended a colleague, a very good analyst in my judgement, for her to continue her treatment with him. Some years later I ran across this analyst at a party. 'How is Marianne?' I asked him. 'Very well. I'm very pleased with her treatment. You sent me a very good patient.' 'She must surely have done anatomy by now?' 'No', he replied, virtually in disgust. 'She left medicine some time ago, but she's expecting her third child.' Neither Dr X nor I were aware then of what W.R. Bion had said in 'Notes on memory and desire' (1967) about analysing without desires for the patient. But at any rate, I believe it is impossible. This case is a good example to demonstrate how every analyst, often without realizing it, projects his desires for the patient's future and acts – in good faith – in such a way that the analysand oftn fulfils them to a tee. However, in other cases, as usually also happens with our own children, the patient does exactly the opposite of what we desired for him. A lot depends on his character and the type of transferential link that develops.

EG: In this case how would you define your, and your colleague's, ideology?

ML: He was a conservative family man, who didn't want his own wife to go out to work, but to dedicate herself to the home and the children. For my part, I have my feminist criteria and I believe it's very important for a woman to develop her capabilities and not be economically dependent on her husband. In order for Marianne to have reacted so flexibly, carrying out the wishes of one person and ten another, she must have been hiding, and in conflict over, her desire to study as well as staying at home and having another child.

EG: For me there is no doubt that the neutrality of the analyst is fictitious.

ML: Me neither. But in 1970, when I gave a paper on this at the Rosario Congress in Argentina, it became the focus of much discussion and controversy.

EG: Also a large part of Castel's criticism of psychoanalysis revolves around the theme of neutrality.

ML: That's right. I want to quote a couple of sentences from Castel's *Psychoanalyse und gesellschaftliche Macht*, which contain his two fundamental objections: 'The "analysand" is at the same time encouraged and enticed by the process of subjectivization, induced by the analytical situation, to put the political and social dimension into parentheses. The psychoanalyst directs this process from his position of "neutrality" ' (Castel, 1976). In turn, we psychoanalysts who left the Psychoanalytical Association do not believe in this neutrality but define the neutrality demanded by the institution as 'apoliticism' and guardian of the status quo.

The second point on which Castel bases his criticism is the putting 'of the social and political dimension into parentheses'. He talks about 'certain Latin American countries where political arbitrariness and torture reign' and where it would be impossible 'to avoid the importance of non-psychic reality'. However, it was preciselyin Latin America, long before its current dramatic upheavals, that the political reality began to be taken into account. In their article 'Crisis social y situación analítica' ('Social crisis and the analytical situation') in *Cuestionamos*, Laura Achard de Maríe and her colleagues describe how the death of a student, in fact the first political death to erupt in a previously peaceful and democratic country, affects the analyst and analysand. It is compared with the death of the country, a common object, in which both believed up to that point. They mention examples of patients who comment on the event, as well as others where the patient represses the painful reality, while the analyst includes it in his interpretations as something common and painful to both.

I'll quote some of their conclusions, clarifying first that in speaking of the 'common object' they are always referring to their country, Uruguay. Among other things, they say: 'We feel that this common object broadens the analytical field in spatial terms, carrying it beyond the walls of our consulting rooms, to include the outside world . . .' and 'in a country in social crisis, faced with periods of national upheaval, we believe that the fate of the common object as well as the treating of external events both on the transferential plane and in relation to internal objects must be taken up in the session – sometimes as a point of urgency' (Achard de Maríe *et al.*, 1971).

Unfortunately, in Argentina in later years we had many opportunities to resort to this technique. But I'd also say that even without the drama of the extreme situations we went through, for some time now we have been unaccustomed to leaving social reality 'outside'. And if Castel accuses us of not 'having at our disposal the theoretical or practical means of differentiating the political–social', I would say, along with Parin – in other words, this time not a Latin American persecuted by tragic circumstances, but an established Swiss analyst – that, in effect, what we need for this is a knowledge of Marxism.

EG: Clearly, we must utilize this knowledge. That's why Marxism was included as a subject in the Teaching and Research Centre and in the Mental Health Workers' Co-ordinator.

ML: Yes, of course. We need both sciences in order to embrace psychology and comprehend the individual. I totally agree with José Bleger when in his article, 'Psicoanálisis y marxismo ('Psychoanalysis and Marxism') in *Cuestionamos*, he says that 'Marxism as method and ideology not only does not replace psychology, but demands it' (Bleger, 1971). It was Stalin who held that Marxism replaces it.

EG: You still owe me further clarification of the differences between a politically 'neutral' psychoanalysis, in other words supportive of the system, and the other, the theoretical framework and praxis of which began to be defined in the two volumes of *Cuestionamos* and other publications of the time. To begin with, what modifications does the setting suffer?

ML: There were many misunderstandings about this, especially in criticism from a Left which had never experienced the analytical process first hand. It was said to be authoritarian, that the very positions of the analyst seated and the patient lying down dramatized, reproduced and fixed generational and class differences, etc. But first, we should synthesize the function of the setting in order to later examine how it is applied and which are its necessary elements and which are in effect maintained for ideological and even utilitarian reasons. As setting, we understand that the analyst and analysand meet within a fixed schedule with fixed fees in a room in which the analysand generally lies on a couch while the analyst is seated in an armchair behind him. In the classical model the analyst will have advised the analysand of the 'ground rule', that is, the request that the patient say everything that crosses his mind. The analyst will listen to the patient's discourse in a climate of trust and will only intervene to interpret, but without judging or advising.

I won't go into the history, generall well known, of how this 'setting' came about; I will only mention why Freud speaks to us of the 'analyst as screen'. The therapist is requested to omit any observations whatsoever related to his own experience – very frequent in other psychotherapies (for example, the 'I really understand that because it's happened to me, too') – in order for the transference to develop cleanly, since it is the vehicle for the emergence of the situations and pathological ties with the past as memories and transferential experiences. Alexander described the transferential process as an amended reissue of the past – amended thanks to the 'neutrality' of the analyst, who neither judges nor interferes, but rather in contrast to the primitive personalities of the patient, listens, tries to understand and interprets.

EG: You must clarify this: after all you said about the impossibility of the existence of a neutral analyst, you yourself are asking him to be one.

ML: Before clarifying this contradiction I'd like to continue to capture and explain the meaning of setting. First, I'll talk about the abstinence the analyst must impose upon himself: he must not pamper or comfort the patient, except in extreme situations – when, I would add, nearly all of us have done so. The refusal to concede to the patient's requests for friendship, love, extraclinical contact, etc., is necessary, because the satisfying of his transferential – and consequently infantile – desires would impede the emergence of the unconsciously repressed. But moreover, and in my long professional experience I've seen how necessary this is, the aove also functions as protection for the analyst because faced with the patient's needs he is often tempted to abuse the transferential situation. For example, sexual abuse occurs with a certain frequency between a male analyst and female patient, though rarely between a female analyst and male patient, and usually has disastrous psychological consequences – marriages between analysts and patients are usually a disaster. There is also abuse from other perspectives, for example the accepting of favours from rich and powerful patients.

EG: I agree with what you say with regard to the economic aspect, but couldn't it be that an amorous relationship between an analyst and a patient is not necessarily an abuse on the analyst's part?

ML: It will always be an abuse because the patient is in an infantile and dependent position. It's true that inexpert analysts often believe themselves to have fallen in love 'pygmalion-like' with their patient, just as the patient falls in love with the analyst in gratutude for all his help. One has to have the lack of narcissism Freud had in order to have discovered that if all his patients fell in love with him, already an older man without great physical attraction, this 'transferential' love simply formed part of the process. Marriages between analysts and analysands usually end badly, because, while she soon discovers that her real husband has nothing in common with the ideal figure she imagined, he will soon realize that he fell into the trap of seducing his beautiful invalid as well as that of countertransference and his own narcissism.

EG: Many of the criticisms of the setting are directed at the couch, which Freud introduced because it bothered him to work for hours under the inquisitive gaze of his patients.

ML: Yes, that's the historical reason. But the reclining position and the gazing into space also facilitate the regression sought to allow the emergence of infantile material, since it brings with it certain sensory deprivation. The discovery of the consequences of this came much later than Freud, who had applied it intuitively.

EG: But the setting is one thing and its exaggerations another. Your friend Emilio Rodriguep̃ ridicules the orthodox analyst who won't even tell the analysand the time if his watch has stopped.

ML: I agree with Emilio in many aspects and I regret he's not here to take part in this conversation with us. I don't defend the excesses of the setting either; rather, I attempt to clarify the reasons for its existence and its usefulness. I'd like to emphasize here: what always differentiates analytic therapy from behavioural therapy is that by our 'neutral' attitude we carefully avoid the system of reward and punishment.

EG: Once again you are entering into the contradiction of denying the possibility of analytic neutrality and demanding it at the same time.

ML: To clarify this dilemma I'll turn to the *The Language of Psychoanalysis* (Laplanche and Pontalis, 1967) and quote the three positions of neutrality demanded of the analyst: first, 'the analyst must be *neutral* with respect to religious, moral and social values, in other words, not direct the cure on the basis of any ideal and abstain from giving any advice whatsoever'. You see, I don't believe that this neutrality is possible, even if we abstain from giving advice. But rather, as we said earlier, our ideology will influence the aim of the treatment and this in turn will affect the material we select, the way we interpret it, etc. While I doubt the feasibility of the first, I am in agreement with the neutrality demanded in the second in relation to transferential manifestations, usually expressed as the principle of 'not entering into the patient's game'.

To me the third point is linked to the first and therefore also unsustainable; '*neutral* in regard to the analysand's discourse, that is, not conceding *a priori* preferential importance, by virtue of theoretical prejudices (I would also add, ideological), to a specific fragment or specific types of signifiers'. In fact, our current theoretical interests will impact, as will our *Weltanschauung*, on the material we choose for interpretation, naturally together with our technical criteria about which are resistential elements, which points of urgency, etc.

EG: You are defending the classical setting and explaining its usefulness. All the same I'm aware that you don't use it at present, the way you did during your lengthy membership in the APA.

ML: That's right, and here we could talk about various differences. But first I want to refer to three important modifications that in general already existed in the APA under the Kleinian influence. The first is with respect to object-relations interpretation. We interpreted much more at the object-relationship level than the merely instinctive and this has its social implications. The second and third modifications humanize the setting and prevent the analyst from being perceived as a computer or distant god. The second refers to the dialogue with the patient, in contrast to the silent analyst, who with luck says a few words at the end of the session. Freud did not work like that but many of his followers sang the praises of the analyst's silence; the third is related to the use of counter-transference, transforming it from an obstacle into an working tool. In Argentina this was achieved primarily due to the work of Heinrich Racker.

EG: But I suppose that shortly after you left the APA you frequently abandoned the couch.

ML: Yes, as well as rigidly seeing an analysand four times per week. Both measures are required by the International Psychoanalytical Association in order for a treatment to be called psychoanalytic. During my time in the APA I almost exclusively analysed candidates, that's to say, doctors in psychoanalytic training, so I had no choice. But once outside the institution, I followed strictly clinical criteria, both in the frequency of sessions and in the choice of the couch versus the face-to-face position.

EG: In other words, you take into account what seems clinically best for the patient.

ML: Certainly, and also for the likelihood of my doing a good job. For example, I believe that I analyse erotic or aggressie transferential fantasies with more ease when sitting behind the patient. But those fantasies can also be interpreted face on. It's fitting to analyse a very obsessive, very controlling patient reclined on a couch but if you are analysing a 'borderline' or a psychotic with little connection to reality in this position, this slight connection is even further diminished. Also there are patients you can analyse very well with fewer than four sessions a week and even some you can achieve a lot with in only one per week.

EG: I suppose that this absolute requirement of four sessions responds more to the economic needs of the analyst than to the clinical needs of the patient, or perhaps because the analyst was taught that that's the way it should be

ML: Exactly. And to the comfort of being able to work to the full with a relatively small number of analysands.

EG: We've arrived at a very controversial subject. The analyst's high fees and the supposed impossibility of analysing free of charge.

ML: Yes, the most unlikely things have been said on this subject. For example, David Liberman, a very intelligent and creative analyst, in an article along with G. Ferschtut and D. Sor wrote that 'the amount of the fee is an indicator of the reality-quantity of the analytical bond with which is contrasted the figure-transference, which must be analysed' (Liberman, Ferschtut and Sor, 1961). On the basis of this, Baremblitt (1974) comments, 'the authors, directly or implicitly, arrive at the affirmation that the act of charging constitutes a therapeutic instrment as important as interpretation'. This is totally absurd. What's more, how would it be possible to analyse little children, as yet unconnected to the concept of payment and money, or psychotics, if this were true? In both cases, it is the relatives who take charge of the payment.

EG: Liberman supports his argument with a paragraph from 'On beginning the treatment' (1913), in which Freud says that the experience he acquired in ten years of analysing for one or two hours daily free of charge showed him that 'free treatment enormously intensifies some of the neurotic's resistances'. He gives as an example the intensifying of erotic transference in young women as well as transferential rebellion against the father on the part of men.

ML: Yes, he said this in 1913. However, only a few years later in 1918, speaking at the Budapest Psychoanalytical Congress – it is true that perhaps he was influenced by the brief existence of a Communist Hungarian government which was sympathetic towards psychoanalysis – he literally tells us,

. . . it is possible to foresee that at some time or other the conscience of society will awake and remind it that the poor man should have just as much right to assistance for his mind as he now has to the life-saving help offered by surgery; and that the neuroses threaten public health no less than tuberculosis, and can be left as little as the latter to the impotent care of individual members of the community. When this happens, institutions or out-patient clinics will be started, to which analytically-trained physicians will be appointed, so that men who would otherwise give way to drink, women who have nearly succumbed under their burden of privations, children for whom there is no choice but between running wild or neurosis, may be made capable, by analyis, of resistance and of efficient work. Such treatment will be free.

I emphasize 'free', Enrique.

EG: What has been your experience in this regard?

ML: When I was doing my training in Vienna in the mid-1930s, each candidate still analysed his two supervision patients free of charge. Every analyst who had completed his training also analysed two people free. The Association had a clinic for people with limitd resources who needed analysis. What's more, every teaching analyst had two scholarship candidates in analysis, who were talented but lacked the economic means to acquire their training any other way.

EG: And that was in spite of what Freud said in 1913. But how did you deal with resistance and problems in practice, the ones Freud refers to in the article I quoted previously, which he himself contradicts?

ML: I left Vienna before I was able to gain any experience in this so I'll tell you about what I observed in Argentina and Mexico. But before that, I'd like to talk about the importance what Freud said in Budapest had for me and many others. It became our motto. Many of us believed in this goal when we started group psychotherapy and when we founded the corresponding Association in Buenos Aires. It was the same aim as we had when we started the Enrique Racker Clinic in the Association, whose first director was David Liberman, curiously enough. It was he who suggested we should accept only 'socially relevant' patients, such as teachers, nurses, etc., since their mental health would be important to a whole nucleus of people.

As we've already mentioned, Wilhelm Reich was the first to attempt to apply psychoanalysis to the working classes, grossly overestimating its political effects. Now Freud, in his lecture in Budapest, was certainly not thinking along these lines.

EG: But you, or rather we, in Buenos Aires were.

173

ML: Not at the beginning and not all of us. When we started group psychotherapy we didn't think beyond Freud's lecture in Budapest, but we did later. Those of us who worked at the Avellaneda Hospital or in the Clinical Psychology Faculty, as well as those who taught at the Teaching and Research Centre, included class consciousness in our analytic therapy goal of acquiring consciousness. And those of us who left the APA stated this explicitly in the declarations of the groups known as Plataforma and Documento.

EG: That was when you abandoned the myth of neutrality.

ML: Yes, both in institutional work and in private practice. The patients who sought us out knew who they were coming to; they made a conscious choice.

EG: Before going on with the subject of the characteristics of free institutional treatment, I'd like to know whether you came across the resistance Freud describes when you analysed your private patients free of charge.

ML: I've always treated patients free in emergency situations but I've never carried out a complete psychoanalysis in this way. I imagine that what Freud describes happens, and in addition the analyst is idealized and there is a certain difficulty in expressing hostility, which is part of negative transference. This occurs if the patient experiences the situation as being philanthropic. But I think all of this can be analysed. Without referring strictly to classical treatment, but rather to analytic psychotherapy, I think we have to differentiate between two situations. It is totally feasible to treat a *compañero* or a militant successfully, without charge, because of the bond of solidarity that unites you and justifies spending your time on him. On the other hand, in a hospital situation, there is no particular difficulty in this respect because the patient, apart from having the right to adequate attention, since this is what he pays taxes for, also imagines you are being paid for your work. So a 'philanthropic' situation does not exist here either.

I'll give you another example. It's true that I have never carried out a full individual psychoanalysis free of charge. But at the moment, in my role as a lecturer in the master's and doctorate courses in clinical psychology at the UNAM, I'm working for the second time with a group which is in fact both didactic and therapeutic. The only difference between this and a private group is that it has a maximum length of two years. But in two years one can both change and learn a lot. This group is in fact free, since I receive my salary as a lecturer for those two hours a week and the post-graduate students who attend the group do not pay for it specifically. However, since they feel they have the right to attend this group, there has never been a problem in this respect.

Perhaps it would also be worth giving an example of an instance where analytical therapy was given in the kind of emergency situation I mentioned earlier. During the first few years of our stay in Mexico many Argentinians arrived traumatized by the loss of their loved ones, by having been in prison, by having to become exiles and by everything that had happened to them. Most of them were in a very precarious economic situation. We managed to organize things in such a way that everyone was attended to, and the patients, who were mostly middle class, accepted this free treatment quite naturally. It was only when they managed to find work and adapt to Mexico that they began to pay. This was useful in a therapeutic sense because, even though they were *compañeros*, the analytic process was made easier when they were able to pay for the analyst's work. In short: we live in a society in which services received are paid for in one way or another. The psychoanalyst should not try to present himself as Maecenas or pretend that he doesn't need to work and earn money in order to live. However, the fact that the economic need of the analyst has become a technical rule, as emphasized by David Liberman, or that the patient might not appreciate free or cheap treatment, as Freud himself says, is a rationalization on the part of the analysts. The amount of the fees and the issue of free treatment ought to be evaluated clinically.

EG: Free treatment is not usually the only objection to hospital therapies from the psychoanalytic point of view. I remember an article by Raúl Usandivaras, 'Comunicación terapéutica y clase social' ('Therapeutic communication and social class'), which provoked a great deal of debate in its time. The author, who was a well-qualified analyst from the APA, belonged to the Argentinian upper class and lacked any Marxist background, describes how he was unable to establish contact with his poor patients who lived in shanty towns. The difference in class and cultural backgrounds turned his difficulty in finding a common code into an insurmountable obstacle (Usandivaras, 1968).

ML: Yes, I remember that article well, since we quoted it in two publications that describe our experience in the Avellaneda Hospital (Langer and Siniego, 1977; Langer, Siniego and Ulloa, 1979). In it he talks about the impossibility of arriving at a diagnosis with these shanty town patients. I quote, 'We were never able to discern whether our patients suffered from psychosis, psychopathy or mental deficiency.' Usandivaras holds that a poor person is incapable of conceptualizing, and, basing himself on a North American publication, he finds that there, as in Argentina, the co-operation of working-class patients is nil as long as the analyst resorts only to the spoken word.

175

EG: Nevertheless, you and your colleagues managed to work satisfactorily in these areas.

ML: It was a highly satisfying experience, even with all the inevitable frustrations. It was made possible because we had the full co-operation of Silvia Berman, the head of the department, and also because of the political moment we were experiencing, both ourselves and our patients. In the therapy itself, in contrast to what Usandivaras said, we did not encounter

specific difficulties in applying our psychoanalytical knowledge. The patients understood our interpretations: they had a greater or lesser ability for insight, just as happens with bourgeois patients; they were just as capable of thinking and talking in place of acting as our analysands in private practice. And some of them, who were very deprived, really needed that hour in which they had the right to listen and to be listened to. That someone was interested in their fate and was witness to it, was much more unusual and therefore more appreciated and therapeutic than it is for our private patients. However, when they lacked even the minimum means for subsistence we failed (to help them).

EG: Did you follow the technique that you, Grinberg and Rodrigué explain in your book or did you make any modifications? From what you say in the prologue to the third edition, you obviously did.

ML: Naturally, at that time I already approached therapy in a different way. I mentioned this when we talked about the criteria for treatment, in any case all institutions impose certain modifications. With respect to the special case of the Avellaneda Hospital, I would say that we used to take the socio-economic and cultural situation of each member of the group into account. For example, you cannot ask a housewife to leave the house, spend money on transport, ask the neighbour to look after her children and have her husband prepare the meal very frequently, or over a long period of time. This time variable, and the demands and pressures our patients were subject to, led to our avoiding very deep regression. We never used to remain silent, Bion-style; we interpreted very little in transference, but we didn't hesitate to do so if it was a question of making conscious the resentment felt towards the therapist or other members of the group, or an idealization at the service of infantile dependence. We focused more on day-to-day problems, without leaving out each member's personal history as a result.

EG: It must have been in this hospital work that you strove towards and partially achieved a valuable praxis – in other words, an integration of Marxism and psychoanalysis in practice.

ML: Indeed, that was our aim. We agreed with Pichon Riviere that any curing process implies learning. But in order to achieve this, and enable the person who at a given moment needs therapeutic help to go ahead later without therapy, he should not only have acquired insight into the psychological problems which led to his illness but also the instruments necessary for understanding how society and his place in it have conditioned his own life. And this awareness will not be operative if he does not simultaneously manage to break out of his isolation and create bonds of solidarity beyond his small, private world. This process was especially important for the working-class housewives who made up roughly one-third of our patients and who usually live in total isolation. We were able to observe how the group's therapeutic process evolved at the same rate as the supportiveness among the members emerged and was consolidated, regardless of the rivalry, tension and ambivalence that existed. In the groups, we set supportiveness against the unhealthy competitiveness of the system.

EG: How was this supportiveness manifested in practice?

ML: For example, in the get-togethers we had in a café after the session, when everything was gone over again, and where we planned how to help this or that patient concretely. I remember that thanks to this supportiveness we managed to help a patient who was in danger of committing suicide.

EG: Your aim went much further than the curing of symptoms, even though because of the limited time at your disposal you were unable to exact the famous 'structural change'.

ML: I'll explain our goals by quoting once more from one of the publications:

> Apart from bringing about symptomatic improvements, our aim was to help our patients lose, or at least diminish, their sexual and social prejudices and to liberate themselves relatively speaking from the ideology of the dominant classes. It was also to achieve unexpected revelations in the weakening of repression and unconscious guilt feelings. The latter were often derived from a conviction on the patient's part that they were the only ones responsible for their failures. We tried to help them to be able to discriminate between their responsibility for their personal history, and that of their family's and society's. We tried to enable them to reach consciousness, and have a different vision of themselves and the world, and to understand how they had been conditioned to occupy the place that society had allocated them and to make decisions which would offer them a way out of their situation. (Several of them began studying and some became actively interested in the social process.)

EG: However, your work might be confused with indoctrination. Could you cite some clinical material?

ML: I hope it won't take too long, but I would like to talk about Maria Elena.

She was a thirty-two-year-old woman, the mother of a fifteen-year-old daughter and a thirteen-year-old son. She was being treated for depression and was sent to us by the Department of Gynaecology. Her daughter had gone to a doctor about the outcome of an abortion. When Maria Elena tried to find out who had made her adolescent daughter pregnant, her daughter replied, 'I won't tell you, I don't want to destroy your marriage.' It turned out that the daughter had been her father's lover for several months. Faced with the realization of the father–daughter incest, Maria Elena went into a deep depression, blaming herself for everything that had happened, since as she worked outside the home she hadn't been able to look after her little girl. During the first sessions, she constantly repeated, 'My poor husband, it's not his fault. He was brought up in an orphanage, he doesn't know what a family is. What a way to end up.' Then she would burst out sobbing and refuel her guilt feelings. 'I can't leave him . . . even though my daughter will be an embarrassment to everyone.'

Maria Elena had left primary school after third grade. She tried to make up for all the severe deprivation she had experienced in her childhood in the way she ran her family. Her husband was a thirty-four-year-old man, a worker who was greatly admired in the shanty town because of his supportive and co-operative attitude to the inhabitants' needs.

At the beginning it was necessary to give Maria Elena a small dose of anti-depressants, not to negate her depression, but to facilitate communication and the creation of new bonds within the group, since she was inundated with guilt and shame.

Her personal history enabled us to understand that with her unconscious complicity her daughter had repeated her own Oedipal drama. Maria Elena had never known her father, but the different men who had lived with her mother had frequently taken advantage of her sexually in the only room the family had. What's more, from a very early age she had spied on her mother's sexual relations. In this context, it was important for Maria Elena to realize that her personal history was not the result of her 'sinful badness', but rather of many factors, including undoubtedly the impoverished conditions in which she'd been brought up.

Probably for this reason alone she idealized so much the 'stable family' she had created. She experienced the 'unexpected revelation' of the father

–daughter incest – which she should have detected much earlier – as just punishment from God for her own sins.

In analysis we were able to show her how she had actively participated in the situation as a result of unconscious guilt feelings. Even though they had two bedrooms, Maria Elena often shared one with her son while her husband shared the other with her daughter. While she was no more than affectionate with her son, she made her daughter act out both her realized and frustrated Oedipal desires, since a step-father is not a real father.

The work of the group with her was intense. Far from provoking rejection and horror, Maria Elena aroused feelings of compassion and sympathy. The transferential Oedipal bond which she established with one of the co-therapists on the team allowed for competent interpretations and helped her remember repressed episodes from her childhood and link them to the present in a fine elaboration. Maria Elena stayed with the group until the end and developed very favourably; she overcame her acute depression which enabled her to do without any kind of medication within a year. In the same period, she separated from her husband and went to live in another neighbourhood where no one knew her painful story. In the end, she was able to remake her life and establish a new emotional relationship. Even before this she had enrolled at night school in order to finish her studies.

EG: In less than three years with this patient, from another social class, you managed to achieve more than one usually does in individual, expensive, private psychoanalysis. This raises several points for discussion. What other interesting cases can you tell me about?

ML: First of all, I'll tell you about a short but successful course of therapy, and then about Ramiro. Maria, a married housewife, was sent to us by the Paediatric Department since she treated her children badly because of her 'nerves'. Things were not going well with her husband either, as she had become frigid over the last few years. 'She is not interested in sex, she has other more serious things to worry about.' The only thing she was interested in was her sister's health. She took care of her sister, who was much younger than her and suffered from aneurism. She could have had a serious attack at any point.

Maria did not feel comfortable in the group and didn't want to continue in it. 'What was the use, if her problem could not be solved with words?' Also, what the others talked about didn't interest her, since she felt that their concerns were totally foreign to her. Then, as the result of an experience of one of the other members of the group (the birth and death of a baby boy with a serious congenital malformation), she suddenly thawed and started to participate and talk – rather coldly at first, then later painfully – about a part of her life which she had never before mentioned. We discovered that beneath the absorbing and unhealthy interest in her sister was the mourning for the death of a little son of hers who had been born with a heart malformation. The final illness and death of this little boy had occurred years earlier in very special circumstances. The staff of the children's hospital where her son had been hospitalized had been on strike. This lack of attention had perhaps hastened the course of events.

Maria and a group of other mothers agreed politically with the strike and did all they could to supplement the lack of staff. The solidarity that developed among these mothers added up to a very gratifying experience for Maria.

But also – and this was what she found most difficult to admit – she felt relieved by the death of her son, who was an incurable invalid. (That was why she treated her healthy children badly afterwards and was only concerned about her sick younger sister, her cardiacal son's successor in her unconscious.) This conflict was beyond Maria's capacity for elaboration and was therefore repressed – giving rise to arrested grief, which paralysed her development and essential skills, substituting these with a constant preoccupation with her sister as punishment. This unconscious process was dramatically resolved and, once she was able to understand and work through the whole situation, the change Maria went through was spectacular. In a very short time, she managed to regain her former personality, and her political militancy as well. From being someone wrapped up in a fixed problem, both restrictive and insoluble, she became someone interested in her husband, her children and the world once again.

She soon decided she no longer needed therapy, but when she left she gave each of us a leaflet about the Party she had rejoined.

After a few months Maria had declared herself cured. But, do patients have the right to do this? In classical analytic terms, this would be resistance to dealing with multiple interpretations. Our criteria are different. If we try to make the patient independent, if we trust that he has learnt something from the group, then we consider that he has every right to decide for himself. However, and this is important and makes the separation less risky, he also has the right to turn to the group again when he needs to.

Now I'll tell you about Ramiro, a metal worker whom we were unable to help. He was sent to the group by the Neurology Department after having been diagnosed as a malingerer. He had no income and dragged one leg pitifully. He was a defeated man, who looked much older than his forty years. He had no family, and his wife had left him, taking the children with her. He was usually very quiet, although he had sudden violent outbursts.

He recognized his class background twice. The first occasion was in a heated discussion about the 'execution' of a powerful and corrupt trade union bureaucrat by a group of guerrillas. He intervened brusquely when a member of the group defended the dead man because he was the father of a family. In an extremely violent manner he told us how this same trade unionist had humiliated and betrayed him, and his union, twenty years before. The second was when the same woman, the niece of a small factory owner, offered him a job as a night watchman. He accepted the job with pleasure, but resigned abruptly a few weeks later, 'because it wasn't a dignified job, since in practice it was police work and he had to spy on his workmates'. We were unable to help Ramiro, because his practical needs were too pressing and in effect could not be satisfied with words. He soon began to miss sessions and eventually he disappeared from the group.

In general there was a lot of absenteeism and dropping out. In some cases our achievements were limited to treating the symptoms.

EG: But often, as Maria Elena's case shows, you managed to achieve more than this and carry out psychoanalytic therapy within Freud's definition, since you took into account transference, resistance and infantile sexuality. Now, how did you deal with 'external reality'?

ML: I've already mentioned that in part. Without realizing it at the time, we adopted Paul Parin's criterion; that is, facilitating the patient's awareness of how this reality functions, and of the rules of the game hidden behind it. Also, we did not put social reality in parentheses as Castel accused us, and, in any case, even if we'd wanted to do so it would not have been possible. In those critical years in Argentina, reality was imposed upon you, and our supposed 'neutrality' would have become absurd.

EG: What repercussions resulted from the fact that the patients were from a different social class?

ML: When we talked about Usandivaras's article I said that the difference was not a technical obstacle, nor is there any reason for it to be one. None the less, you have to take cultural differences into account. I have already observed the same thing in my work as a supervisor in Mexico.

EG: With reference to what?

ML: I'll give you a specific example: in the case history of the Wolf Man, Freud bases the origins of his severe neurosis on the fact that he probably, on only one occasion and as a very small child, observed his parents' sexual relations. I mentioned earlier that observing her mother's sex life had an influence on Maria Elena's later neurotic behaviour. None the less it was not a determining factor, and one of the social variables that we have to take into account when we analyse patients from another social stratum is the lack of intimacy in the sexual life of adults, owing to the lack of space and the precariousness of their housing situation. If the mere fact of observing the parents' sexual relations in childhood were unhealthy, then there would be no adults from the working, peasant or marginal classes who would not be neurotic.

EG: Yes, these are the socio-cultural factors which Freud was not in the habit of taking into account.

ML: Look, at the beginning he took them into account. In *Introductory Lectures on Psycho-Analysis* (1916–17) there is a description of how the same infantile sexual activity does not make a working-class girl ill, while her little friend who went through the same experience but is the 'daughter of a good family' will later become ill as a result of having been brought up in an atmosphere of 'purity' and sexual repression. Unfortunately, Freud did not continue along these lines.

EG: Surely one reason for this omission must have been that both he and his followers tended to analyse only members of the same class as themselves, which must have caused them to gloss over certain problems.

ML: Obviously. We only realized this when we had the opportunity of analytic contact with proletarian and marginal sectors. But what might have been a discovery for us is a truism for the ethno-psychoanalysts.

EG: Pichon Riviere emphasized the importance of including people with different backgrounds and from different social strata in his working groups. He contends that the group becomes more creative in the degree that it becomes an expression of different perspectives and points of view.

ML: Yes, I agree with this if the differences are not too great. Also, if we do not try to eliminate the differences.

EG: I was thinking of something else: Pichon Riviere's concept that in working groups dilemma should become dialectical.

ML: The famous dialectic spiral, consisting of thesis, antithesis and synthesis which once again becomes thesis. This is feasible in a working group where the members have or acquire a common goal, but not if there is real antagonism based on class consciousness.

EG: To require the feasibility of always being able to go from the dilemma, that is, from the antagonistic to the dialectic would – in spite of the Marxist nomenclature – be an idealistic proposition.

ML: I'd say so. This proposition reminds me of the US-style encounter groups. I once read a very flattering article on these groups in a North American magazine which insisted on how important it was that its members should learn to hate each other openly so that once the encounter group was over they'd be able to love each other and say goodbye to each other very affectionately. It's important for us to be able to love, but not indiscriminately. This is what Freud insists on in *Civilization and its Discontents* (1930) when he criticizes the Christian requirement of loving one's neighbour as oneself, and at that indiscriminately. Also relevant to this is the criticism of the T-groups (Training groups) which were carried out in an armaments factory. Speaking ironically, the journalist who made the criticism remarked on how wonderful it was that when the group encounter ended the executives, employees and workers, who produced the napalm or tanks which were sent to Vietnam, should all love each other and should have learned to love their neighbours. The problem was their neighbours were not Vietnamese.

EG: But what would Pichon Riviere say if he were here now?

ML: I'm sure that he'd defend his point of view intelligently. Enrique Pichon always held his complex ground: he was a Marxist by training and education, an anarchist out of passion and because of what he'd done in his youth, and he was convinced that his working groups and his psychology were revolutionary.

EG: You could say something similar about what we were saying with regard to Freud: Freud was a revolutionary as far as psychology was concerned, but not in the political-ideological sense.

ML: But Freud didn't try to be either, whereas Enrique did. And for the last fifteen or twenty years he devoted all his scientific efforts – and also his Marxist ideology – to social psychology and learning about this in working groups.

EG: The concept of the psychologist as an 'agent of change', criticized by many, arose in and was disseminated by his school of social psychology. In my opinion this concept became rather reformist in that it encouraged the idea that change could be brought about through psychology and that the psychologist was 'revolutionary' by the mere fact of his being a psychologist.

ML: In fact, at one point in Buenos Aires we frequently discussed the term 'agent of change'. I'll mention what I learned precisely from Pichon himself; in the face of all change we must ask ourselves the following questions: *why, what for and for whom?* The psychologist can be an agent of change in a progressive sense. But if you remember that the North Americans started community psychology in order to obtain greater control over the population, then you come back to that famous and often-repeated phrase of Lampedusa's in *The Leopard*: changes are often sought in order for things to remain the way they are.

EG: To return to the hospital groups: I was struck by the fact that you mentioned transference with a co-therapist, when at the time it was still customary to work with 'a silent, non-participating observer', as they were called in the Pichon Riviere school.

ML: We did it for training purposes. It was very useful. We used to put several beginners together with a couple of experienced therapists, with instructions that the beginners had every right to intervene. This way each of them learnt to interpret gradually, at his own pace. We established two conditions for their belonging to the team: that they should be or have been in individual or group analysis and that they should attend the theoretical and practical courses at our Teaching and Research Centre which had been set up by the Mental Health Workers' Co-ordinator. In addition, we used to meet once a week in a group for reflection which supervised the work in common. In this way we were able to provide young psychologists and psychiatrists with alternative training which was practically free, non-élitist, and therefore, non-institutionalized.

EG: How did the patients accept such a large team?

ML: We were careful, of course, never to have more therapists than patients. We also made it clear that the young people were there because they needed training. This helped, as did the fact that we openly discussed differences of interpretation, in order to demystify analysis. We did not present an image of a knowledgeable, homogeneous block, but rather we sometimes contradicted each other and sometimes complemented each other in our interpretations.

EG: You've obviously changed considerably since you wrote the 'classic' with Grinberg and Rodrigué.

ML: Without a doubt. Besides, I learnt a lot in this hospital work and I also brought these changes to private consultation. I don't distance myself as much as before and I'm much less silent. I'm not afraid of being addressed informally, nor do I worry about sign language any more. In short, I think that both the patients and I have become more spontaneous.

EG: Since you're talking about the changes you have gone through as a group therapist, what do you still maintain and what would you retract in relation to your book?

ML: I'll begin with the latter: I would no longer talk about the Group, with a capital G, as a new creation which leaves aside each member's individuality. Whereas today it appears to me to be an idealistic approach, at the time we thought of it as something belonging to the future and science fiction.

EG: Rather like what Sturgeon proposes in *More Than Human*?

ML: Yes, at the time we used frequently to refer to *More Than Human* (1986) and *Homo Gestaltensis*, the successor to *Homo Sapiens*. But the Group as a totality is a fiction that runs the risk of leaving behind the reality experienced by each member of the group. At the moment, I support Fernando Ulloa's idea of taking group interpretation more as a desideratum which can be reached at the end of a session, than as interpretation which is possible from the beginning but often forced.

EG: In the most recent prologue, you already confirm that the group is not a micro-society.

ML: Of course not, more so because all patients in private practice belong to the same class.

EG: But in a hospital the patients belong to the opposite class from the therapeutic team, if you can put it in such a way.

ML: Yes, and that's where it's more like a 'micro-society', although there is no dependence relation between them at the level of direct links to production. I'm going to quote what Ulloa, Siniego and I said in this respect in a German publication:

> A therapeutic group in a hospital reproduces the class conditions of society since in fact in a hospital the patient and the therapist belong to different classes and tend to establish the asymmetrical and submissive bonds already implicit in the doctor–patient relationship. This asymmetry has to be clearly dealt with in the presence of the patient because of the invalidity bestowed on him by his illness and by his class limitations; this technical attitude determines the degree of reciprocity. In other words that the patient should expect that this asymmetry be corrected, not because he is to a certain extent the therapist, but because he will recuperate his validity in the form of health and possible consciousness. Then from that point on he will tend to destroy crystallized situations of domination. (Langer, Siniego and Ulloa, 1979)

EG: After that quote it would be rather redundant to insist any further on your prologue and your discrepancies with the text, written by three authors several years ago. Even so, there are still a few points to clear up.

ML: What are you referring to specifically?

EG: The supposed 'neutrality' has been clarified with respect to the psychoanalyst. But in the book you attribute this quality to the industrial psychologist. You say that he enters a factory without taking sides. It's impossible for it to be so.

ML: We were specifically referring to a pilot project carried out by Elliot Jacques. He based the psychologist's neutrality on the fact of his having been contracted and paid by the management and the trade union of a factory where there was a dispute to carry out group work with the aim of resolving the dispute. He achieved his aim as far as arbitration was concerned. All the same I don't think that he wouldn't have 'taken sides', consciously or unconsciously, at the level of counter-transference. In any case I would be more suspicious of industrial psychologists who are paid only by the company.

EG: Another point which isn't clear is what is called the therapeutic impact of the group. You say that, among other objectives, 'it tends towards the integration of the members into the group and by extension, into the society in which they act'.

ML: I presume that when we talked about 'active adaptation' as a health objective, I clarified my concept of adaptation.

You ask me what I still support in this book. I'd say, a lot. It's used as a set text in various places. As such, I would like it to be read critically. Then it can contribute something.

EG: Would you add anything from your new experiences?

ML: Yes, primarily with respect to the indication for therapy, an indication which shouldn't depend on economic or institutional motives.

Along with the likelihood of solving such and such a symptom and perhaps, in the long run, bringing about a structural change, group therapy provides something very important: a group to belong to. A group in which you can express yourself with total sincerity and learn to give and receive support. When the exiles came to Buenos Aires – first the Uruguayans and then the Chileans – we recommend those who asked for therapy to go into groups if it were possible, and this wasn't just for economic reasons. Group therapy was suggested because it could offer them a sense of belonging and allow them to create ties in a country and ambience they were unfamiliar with.

EG: In what other circumstances would you recommend group therapy as a first option?

ML: For an adolescent, to provide him the possibility of meeting members of the opposite sex in an atmosphere of trust and sincerity. It would help him a great deal to get rid of his own anxieties when he became aware of other people's. I'd also recommend group therapy to an adult who is very isolated and lonely inside, even if he were able to pay for individual therapy. But I'd also recommend it for a very pushy person, or for someone who was unbearable – although this doesn't sound very scientific – and didn't realize he was. The group would act as a mirror and would make him understand how he actively causes his conflicts with others better than in individual therapy. But this kind of indication is described in the book. Another change is that I no longer see any reason for not accepting a homosexual in a group. At that time, this was one of the criteria. But I think that in general it changed.

EG: What counter-indications would you still maintain, then?

ML: People with acute needs who are in possible danger of psychosis or suicide; people who are very narcissistic, such as hypochondriacs who don't know how to listen, and also people with very early, severe deficiencies. They need the bi-personal bond which individual analysis provides.

EG: It is often held that group therapy has more prospects for the future than individual analysis.

ML: That depends on the circumstances. From the point of view of hospital practice, group therapy is already being given preference because it requires fewer staff, less time, etc.

It will also have more prospects in a socialist country for ideological reasons, as is happening in the German Democratic Republic, where group therapy with a psychoanalytic approach is already being carried out. In other words, while psychoanalysis has been practically eliminated in the mental health institutions of socialist countries, it has managed to gain entry and establish itself in the form of group therapy.

EG: Beyond the clinical, what do you think psychoanalysis can contribute to society?

ML: Basing myself on an article by Rudolf Eckstein, 'Psychoanalysis and social crisis' which was published in the *Bulletin of the Menninger Clinic* (1969), I'll tell you about the preoccupations which already existed during my youth in Social Democratic Vienna. I think that, in spite of its political blindness, psychoanalysis had a far more social orientation then than it does now. At the time everyone in Vienna agreed that psychoanalysis should be applied to the educational system as well as to the legal and the penitentiary systems. When talking about Reich, I mentioned the family advice centres which were already concerned with offering guidance on contraception.

EG: Everything you describe seems to me to be very useful and relevant, provided that it really is in the interest of the masses and doesn't merely serve to support the system so that, as you said earlier, everything changes so that nothing changes. In Argentina too, during our period of quasi-democracy, mental health workers dealt with very important topics. I think it's extremely necessary that psychologists, like any other professional in medicine, engineering, etc., contribute their specific knowledge through interdisciplinary work to the struggle of the working classes.

ML: Naturally. This happened, as far as was possible, in Argentina in 1973 and 1974. I've already mentioned the important work which was done at the Department of Industrial Medicine where, to quote your paper presented at the Latin American Congress on Psychoanalysis and Social Context, in Querétaro, 1980, it was possible to 'reverse the meaning (of industrial psychology) when its observations and conclusions, carried out from a perspective obviously different from the traditional one, are employed as an instrument of conscientization of the effects of work itself and are handed over to the workers and their organizations as a weapon of struggle'. In the Department, doctors, psychologists and sociologists worked in an interdisciplinary team, doing serious research on the physical, psychological and social damage done to workers in specific industries and handing over the conclusions to the respective trade unions, thus providing them with the possibility of demanding the necessary modifications.

Within the Mental Health Workers' Co-ordinator we worked with the lawyers' society. However, the area of mass communications was where there was a lack of work in common. As we're in complete agreement with respect to this, let me quote from your paper once again:

> Propaganda is another forgotten yet vital area. The well-known heaviness, dullness and lack of quality of the propaganda material of the working-class sector – at a total disadvantage to that of the ruling-class sector – is obviously not the fault of the mental health workers or the psychoanalysts [from my own experience, I would add that they do not even let us participate], but it is just as true that they can contribute towards some change in this direction – even though they may not be able to solve the problem by themselves – and also to the job of clarifying the contents for the dominant media.

However, let me return to my area, the clinical field. In times of peace, in hospitals and in health centres, we've contributed our psychotherapy within an analytic, individual or group framework. This happened in Argentina, is occurring in Mexico and, if we manage to overcome the mistrust of the respective authorities, it will also happen after there has been social change. We are complying with what Freud asked us to in Budapest in 1918. Already being used in training is the technique of working groups, created by Pichon Riviere, in whose frame of reference psychoanalysis occupies an important place.

EG: If we don't shut ourselves up in our ivory towers once again, I'm sure that all these experiences could be used at a later date in liberated countries or countries where reconstruction is taking place.

ML: Yes, and in effect this is already happening. As an example of a valuable experience which can result from co-operation with an educational psychologist, let me mention the work which Adriana Puiggrós recently did in Nicaragua, when she 'de-ideologized' school textbooks by removing their imperialist content. That year Armando Bauleo and Marta de Brasi also carried out an important task in Managua; every day for a month they organized working groups of colleagues who were preparing to work with peasants in agrarian reform. Through the working groups they were able to adapt themselves suitably to their future task, by recognizing their own shortcomings and difficulties, converting them into instruments of insight and creating an adequate strategy and tactics.

EG: We will have an enormous field provided we are aware of it and are seriously prepared to deal with it. And what about during a revolutionary struggle? Why don't you talk about the very brief but important experience that we shared: our psychotherapeutic encounter with the Sandinistas in political asylum in Mexico?

ML: It was a wonderful experience. Chayo, a Nicaraguan doctor, approached a group of us mental health workers to ask us for our psycho-therapeutic assistance. A large group of combatants, who until a few days earlier had been in political asylum for months in the Mexican embassy in Managua, had arrived in Mexico City. They were disconcerted by the huge city they had landed in and worried about their relatives and the repressive fate they might face. They were also frustrated at being excluded from the struggle for the time being and demoralized by their lengthy, overcrowded stay at the embassy (they would've left earlier but Somoza's government took a long time to give them the necessary safe-conduct passes). For its part, the Mexican government received them with its characteristic generosity, putting them up at a hotel in the centre of the city, paying all their expenses and giving them the right to stay here and work, a right which no one exercised. I asked Chayo how much time we had at our disposal for therapy – a year, months, weeks? 'Weeks', she replied, and that's the way it turned out: they all went back to fight.

We made the appointment in a house belonging to an institution. Many arrived, perhaps fifty or sixty, nearly all of them very young men, though there were a few girls among them. They came with their respective superiors. They didn't know why they'd been brought there, so as a result things were not easy at the beginning. We introduced ourselves all the same and an assembly-type discussion began. One, the most 'Marxist' among them, rejected any psychological explanation whatsoever; to him, if there were any conflicts they were because of a lack of revolutionary ideology. Another was mistrustful: we shouldn't talk about problems, for surely there were infiltrators in the meeting. (In fact it was later confirmed that there were.) At the same time the problems began to surface. The main problem was the choice between the struggle and concern for the family. After two hours of collective discussion we told them that we were going to step down and that if any of them wanted to talk to us on an individual basis either then or later, in any place, then we would be available. We said this with little conviction that anyone would want to. They were in agreement, but first they wanted to sing. They got their guitars and sang us some beautiful protest songs, two of which were dedicated to women guerrillas. I had often listened to protest songs when they were in fashion and was frequently aroused by them, but I was always wary of falling into the trap of a sterile, manipulated emotion. But this time the songs sung by these young people were real. We stepped down, and it turned out that many of them wanted to talk to us on their own. I talked to five of them. I'll comment briefly on two cases in which both of us, patient and therapist, were seated on the floor of a corridor. The first was a handsome, shy, seventeen-year-old boy whose moustache had just started growing. He had become a militant and had had to seek asylum, but while in the embassy a problem had arisen: another boy had seduced him, had persisted and had played the woman's role with him. And now, what was he to do? He had no other vices; he sometimes drank a few beers and smoked, nothing else. But then this happened. Yes, he had a girlfriend whom he was writing to. He had tried to find a girlfriend here too, but the other boy provoked him, wouldn't let him go, kept insisting. I felt very maternal towards this anxious young man and I really believe I helped him during that brief interview, by explaining that it wasn't his fault, that these are things that could happen to anyone and, in the end, by giving him 'absolution'.

Then there was Maribel. I saw her about four times before she went back. Sex was mingled with revolution for her too. The daughter of a nurse and a language teacher who was a Communist, but a *macho* all the same, she had been in secondary school until the year before. She had become a militant, they had discovered her and she'd had to leave school and live semi-clandestinely. Then that year, when there was another insurrection in Estelí, she had asked for a gun and had participated in an assault on a police station. She had had to ask for political asylum. In the embassy she had fallen in love with a boy from another political tendency and they'd had a sexual relation-ship. They came to Mexico. She was concerned about her mother and about the possibility that she might not be able to go back along with her young man. She didn't doubt that she would go back and join the struggle again. The last time I saw her, we talked about how strange she felt here, away from her country and in conditions so unfamiliar to her. I tried to explain to her in simple terms, that it was what was called 'depersonalization'. 'No,' she said, 'it's not that. Do you know what it is? I'm going to be fifteen next week. Just a little while ago I was a girl, and now I'm a woman.'

And the others? Several of them told of horrible experiences, of torture and relatives being killed. But nobody complained about their fate and it seemed that for them, militancy, with all its tremendous risks, was something natural.

EG: There are two specific things that I think about this: in the first place, as a result of this experience it became clear to me that therapeutic practice in these cases is in fact different from classical therapy – from the objectives, to (at times) the techniques and the methods of approach – and that there is a lot to learn and develop about this. Secondly, in this particular case the 'patients' were participants in a massive insurrection and were all young people from the mass sector. The latter is what differentiates them from the militants/patients we saw in Argentina in the highly-politicized early 1970s. I remember that there we observed and discussed the 'neurotic' characteristics of some militants.

ML: As I've already said: for me militancy is always multi-determined.

EG: In any case, we need a theoretical response to this problem and I think that the consequences of this lack are also a manifestation of the difficulty of finding a link between psychoanalysis and Marxism. To some extent, it is possible to understand a person's artistic activity, but not his political activity. At least, not in terms of psychoanalysis.

ML: Freud insists that artistic activity can be partially explained, but that analysis does not attempt to explain genius. On the other hand, political activity is also creative.

EG: But, as in the case of art, the issue is the boundary between creativity and pathology and the latter tends to have very serious consequences in militancy.

ML: I view 'non-neurotic' militancy as the need for transcendence, and to be involved in a project which is not merely personal. And therefore I consider it sublimation and reparation activity.

EG: To the extent that one locates oneself within the historical context and alongside the exploited sectors of society.

ML: Exactly. It's a question of a need which has not been explained psychoanalytically, although we think in terms of narcissism, the ego ideal and the super-ego. The topic has concerned me for some time. When I raised the issue last year at the Psychoanalytical Seminar in Zurich, there was a lot of discussion but we didn't get very far. Now that I am an old woman, I understand it more as the need to survive individual death. Freud, in *Civilization and its Discontents*, tells us that there are few remedies for saving ourselves from this malaise and mentions sex, science, drugs, art and faith (if one has this, it's through grace, according to the Catholics).

Curiously enough, he does not mention politics. Politics is precisely that for me: what to do about your transcendence faced with the certainty of death, without a hereafter. What do you do about your 'being in the world and for what', as the Existentialists would say, if you cannot find something to outlive you? For me and for many others, it is to be – and I'm not attempting to define this analytically – on the side of history: you are born at a determined historical moment, you are part of what existed beforehand and you live out your cycle, either with history or against it. At one point it is your turn to die, but if you have lived on the side of history then you will die with the feeling that you will remain part of it, that you will exist beyond your personal life and that you have contributed to the future, to however small a degree.

CODA ON THE SUBJECT
OF WOMEN

A feminist is someone who attempts to better women's condition in the world. Any woman or man is feminist if they are conscious of the oppression women are the object of.
Yvette Roudy

WHAT I AM about to say now will not be new to the readers of feminist literature. Perhaps it contains a minimal share of originality; maybe it's all been said or written before. Its newness is less important to me than that it might have some value for those readers who have never before defined themselves as feminists and who now recognize themselves in the Yvette Roudy quote.

I will attempt to make a brief outline, perhaps superficial or hypothetical, which for me contains an explanation of the rise of patriarchy, and why it is only now that there exists the likelihood of ending this period and of the appearance of a society in which woman will no longer be marginalized.

I will begin by referring to Ernest Bornemann, a researcher who is convinced that a matriarchal society existed in prehistoric times. One of his theories, which appears to me to be central, is based on the transition from a community sustained by hunting, fishing and gathering, which was matriarchal, to a pastoral patriarchal society. Indeed, according to Bornemann, the appearance of domesticity brought with it the beginning of patriarchy and private property. (Cattle, easy to count and distribute, created individual possession and are the basis of the appearance of money. *Pecunia* from *pecus* = cattle, means money in Latin.)

Well, being a herdsman allows you to make a fundamental observation: while adult male animals' bodies do not change nor do they breed, females, once crossed, become pregnant and give birth to new animals. (Bornemann supposes that in this way cattle were transformed into the first interest-producing capital.) Simultaneously, cattle demonstrated to man the relationship between intercourse, pregnancy and birth – unknown until then in many places – and constituted the first private capital.

In *The Origin of the Family, Private Property and the State*, Engels maintains that only with the existence of excess production and the creation of a surplus product does there begin the possibility of inheritance, as well as that of making slaves out of members of other communities captured in battle.

We are already familiar with this in the Old Testament figures of the patriarchal herdsman and warrior, but Engels also affirms that patriarchy, in other words the domination of women, has its origins in the desire of man to leave his goods in inheritance to his own offspring. I am not convinced that the 'legitimacy' factor would have been decisive. It seems to me that this is a modern psychological need related to our society and ideology projected on to a period in the past. In Rome, for example, one left one's fortune, or the empire itself, in the same way to one's biological son or the biological son of another, one's adopted son.

The origins of women's domination can be viewed in a different manner: if the slave is valuable because he produces more than he consumes, then so is the child. The woman, capable of bearing children, is transformed from a free being ino 'capital', just as with female cattle. That is to say, she produces 'interest' and as this 'interest' is a product of her sexual relation-ships it is necessary to own her and restrict her freedom and desires in order to be able to enjoy the fruit of her reproductive capacities. Little by little, she will be confined to the domestic sphere, and subjected to strict 'moral' standards so that she will put her eggs in the appropriate nest. This is, as I understand it, how her capacity to give birth to the men and women of the future was transformed from a power – something that was her strength and in keeping with her elevated position in primitive society – into the cause of her ruin and subjugation. Along with the woman the child is repressed: the *pater familias* is absolute master.

According to Bornemann, patriarchy emerges with the transformation of hunters into herdsmen. Obviously, this transformation did not occur in all those places in which we recognize that patriarchy exists, even though we may also come across the existence of earlier female rule or a matriarchy from the rites and figurines of fertility goddesses. On the American contin-ent, for example, particularly in Mexico, we are aware of the severe sexual restrictions pre-Hispanic societies imposed on women, confining them to their reproductive function. (Among the Mexicans only death in childbirth could put women on the same plane as men and fallen warriors in the other world.) When in the Teotihuacán fresos we see the priest watering the soil with his semen to fertilize it during the ceremony that marks the beginning of the sowing season, we know that pre-Hispanic man had already discov-ered what the herdsman knew. In these communities, perhaps we ought to relate the coitus-pregnancy-birth discovery to agriculture, around which almost all myths revolve.

Whatever the case, patriarchal man attempted to erase all traces of primitive female power. He appropriated her capabilities: Eve was made from Adam's rib and Pallas Athene emerged from Zeus's head. This is why in Ancient Rome and in many other cities a child is considered part of the family only when the father lifts him off the floor and, raising him up, 'gives birth to him'. This is why the 'couvade' (while the woman is giving birth discreetly at a distance, her partner, surrounded by friends, complains noisily of a spectacular and imaginary labour) still exists in many communities. It is also why Napoleon defined woman as a tree whose fruit belong to man, her gardener. This is why . . . and we could add an infinite number of 'reasons why'. And if for a moment we think about Genesis we should perhaps interpret Jehovah's condemning of woman to painful childbirth as the envy man feels towards woman's natural creativity.

Did a matriarchy really exist? Do we have sufficient proof? Since Darwin, Bachofen and Engels it has become a tradition of the Left to believe that at the least there was a matriarchal society at the beginning of the history of mankind. We still do not have a body of research to complete Marx's reflections in *Precapitalist Economic Formations* which would doubtless allow us to move more confidently in this area. On the other hand, our feminist enthusiasm (invaluable in the struggle) often leads us to make affirmations which are not totally scientifically valid. The most recent historical evidence is not always favourable to the hypothesis of the existence of a matriarchy. We can say that woman was not always submissive; we can also say that, while matrilinear systems of kinship do not mean a prior matriarchy, they do speak of the importance of women in the societies where they were practised. But, above all, we can be absolutely certain that in historic times the role of women in many highly civilized societies was not always a secondary one. The Hamurabi Code was based on the principles of great equality and independence for the Babylonian woman. (Might not the scandal that the 'licentiousness' in Babylon caused among other peoples of the time have been produced by the sexual freedom women enjoyed?) In Greece, woman's role degenerated from Homeric times until the Classical period in which woman was merely a birth-giving slave and an object that formed part of the household furniture. In ome, in spite of the historical importance of so many women whose names we are familiar with, a woman was treated as an 'imbecile' in the face of the law and could not sign a contract or serve as a witness, much less occupy public positions. However, if we are to believe Herodotus, things happened very differently in Egypt; women were the dominant sex and the number of Egyptian queens would seem to prove this. In Sparta, there was almost total equality between the sexes: women could mix freely with men anywhere, and they had a voice and vote in public affairs.

The Middle Ages followed the Roman model (did this follow the Greek and Etruscan models?) which ended up dominating the customs of all the communities whch populated mediaeval Europe. Christianity, perhaps as a trade-off with Roman power, served only to reinforce male domination in spite of recognizing that woman had a soul; one only has to remember the terrible things St Paul wrote in order to confirm this: man does not cover his head in church because he is the glory of God – woman is the glory of man and must not speak in the church, etc.

In America, the subjugation of woman seems to have had basically the same characteristics as in Europe and Asia; however, there is no lack of communities where women have rights. In synthesis, it could be said that there have been historical periods in which woman has shared the rights of man, as in Sparta, Egypt or Babylon. (Nevertheless, I would tend to agree more with Bornemann when he says that we can observe the traces of matriarchy in these societies.)

I have said that we do not have at our disposal a sufficiently large body of research to prove the existence of a matriarchy, but nor do we to disprove its existence either. Be that as it may, and even though I doubt the validity of *Totem and Taboo* because Freud bases his reconstruction of our prehistory on the Oedipus complex of a small boy at the beginning of the twentieth century, one could claim the same validity in order to demonstrate the existence of a matriarchy in the past. Or conversely, to maintain, as does Marina Moeller-Gambaroff in *Emanzipation macht Angst* (1977) that 'at least on the psychological level matriarchy exists before patriarchy'. We could interpret matriarchal history as a myth arising from the personal experience of each of us, in whose lives – after an all-powerful mother who nourished us, not according to our merits but according to our needs (a condition which defines the future success of a Communist society and which would supposedly have governed a matriarchal society) – the father made his appearance as the embodiment of law interrupting our idyll with her.

What is certain is that from a specific moment, which might have occurred at different points in history depending on the society, woman was confined to the domestic sphere, to doing, as Isabel Larguía says, the 'invisible work'; in other words, to producing children and restoring her partner's work capacity on a daily basis. What happened to her sexuality? Masters and Johnson maintain that primitive woman's ability to experience pleasure was unlimited (a reflection of this capacity is the myth of tiresias, who, having been both man and woman, in a debate among the gods affirms that it is woman who finds most pleasure in love). In order to build a society based on the family, paternal authority and the prohibition of incest, woman's sexual avidity had to be repressed so that she would become docile. This repression coincides with the origins of 'civilization' and written history. Was it necessary for a son to repress his desire for his mother, also for her to be obliged to repress her sexuality and, as a result her desire for her son, thereby facilitating the repression in the male, in order that written, patriarchal history should appear?

By favouring the reproductive function, sexuality and woman's capacity for pleasure became superfluous because they could lead her to infidelity and to abandon the home. It is true that woman became a highly sexualized object, but as a sexual object of and for man. This explains precisely why in the East where *A Thousand and One Nights* tells us there was an intense eroticism, women led extremely restricted lives and were destined to provide man with children and pleasure and even, should it be necessary, work for him. The fact that woman's own pleasure was of no importance is demonstrated by the practice of the clitoridectomy which is common in Muslim societies. This is the ritual amputation of the clitoris, woman's most highly erogenous organ, the sole function of which is sexual stimulation and pleasure. In this way woman will be less tempted to be unfaithful and man's pleasure will not be perturbed.

How did it come about that women acceptd this position designated them, that little by little they would evolve in less favourable psychic and mental conditions? How did the majority finally admit to this supposed 'natural inferiority' and become 'colonized from within' (to use Frantz Fanon's terminology)?

Wilhelm Reich would say that this passive acceptance was a consequence of the sexual repression to which they were submitted . . . But we said at the beginning that human psychology is the result of two forces: the sociological and the biological. While the latter was ongoing and supposedly unchangeable, women's social position, the family structure anyway, underwent numerous changes throughout the course of history in every society; none of these, however, was as definitive as that provoked by men's conquering of patriarchal dominion.

Yes, throughout history the majority of womn accepted their position and considered it, just like men did, to be 'natural', that is, biologically determined and also an expression of divine will. But not all of them respected the system, and the majority of those who rebelled had to suffer the consequences. I will only mention the extreme case of Olimpia de Gouges. During the French Revolution she drew up the *Declaration des droits de la femme et citoyenne*. However, believing that the revolutionary slogan 'Liberté, égalité e fraternité' also included women cost her her head at the guillotine.

There were more persuasive ways of keeping a woman in her place or making her return to it if she had left it for economic reasons. In England, proletarian women of the last century who worked in factories had to leave their children at home neglected or take them with them to work. It did not seem wrong to anyone in the dominant classes that they should do this, but it did that they had so many children. Malthus maintained that the number of poor people in a country should not increase because their reproduction could cause wars and famine and the degeneration of race; two children per ouple was the desired number. Does this not remind us of the time MacNamara wanted to limit United States aid to Latin America to those countries which were prepared to accept family planning?

Anna Davin in her article, 'Imperialism and motherhood' (1978), describes how these criteria changed radically when war broke out betwen the British Empire and the Boers in 1899. A great number of soldiers were needed, soldiers who came almost exclusively from the poorer sectors of society. Precisely because they were poor, many of them presented themselves as volunteers; the war offered them their only chance of good food, good clothes . . . But it turned out that only two out of every five volunteers were in good enough physical condition to resist the rigours of war. A huge campaign was started to educate and enlighten the 'ignorant' and guilty mothers, since, by neglecting their children and not feeding them well enough, they were harming the future of the Empire and the race.

At the beginning of our century, Malthusianism as a state ideology had been transcended and all governments were demanding that women have a lot of children. In order to convince them, according to John Burns, a Liberal MP of the time, it was necessary to 'lend dignity and purity to motherhood by every possible means'. This was how it was attempted to obtain women's consent so that they would accept their 'natural destiny'.

The rebellion against this fate began towards the end of the last century. Linda Gordon in her article 'Maternità volontaria' ('Voluntary motherhood') talks about the 'voluntary motherhood' movement which emerged at the time in the United States (Gordon, 1978). Women demanded the right to plan the number of children they would have, but since they thought that the use of contraceptives, which were rather primitive and unreliable at the time, was immoral, they proposed sexual abstinence. Two tendencies in this movement explained that this implied the same degree of sacrifice and discipline necessary to control their 'animal' instincts for them as it did for men, in other words, they had the audacity to hold that women too felt desire.

Yet, if war had forced women – as the providers of future soldiers – into constant motherhood and tied them to the home, it was, paradoxically, during another war, the First World War, that the liberation of women began, or, to be more exact, the liberation of the women who belonged to the ruling classes. However, it is these classes which produce the 'dominant' ideology in a society.

In the first edition of *Maternidad y sexo*, I described this change:

> ... suddenly, women from various warfaring countries, whose only sphere of action had been their home and their social nucleus, whose sole function was to have children and to bring them up, and who were economically and socially dependent – at first on their fathers and later on their husbands – were encouraged to occupy man's place in all areas. They successfully carried out tasks which until then had been considered unrealizable for them and, along with their being included in the work process, they achieved full independence and responsibility. Once the war was over, the change had become irreversible.
>
> The middle-class woman in 1914 (in the first part of the book, I describe how my mother and her friends experienced this situation) responded enthusiastically to the authorities' call to leave her home and start working, not only out of patriotism, but because she was both psychologically and materially availabe. The previous generation, in its time, occupied with numerous pregnancies and the difficulty of bringing up several children, would not have been able to do it. But the bourgeois woman of the turn of the century had a smaller number of children and felt wasted in her empty house. Medical progress had brought down the rate of infant mortality and made fairly effective contraceptive methods available to couples, and even provided abortions with fewer physical and legal risks. (Langer, 1951)

What I have said about the change in woman's situation is true but nevertheless, throughout the entire first half of this century, motherhood continued to be idealized as, if not the only, certainly the most noble female function. Of course, these concepts changed according to the economic and political situation of each historical period. Whilst Hitler, for example, initially urged women to produce several Aryan children (once more there is the question of race, already a concern of British imperialism), and to devote themselves to them totally, as the war went on and food and labour began to be scarce he urged them to leave their homes once again.

Juliet Mitchell describes the post-war situation in England and the United States. Men came back from the war to find their jobs had been taken over by women. How to make these women go back to their homes and their children – many of whom, until then, had been looked after in nurseries and day-care centres – after they had done such important jobs so efficiently? Mitchell maintains that it is no coincidence that just at this point Spitz's research appeared; it describes 'hospitalism' and shows how any institution, however well run, damages the small child if he lacks sufficient maternal affection. Of course, he also says that this affection can be substituted by the relationship with a nurse or another person who provides the child with steady affection. However, this part of the research tends to be forgotten. Meanwhile in England, Klein and Winnicott discovered the enormous importance of the early mother–child relationship for the future mental health of the child. I do not doubt the good intentions of these researchers, or the value of their discoveries, but they – like the scientists who talked about the 'schizophrenia-producing mother' during the same post-war period – were used, and unwittingly and unknowingly suported the same position as those researchers (mentioned by Anna Davin) who accused working-class mothers of being responsible for their children's hunger, their precarious state of health and the defeat of the Empire.

For Juliet Mitchell the culmination of the importance of the mother–child relationship is an example of how science is not neutral either, but rather adheres to current political interests and the establishment in its research. (Bruno Bettelheim's study of an Israeli Kibbutz, *Children of the Dream* (1969), which shows that the children who are separated from their mothers during the first few days of life and then brought up in small groups with other similar children are different from our own children but certainly not more unhealthy, received far less publicity.)

Elisabeth Badinter in her article 'L'amour en plus, histoire de l'amour maternel' holds that the blaming of mothers, which for her is also dependent on economic factors, has its roots deeper in the past (Badinter, 1980). For her, Rousseau, through *Emile*, was the first ideologist to condemn woman to total sacrifice in the pursuit of motherhood, declaring her to be practic- ally the only one responsible for the child's mental and physical health. Rousseau gradually convinced philosphers, theologians and women that they should 'naturally' and instinctively be devoted, sacrifice themselves, and take pleasure in their sacrifice. According to Elisabeth Badinter, Freud was the last ideologist of this school one hundred and fifty years later, and afterwards so were several of his followers. She mentions Helen Deutsch, who describes childbirth as a masochistic orgasm, and criticizes Melanie Klein and especially Winnicott, because of his insistence on the importance of a mother faithful to the model of Sophie, Emile's ideal wife. She also criticizes Winnicott for leaving the father completely out of a child's upbringing. She underlines the fact that from Freud to Lacan, a great deal of importance is given to the role of the father, but a father who legislates, rewards or punishes, a father dedicated to the outside world. In the last instance, he is a father who is a symbol of struggle, progress and success; he is a father with a symbolic function, representative of the word and the law.

The above are two feminist opinions on why we mothers always feel guilty. But there is also a psychoanalytic explanation with which I agree, since all of our emotions are multi-determined and not only the result of ideological factors. From the analytic point of view, we would say that a mother is believed to be guilty because of the unconsciously repressed – but still active – rancour the adult felt as a very small child against the omnipotent mother of his early childhood, as a result of the inevitable frustrations or deprivations she imposed on him; or those he blames her for even though she was not the one responsible.

But let us return to the social aspect: if during the first half of this century woman had the opportunity to demonstrate that her abilities were not inferior to man's, it was only during the second half, with the preoccupation with the 'population boom', that there was a massive attempt in the developing countries to encourage women to limit or even give up their motherhood, which at the same time began to lose its prestige. It was then that those in power decided to allocate large sums of money for research into cheap, easy-to-use methods of contraception. The practice of sterilizing women by tying their Fallopian tubes spread. This was often done against their will and is still irreversible. The corresponding technique for men is rarely used. The pill was created, with all of its physiological and psychological consequences, depending on the individual, of course; but thanks to the pill and the IUD 'voluntary motherhood' became a practical reality.

From then on coitus for the woman was as free of consequences as it was for the man. For the first time, for her too pleasure and love could be separated from procreation. And motherhood – which, if we are correct, had been the object of man's envy and had provoked his avidity thus bringing about the downfall of woman – became much less sacred and admirable, and in addition controllable according to the wishes of the woman or the couple. It has become much more of a shared thing.

The autonomy of the sexual act with respect to motherhood is in fact the equivalent of a biological change in women. That is why it is *today* – along with the increase in technology which removes the importance attached to the difference in physical strength between the sexes – that the conditions exist for a real equality of rights and responsibilities between man and woman, and for a true companionship.

But if psychology is the result of the biological and the social and if there have been significant changes in both areas, then how has woman's psychology changed? It is impossible to tell and difficult to generalize, because all of these changes vary from one society to another and from one social sector to another. While Simone de Beauvoir still maintains that a woman needs to forsake motherhood in order to be fulfilled, younger mothers generally do not think like that. It is true that, especially in the developed countries, many women renounce having children, but it is also true that the majority are not prepared to do so. A new phenomenon has arisen in Europe, and also exists in Mexico: that an unmarried professional woman generally decides to have a child when she is about thirty-five.

But is this 'new woman', who has opportunities her grandmother never even dreamt of, happy? After several years of psychoanalytic practice I know her inside out. I would say that in any case she is happier than Freud's patients were. But she does have conflicts and I would ask young psychoanalysts and psychotherapists, especially male colleagues, to help her solve them. Do not tell her – as the previous generation of psychoanalysts did, basing themselves on Freud's concepts – that penis envy is the reason why they want to undertake such-and-such an area of study, or take on this or that responsibility outside the home. Do not load her with guilt if her child is sick or aggressive in the kindergarten, or wets his bed. It is true that it may be because she works or because she is getting divorced, but many children of old-style mothers do the same. Besides, we are not perfect – not us, nor our parents, nor our children. And, what is more, as Freud always insisted, we are the result of our biological heritage, our temperaments and, yes, also of the events of our childhood. So, do not blame mothers for everything, but try and make a better analysis of the resentment you feel towards your own mothers, a resentment which is sometimes displaced on o your patients through counter-transference. Yes, mothers always seem to be the guilty ones – women in general, in bed too. I hope that even before reading this text, you will have been convinced that a woman does not have to forsake the pleasure she can derive from her clitoris, and that she does not have to sacrifice this, as Freud believed, in order to be 'truly feminine'.

The women whom we see in analysis (and also those not in that situation) easily feel guilt precisely because of their achievements. It is because of the 'tradition-prejudice', to use the term Isabel Larguía employs in her article 'El sector mas explotado de la historia' ('The most exploited sector in history', 1980). They feel torn by so many different demands placed on them. But how is it possible to do a job well and be lucid at work, if your mind is on the child? Take today, for example, Monday: will the maid have come back after her weekend off? Will there be a problem with the school bus? Fortunately, her partner is not a chauvinist, he shares some of the responsibilities, but, at the same time, he sometimes implies that his mother was a rather better cook, that when he was a boy the house, even though they did not have as many appliances, was sparkling clean and his shirts were always neatly pressed, with every button in place. How many arguments there have been about those blasted shirt buttons, when the most feminist wife in the world would never dream of reproaching her husband for not sewing up the hem of her skirt!

So please, therapists and analysts, since she is not castrated, even though she may be unsure of her rights and abilities, don't you castrate her. An important aim in the analysis of this woman would be for her to understand, as Freud explained it to us with regard to the male child *vis-à-vis* his father, that a daughter also feels guilty for having managed to surpass her mother. It is this displaced guilt which is rationalized when a woman thinks she is much worse as a wife and mother than her own mother was. This guilt is derived from the old rivalry with 'mother', who has now been defeated. In order for this victory not to be too resounding, it is better to become embittered and to say that because you cannot sew or cook like her, you are worth nothing. Another goal would be to help her to realize that maternal affection cannot be measured quantitatively but rather qualitatively. Or, to put it another way, an embittered mother closed up in her home and irritated by her children, who are practically her only company and objects of control, tends to give less than a woman who comes home full of outside stimulus and dedicates only a limited amount of time to them, but well-dedicated time.

Let us talk about another patient, one of the old kind: the fifty-year-old housewife who is going through the infamous 'menopausal depression'. How could she not be depressed if her goal in life, and her only 'visible product', was the children who have already left home? Where she – finally with nothing to do – waits every day for her husband, who is no longer particularly interested in her, to come back from work.

Please do not send her to psychiatrists, so they can give her medication, or to the gynaecologist for him to try magically to rejuvenate her with hormones. Try to understand her and help her so that she understands herself and perhaps she may still find some other alternative, something to do outside the home, so that she can feel she is doing something useful in this world.

But let's leave the psychological approach for a moment and go back to the social: in spite of what modern woman has achieved, her participation in managerial and decision-making positions is still minimal. It is true that some women, Margaret Thatcher or Golda Meir for example – I am purposely omitting those who got their positions through being the widows or daughters of famous statesmen – have managed to get into power, but it is also true that they are exceptions.

How to achieve real equal rights and opportunities that satisfy both members of the couple? Most, but not all, feminist movements have tried to do this. There are those that have concentrated on the struggle against men. Psychoanalysts may help us to understand this attitude and to try to change it. Marina Moeller-Gambaroff defines hostility towards men as a symptom, that is, as a compromise between the repressed and the defence. She holds that the anxiety and hostility provoked by the attempt at emancipation is derived from the early relationship with the mother, secondarily displaced on to man. But she also maintains that it is only by working through this first conflict that woman is able to achieve true emancipation and combat the patriarchal system effectively.

According to her, mothers who provoke this constellation in their daughters are, on their part, repressed women held back by their situation in life. This leads them to abuse their omnipotence with respect to their daughters – also their sons, but that is another subject – in order to protect a position of authority that provides their self-esteem. Thus, they intensify the hostility inherent in any relationship of dependence and, therefore, the necessity for repression.

The struggle against patriarchy should not be confused with the struggle against men. The woman who rejects men, and who sees the only possible relationship as that which could exist with another woman, is going back to the pre-oedipal relationship. Once installed in this kind of relationship, she attempts to re-establish her idyll with a generous, all-powerful mother, denying her own hostility and the other image of the terrifying, omnipotent mother. She displaces this image on to man and simultaneously pacifies her internal mother by renouncing, to this end, her vagina and her capacity for emancipation and autonomy as well as her motherhood; in short, she renounces man, the father's heir, and everything that he could give her.

I have promoted feminism in these pages, but certainly not that tendency which is hostile to men. Why are feminist movements necessary, if left-wing parties defend women's rights and if the feminist struggle divides and therefore weakens the fight against the system? This once-classical and virtually irrefutable argument is no longer sustainable. There are now many of us women – and men – who maintain that feminis cannot bring about structural change without Marxism, but also that Marxist parties alone are not enough to fight for the rights and needs of women. Proof of this is the fact that women are a total minority in the directorate of Marxist parties in both capitalist and socialist countries, with the result that the social needs of women and especially mothers are insufficiently attended to.

Why does this happen? In no way because men are 'bad', nor because they are guilty of bad faith. In theory, as is evident in writings from Bebel to Fidel Castro, they were disposed to obtaining equal opportunities ad rights for women at all levels. And in revolutionary practice this did in fact happen. We are all familiar with the active participation of women in the wars of liberation in Algeria, for example, or in Latin America. Among the first measures the Soviet leaders took in 1917 was the complete modification of legislation with respect to women and their rights. Without a doubt Lenin was a feminist, although he would not have accepted this definition. But once the new system was consolidated, everything seemed to go back to the situation that had existed before. With the exception of a small group of intellectuals, Algerian women took up the veil once again. This happened because the leaders, and also the people they represented, had been brought up in the old way, in traditional families. As Lenin says, it is difficult to change customs, and, as Freud shows us, our super-ego: in other words, our norms, evaluations and ethical prejudices are inherited from our grandparents, from generation to generation.

You have to be a woman, and to have experienced in your own flesh and blood our insecurities, doubts, burdens and marginalization, in order to be able to identify all that has to be changed. What should we do then, and how should we organize ourselves adequately, without leaving aside, but rather joining with our companions, our natural allies?

In Italy and Spain I was told about an interesting phenomenon. From the beginning of the upsurge of the Marxist parties of the last few years – in post-Franco Spain, and in Italy where the Communist Party is supported by a virtual majority – women voted for them massively because during the pre-electoral struggle their leaders had promised to defend feminist demands, such as the decriminalization of abortion, the divorce law, etc. Nevertheless, once the electoral struggle was over and often won, party leaders dealt first with many other priorities, fearing that their promises to the feminists would provoke the men and also a large number of women afraid of change and their possible greater freedom. Women who had voted for them because of their promises later unfulfilled, began to organize themselves and to take part in feminist movements. In the next elections they refused to vote for them. The Left suffered losses in the elections, partly as a result of this process. Owing to these losses, in the period that followed, the Left took its promises much more seriously and important changes were made. Many women went back to the parties, and the feminist movements, rather anarchistic in their methods, diminished their struggle. Through the wave of feminism an important dialectical movement was produced, whereby the parties were revitalized and motivated to fight for the needs of women.

It was possible to influence the traditional left-wing parties from the outside. Yvette Roudy, a member of the directorate of the French Socialist Party, told us about the laborious process of bringing about changes from inside a party and the trade unions. She also believes that there can be no equality without socialism because patriarchal capitalism – the only kind there is – is a doctrine of inequality.

I was going to end with this phrase, beautiful in its truth and brevity and therefore fit to be the final one in this book. However, when almost everything had been written, I came across Badinter's history of maternl love. I found it just in time to be able to include a few lines with reference to the ideological role of Rousseau and the way his concepts of female psychology influenced Freud's respective theory.

I made two discoveries that made an impact on me and which I would like to comment on. Firstly, I understood my aversion to Rousseau. Naturally, we used to read *Emile* in the Realgymnasium, and that was how I became aware of Sophie, the model companion for the ideal man. Sophie was dedicated, self-sacrificing and totally devoted to her home and to motherhood. She was not overly intelligent, but certainly pactical. She was neither argumentative nor ambitious. Fragile and vulnerable, she found support, guidance and protection in her husband. As women, we should be like her, Jean-Jacques tells us implicitly. It seems that I did not much like this reasoning but I repressed it and forgot it. Now I understand why I always laughed ironically whenever anyone praised Rousseau's famous phrase, 'retournons a la nature' – which to me must have meant going back to Sophie.

Second discovery: my mother, with all her contradictions and rebellions, was a Rousseauian mother. I began this book by talking about my mother and I will end it by understanding her better.

When Badinter establishes the link between Rousseau, Freud, and his followers, especially Helene Deutsch, she emphasizes that the triad characteristic of the 'feminine woman' – passivity, masochism and narcissism – originated one hundred and fifty years earlier. Of course, the reasoning is new. Freud maintains that women's greater narcissism is an attempt to compensate for her lack of a penis. That is why it diminishes with motherhood, since in her unconscious the chld is a phallic substitute. Helene Deutsch argues that female masochism is the result of a 'biological' return of activity which is primitively directed towards the world, herself and within the little girl.

Since I realized my mother was Rousseauian, and also because she belonged to the same generation as Freud's patients, I went over my memories to see if she had the three feminine characteristics. But before that, I want to mention something about narcissism: years ago, when I was writing about women, their limitations and potential, in *Cuestionamos* 2, I maintained, relying on Isabel Larguía's concept of the invisible work of woman, that her possessiveness with respect to her children was due to their being the only visible and abidin product the majority of women are allowed to produce. These children, if they turn out well, testify to maternal validity and integrity. On reflecting upon female narcissism, which decreases with motherhood, it seemed obvious to me that children, as the only product, etc., are burdened with their mother's narcissism. And it made me remember my mother and an often-repeated scene which I found irritating as a child: Mama, feeling me to make sure that I was healthy and robust, used to say, 'This one's turned out well.' I promised to be a strong, lasting product.

And what about female masochism? It is true that my mother was a masochist and always prepared to sacrifice herself for her children. She spent her last years practically in misery, refusing to accept any help, and nursing a small fortune which had been left to her. This was destined for us, as our inheritance and was especially for my sister in her old age. Yes, like many others, this was a self-sacrificing 'maternal' and masochistic attitude, worthy of Sophie. Yet, as I described at the beginning of this book, when my mother had the opportunity to be active and dedicate herself passionately to something outside the house, this masochism disappeared as if by magic. In short, I would say that the feminine triad exists, but as the superstructure of a certain era, already condemned to disappear.

I discovered that my father was aso marked by this triad and its ideology. That is why, arousing both my protests and my Oedipal jealousy, he used to say, 'Gretl is a saint.' My mother, of course, was no saint, and just as well I would now say, but she had a right to that title by the mere fact of her motherhood. And also, it is true, because she was always very supportive and not at all prejudiced towards my father, when in fact she really did have problems, but that is another story. Sometimes, my father would look at the three of us, his wife and daughters, and say very sympathetically, 'Poor women, how you suffer because of what you have inside.' This also came from Sophie. We were genitally fragile and vulnerable. That was why I understood Melanie Klein so well, when I became familiar with her concept of 'female, internal castration', a concept which Freud concealed with the horro of the male castration complex at the sight of woman's mysterious genitals. As a young girl, when I walked through the streets of Vienna, I used to read the plates on the doors which gave the names of the doctors and their specialties. I used to wonder – there would have been no point in asking adults, they would not have told me – why there were so many name plates which said *Frauenarzt*, women's doctor (gynaecologist in English is more discreet). And I used to wonder why there was no *Männerarzt* (men's doctor) and if we really were more unhealthy than they were.

In finishing this book I think I have found the common denominator between Marxism, psychoanalysis and feminism, the three main interests in my life. This common denominator is consciousness – the consciousness to be able to bring about change.

POSTSCRIPT

It is not at all a pleasant experience to grow old, but it is unavoidable. It is not pleasant to experience physical ageing nor can it be easily foreseen. But I refuse to commit the error of living exclusively in the past, which is what any old people do.

Only once a year do I permit myself the luxury of reliving the past. Sterba and I have developed a good friendship and I spend a week with him every summer. He lives and works in Detroit and spends his holidays in Vermont, in a lovely place in the middle of a forest. He is eighty-five years old, but still we go riding every day – very grand, very amusing . . . I often say it's as if I enter a time machine and emerge a grand lady. I harbour no resentment towards him, although I could say that he terminated my analysis in a very sloppy way in order to be done with it. But I could also give him credit for that . . . When I visit the Sterbas, it is as though I were re-experiencing Vienna, through their customs nd language. With them I'm the youngest, and I become a nice, pleasant young girl as I help Mrs Sterba into an armchair, or fetch her a shawl or some such thing. So, I am young!

Melanie Klein has written a very good article about old age and solitude, which I find very convincing: if you have good inner objects, then you are fine. Melanie Klein is my model for growing old. She was over eighty when she suddenly became ill on a trip she had gone on by herself. It turned out to be cancer, and within a week she was dead. That's the way to do it. But growing old is no fun . . .

What remains is one's profession, politics and – in my case – also children and grandchildren. I don't have a lot of contact with my grandchildren, but that's partly because of the diaspora-like situation in which we live. I have a very good relationship with my children but I would never sacrifice a politically significant task just to see my son. Of course I would gladly give up an analytic congress.

Take the case of Nicaragua, for example. At the moment I travel to Nicaragua once a month in order to help set up a social-psychiatric network. In Nicaragua I live outside time; it's as if we had never lost the Spanish Civil War and were reconstructing Spain. In a strange way it is similar to being with the Sterbas: I am able to rediscover my youth. It is as if something clicks, even physically. A colleague of mine took a photograph of me in Nicaragua. I didn't even know he was taking it. It is during the land redistribution and I am wearing a straw hat because of the sun. By coincidence I am stnding under a billboard with an image of Sandino on it. I look so triumphant and young in that photograph . . .

So, if you can find something meaningful, old age loses its significance. And therefore – which is the whole point about politics, and previously religion – you must find something ongoing. But it must be ongoing . . .

PART THREE
From Buenos Aires to Managua

Marie interviewed, Mexico, 1983

NICARAGUA

IN 'A FEW WORDS' at the beginning of this book, I talk about the difficulties I had separating myself from the book. This separation took place in January 1981.

I did not know then that I would have another opportunity to be 'on the side of history', as I put it somewhat pompously at the end of my conversation with Enrique Guinsberg.

This happened in the following way. After the Sandinista victory I said to my friend Sylvia Berman from time to time: 'Silvi, let's do something. Let's go to Nicaragua.' Sylvia had worked in Nicaragua as a medical doctor in one of the brigades, though not in mental health. Towards the end of the civil war they were in a clandestine, improvised landing field in Diriamba, which was already liberated territory by then. When Sylvia left for the war, I asked myself why I had not gone with her. There were several reasons why I hadn't; cowardice was probably one of them. But besides that, forty years had passed since my experience during the Civil War in Republican Spain; my few clinical and surgical skills were no longer sufficient to the task, as they had been lost through the many years of practising psychoanalysis. So, I decided not to join her and the other Argentinian comrades who formed part of the brigade.

When I asked her again around July 1981: 'And Nicaragua, Sylvia?' she answered, 'Yes, now yes (it's all right).' It all began with a congress of the professional staff in Nicaragua's health services in which Sylvia gave a paper on the psychoanalytic training programmes we had both worked in at the Centre for Teaching and Research (CDI) in Buenos Aires. The dean of the Faculty of Medicine at León at the time, the only one which existed in Nicaragua, was impressed by this work and offered Sylvia a professorship for the training of other faculty members. Mental health was to be included among the subjects, since it had proved necessary to adjust the contents of medical studies to meet human needs.

But Sylvia had binding obligations in Mexico and could not leave, so she proposed forming a working group. The twelve of us would merge into a single element, an almost omniscient teacher – a *homo gestaltensis* teacher, I would venture to say.

In September 1981, three of us – Sylvia, Nacho Maldonado and I, who were responsible for co-ordination within the group – arrived at the Augusto César Sandino airport in Nicaragua. In spite of the tropical air and colours, the atmosphere reminded me of another time in another country: the airport in Santiago de Chile, where I had arrived the day before Salvador Allende became President.

I am not going to attempt to describe this new Nicaragua 'with its violent sweetness', as Julio Cortázar expresses it in his latest book. He is able to create an image of it, I am not. I will only talk about it from a professional point of view, about our meeting with the Department of Mental Health in the Faculty of Medicine in León. The Department was responsible for the teaching of clinical psychology and psychiatry and for the medical care in the psychopathological casualty unit at the university hospital. They had already changed the medical studies curriculum in order to create the kind of doctor the new Nicaragua needed. Field work in primary prevention now became obligatory for every student at all levels; this entailed attending to the local population. Our Department was to be co-ordinated with this part of the training, which was called 'studies and field work'.

The Department of Mental Health, with which we met to discuss our co-operation, consisted of two reactionary psychiatrists who stuffed their patients with drugs and never listened to what they had to say (we thought it fitting that shortly afterwards one of them should be working as a veterinarian in Miami and the other selling cassettes in Honduras), as well as two psychologists – upright Sandinistas – and one female social worker. It was she who most thoroughly understood what was going on among the people. When the psychiatrists complained about the long list of patients, we said, as if with one voice, 'You should try group therapy!'

One of the young psychologists said, certainly, that he had already thought about it and that the following day he would start doing therapy with his first group. We supported him enthusiastically. When I was leaving I asked him which theoretical approach he had selected. He answered as though it was taken for granted, 'The Marxist approach, of course, because we know how relations of production are reflected in the psyche and how . . .' At that point it became clear to us that we had to start teaching seriously the basic elements of psychoanalysis and group therapy.

We made brief notes on the most fundamental points and compiled a sort of ten commandments, a list of concepts and principles that would become the core of our first lectures in psychoanalysis. I want to reproduce them here because on my trips through other countries in search of solidarity and financial support for our project, I found out that some psychoanalysts, and other people working in mental health, were interested in them. So here is our list:

(1) We must be able to listen, to question and to assimilate the meaning of catharsis.

(2) The unconscious exists; this is easily proved through the interpretation of slips, dreams and fantasies. Everything which appears illogical in us has a meaning.

(3) Hence our attitude and actions are over-determined. Our ideology is in part unconscious.

(4) We are a sum of conflicts. We are apprehensive of changes, which awaken our basic fears. Every symptom has a primary and a secondary benefit.

(5) We are a sum of contradictions. Even the mother who loves her baby hates it at the same time (Winnicott).

(6) The history and sexuality of our childhood are important because they are repeated – generally without our realizing it.

(7) Transference relationships are important, because we repeat them.

(8) Counter-transference is important; nobody is neutral. The practice of psychotherapy is a political task.

(9) The sequence of complementary events explains why one person becomes ill in a particular traumatic situation and another does not.

(10) We are all wonderful, but also mad; we are heroes but also cowards (how to cope with fear?); we are loving but at the same time perverse. Feelings of guilt have to be diminished, as they don't help but paralyse.

From the very beginning we simultaneously started supervision with each of our teams. From this first meeting and all subsequent ones, there arose many different tasks that no single person would have been able to fulfil alone: participating in developing a psychoprophylaxis project for pregnant women; training children's doctors towards a better understanding of the problems of children, their mothers and families as a whole; acting in a consultant capacity for clinical psychology; drafting a research project for second-year students within the 'studies and field work' part of their course. The latter was an investigation into the physical and psychological health conditions of fifteen thousand elementary school pupils in León. And there was more involved: sexual education, Balint groups with the doctors and nurses in the Ministry of Health, and a few other things. In addition, there are the courses in the psychiatric hospital in Managua, where we are still responsible for part of the training of future psychiatrists. Furthermore, we attempt to retain behavioural psychologists and to teach them and social workers a different (and, to them, unknown) form of psychotherapy. In Managua we teach a comprehensive course on psychoanalytic theory, a second one on group therapy and another on family therapy. Assessment of the relationship between the individual and the family is based on psychoanalytic theory, the analysis of relationships within the family follows the systemic approach, and the role of the family in society is defined in terms of the Marxist approach.

One person or one teacher would never have been able to handle such a range of knowledge and techniques. But we are not single individuals, we are a team with the somewhat cumbersome name of 'The Mexico–Nicaragua Team of Mental Health Internationalists'. We are twelve specialists, psychologists and medical doctors with psychoanalytic training. We are Argentinians and Mexicans, and one of us is Chilean.

Gradually, new requirements evolved. On each trip there was something else that had to be done or acquired, sometimes the most disparate articles: there's a lack of pens, nappies, books of course, and many other things. So every time the team goes to Nicaragua they take surplus baggage without Aeronica charging for it. On my last trip in June 1985, we took one hundred kilos of luggage, eighty kilos of which were medicines which the Mexican 'Hands Off Nicaragua' committee had donated to counteract the North American boycott, which has greatly affected medical supplies.

But let's go back to the beginning. From this first pilot trip we returned to Mexico, where we were eagerly awaited by an anxious, happy, almost manic team which at the same time was very worried. How would we manage? How should we organize our work to match the expectations we had met?

We decided – every decision we made was supported by the group as a whole – that we would meet every Monday night, that every month two of us would travel to Nicaragua and that all the tasks that had to be done would be prepared by all of us. But we also met in small groups to discuss and decide on very specific problems. And today, almost four years after our first trip, we still follow the same plan.

At the beginning, in some pessimistic moments, we thought that our classes and advice would not come to fruition. But as time went by we were able to observe the first successes. These were achieved with the help and co-operation of internationalist colleagues, such as Tania, a French psychoanalyst who worked for two years in León. At the time she was the only psychiatric doctor who worked in 'Region Two', a region that comprises a quarter of the entire country. Or Bigna, who committed herself to working for a year in the psychiatric hospital in Managua, where she fought against electric shock treatment with such persistence that she finally succeeded (in abolishing it). Her colleague Berthold Rothschild, an old friend and founding father of Plataforma Internacional, worked with her for a few months. And there was also Diana, an Israeli psychologist who had decided to work in Nicaragua but who nevertheless frequently asked herself if she shouldn't be in Israel fighting for the Palestinian cause. And then recently Erika Dannenberg, a trainee analyst from the Viennese Association, came along and contributed valuable work. Estela became involved to enable part of the staff of the psychiatric hospital to collect personal experiences within the framework of group therapy. She is a *compañera* from Argentina, a psychologist with psychoanalytic training, and works in the Ministry of Planning in Managua. The little spare time that she has, she likes to spend in this work.

We usually suggest group therapy, although we propose individual therapy in some cases. But we have never doubted that group therapy is the most suitable medium for Nicaragua – a changing country, a country on the road to socialism. On the other hand we have almost reached the point where group therapy will be phased out and replaced by community psychiatry.

But what are the specific features of the 'Nica' groups, apart from certain healing mechanisms which exist in every therapeutic group? In addition to 'projective and introjective identification', mirror reactions or the avoidance of stereotype role models, it is the socialization of grief for the dead, the permanent burden under which people there have to live and also – why not? – the socialization of the hatred towards the enemy who is invading the country.

With this I want to end my report on our work in Nicaragua. But why have I written it after the book has been published in Spanish and is available for any desired translation? As an old psychoanalyst, of course, I asked myself this question. Did I want to satisfy my narcissism by putting myself on public display? Did I want to show that at the age of seventy-five – my birthday is next month – I am still 'undefeated' and continue to fight? There is certainly some truth in that, but not all of it by far.

I feel very close to Nicaragua; all of us in Latin America and the Third World feel close to it, because the 'crime' for which Ronald Reagan is stubbornly punishing little Nicaragua is its hitherto successful attempt to break out of neo-colonialism and to dispose of its own natural resources and capacities as it wishes. The people of Nicaragua are making themselves 'the masters of their own history and architects of their own liberation', as the Sandinista anthem says. If they succeed in their intention they will be, according to Reagan, a dangerous example for the whole continent.

In this battle – which is, I would like to stress again, the battle of the whole of Latin America – Nicaragua needs solidarity. And with this brief and incomplete account of our work in mental health there I would like to ask you for your solidarity with Nicaragua.

MARIE LANGER
Mexico, July 1985

PSYCHOANALYSIS AND REVOLUTION IN LATIN AMERICA*

MARIE LANGER INTERVIEWED BY ARTURO VARCHEVKER

IN 1971 MANY PSYCHOANALYSTS resigned from the Argentinian Psychoanalytical Association. This was probably the first time that an organized group in a psychoanalytic training institution took such a step for political reasons. Even if this event was historically recent, we can still explore and evaluate it, as its relevance spreads beyond the psychoanalytic context.

Our present times are characterized by rapid changes in society. While these at times are due to creative forces, the inevitable companions of rapid change are uncertainty and a sense of insecurity. Violence is not a new phenomenon of our society; from our tribal origins it has been a daily occurrence. However, what is worrying now is the proliferation of institutionalized violence and our capacity to annihilate the world. This is a very serious phenomenon because it qualitatively changes the consequences of violence and our perception of it. Confronted with it, the individual's psyche feels like a chair standing on two legs, off-balance and disoriented. This is a perverse and pervasive phenomenon that also cripples institutions.

At the time of the above-mentioned crisis in the APA, Argentina was in the grip of a fascist dictatorship which had institutionalized violence, distorted values and perverted truth. If we agree that psychoanalysis is a discipline that deals with mental processes by trying to understand the interplay of destructive and creative forces in the individual, and in its endeavour promotes the search for meaning and stimulates freedom of

*Translated from the original Spanish by the interviewer.

thought, then these values should have been in conflict with those promoted by the political regime under which psychoanalysis was then taking place in Argentina.

Some psychoanalysts maintain a belief in institutional neutrality: that the institution should be kept outside politics and its domain restricted to 'pure' theory and technique. Others consider this stance an absurdity. There are difficulties, none the less. Firstly, how should we integrate the social domain (and therefore ideology) into the praxis of psychoanalysis, its theoretical and technical concepts? Secondly, what are the parameters that safeguard the praxis and the institution from turning into political activities?

Marie Langer wrote in her book, *Maternidad y sexo*, 'We live in very difficult times and in a world that is in constant change. We fail to offer our children the security and also the limitations we had before. However, thanks to Freud and the stimulation his discoveries had on other psychoanalysts and co-workers from other disciplines we have learned how to furnish them with internal security.' In the prologue to the 1972 edition to the same book she wrote, 'Society changes very fast in this, our century, so markedly. Luckily one also changes . . . I knew it before I wrote *Maternidad y sexo*, but I only realized recently that I made a serious omission: I had put it aside – because I didn't know how to incorporate it in a psychoanalytic perspective – that is, the social aspect and the struggle for change. Now, together with many others, I learned and I know better.' Marie Langer didn't find the answer, but with courage and dignity she posed the question in words and in action.

ARTURO VARCHEVKER

Acknowledgement: I would like to thank Paul Caviston for his helpful comments on this Introduction.

INTERVIEW

AV: I have reread *Cuestionamos* (1971, 1973) and it made me remember very important years in Argentinian politics and the psychoanalytic movement there. So my first question will be: Why *Cuestionamos*, for you?

ML: As I say in the Prologue to *Cuestionamos*, the idea came to me when a paper I presented at the APA was not published in their journal, though it's in the APA records. In a way it was with this paper that I left the APA – a strange piece of work! But prior to this I had already returned to active politics. I had a very strange feeling about writing this paper, called 'Psychoanalysis and/or social revolution'. It was like a driving force inside me. It's as if it had worked as a total statement for myself. It took me out of the APA, along with the whole Plataforma group, out of my ordinary life, and finally to Nicaragua.

AV: When you presented the paper, did Plataforma already exist?

ML: Yes, Plataforma had already been formed in Rome, at the time of the International Psychoanalytical Congress in 1969. Afterwards, in a rather confused manner, a Plataforma list was made; people put their names on it, then the list disappeared . . .

AV: A part of the psychoanalytic world was expressing some unease. What is your view of that period? And is this a prologue to *Cuestionamos*?

ML: Plataforma had its beginnings in fact in Zurich. It existed for quite some time there, where it was possible because some training analysts were tolerant, flexible and progressive. There was something of Plataforma in Vienna, but not much, and it didn't last; there was also something in Bologna. This was 1969, after 1968, which was a very important year in Europe.

AV: This means that the student movement in France, Germany and Italy had a part to play in this.

ML: Yes, all of that came into it. And precisely in 1968, there was a mixture of revolt, spontaneity, revolutionary intent of the students, combined with psychoanalysis – the reclaiming of Marcuse and Reich.

AV: The thought of Marcuse contains all the elements?

ML: Yes, as well as Wilhelm Reich, who suddenly became contemporary. At that time I was on the advisory board of Granica (publisher) in Buenos Aires. They brought me the works of left-wing psychoanalysts (Freudo-Marxists) of the 1930s, from the period of the Frankfurt school, to see whether they were interesting and should be translated. When the Plataforma group and later the Documento group split from the APA, they had no common theoretical base at that level, but such writings influenced those who formed the groups that split. It was essentially a European movement in which Argentina participated to some extent, through Armando Bauleo and Hernán Kesselmann. At the 1969 International Psychoanalytical Congress in Rome, they set up a Parallel Congress, which I attended, of course. It was very interesting. Many American analysts attended, deeply moved by the Vietnam War and the 1969 march on Washington.

AV: So the other important element was what was happening in the USA and Vietnam.

ML: Yes, the young people who threw away their draft cards and rebelled, the young (analytic) patients, who asked questions. So, what is it we questioned? Psychoanalysis as such? No, but we questioned the institution. And we questioned certain aspects of Freud himself, and the use of those aspects. I'll give you a minor example, which didn't appear officially in Plataforma's Declaration. Freud always treated someone free of charge, such as the Wolf Man. When I was a student in the Viennese Psychoanalytical Association, I myself had to have non-paying patients. This is done in many institutes, and I believe there is a similar provision made at the London Institute of Psycho-Analysis. In Vienna the members had to have two non-paying patients and the training analysts had to have two non-paying candidates. And that was under Freud – a fact that is not well known.

AV: Isn't this a sort of guilt, or – as Freud did it – a desire to develop psychoanalysis when it began to spread?

ML: Yes, all this is true. And Freud was no revolutionary. But it is also true that the analysts, later the institutions, latched on to what Freud said in two or three brief technical articles: that it isn't possible to treat someone for free, while omitting the fact that Freud's own Association did so. Though, admittedly, four or five hours per week in this fashion could become a burden over the years.

AV: From the standpoint of this questioning which arose all over the world, what is the linking factor or situation which caused it to arise in Argentina and not in other places?

ML: Look, we thought – and take note, as this erroneous thinking cost many lives – that the situation in Argentina was pre-revolutionary. This notion created a certain climate which led psychoanalytic trainees to make revolutionary proposals. In this case it did not mean a call to arms. But it did mean becoming politically radicalized, entering then into a conflict with many members of the APA. I left the APA in 1971, some time after the Vienna Congress that same year.

AV: What would be the standpoint and attitude of a psychoanalyst who had become radicalized and took an active, committed ideological position?

ML: Very complex. For example, for the trainee it was important who his analyst was. In some analyses the situation was dramatic; in others, not. It is said that the child learns from the parents as the analysand from the analyst, but I always say that the parents also learn from the child and the analyst from the analysand. I was Armando Bauleo's and Hernán Kesselmann's analyst. They were the founders of Plataforma in Argentina; of course, this influenced me very much in the counter-transference situation and it didn't create a major conflict in the analysis, just as it wouldn't when an analyst of bourgeois convictions analyses a patient of bourgeois convictions.

AV: It is fine if you can maintain clarity, as things are then analysable within that context. But can you maintain that sort of clarity if you move from one context to another?

ML: Yes, taking into account internal and external reality. Nevertheless, there were serious conflicts which led analytic treatments to break down. Some training analysts reacted furiously, and the analysands had little political experience, at least some of them. They took all this 'too seriously'. My viewpoint was always that Plataforma *was* serious, though not a subversive organization. But some Plataforma members behaved as if it were, and analysands hid all this from their analysts if those training analysts remained in the APA and therefore belonged to 'the other side'. In some cases conflicts increased and analyses broke down.

AV: Was all this an idealization which caused a distortion of the analytic relationship which was not analysed?

ML: Yes, due to a narcissistic idealization. We acted as if we were going to change the world.

AV: You say there were many problems on a practical level, analyses that were interrupted or were unmanageable in that situation.

ML: In the Prologue (of *Cuestionamos*) I describe how the situation came about on a practical level.

AV: Yes, but I want to compare this with a kind of problem that can arise in a 'bourgeois analysis' or any type of analysis. It is common for training analysts to participate in the running of the institution where their trainees train. Consciously or unconsciously, for various reasons, including narcissistic ones on the part of the analyst or the institution, the analyst may promote views which feed into the institutional and analytic situation, perverted or not. The analysand doesn't have the possibility of sufficient discrimination. How would you view this situation?

ML: As I said at the Congress of the Federation of Psychiatrists in Rosario, and as many others now say, the neutrality of the analyst is a fiction. No one can be neutral. Consider the case of a woman who aspired to study medicine (recounted in detail in the Praxis chapter). After she had been in analysis for two years, her analyst told me that 'She is really a good patient and is making good progress.' I said enthusiastically, 'Ah! So she's already done anatomy!' He looked at me in disgust and replied, 'No! But she's expecting her third child.' Here is a clear example of ideology being transmitted to the patient.

If Freud says that analysis is based on communication between the patient's and the analyst's unconscious, and if our ideology is partly unconscious, then obviously our ideology comes into play. For example, Bion says that it is necessary to analyse without memories or aims or plans for the analysand, but I think we always have a certain plan or aim for the analysand, whether or not we want to admit it. And this aim is always ideological.

AV: Which is to say, the analyst's ideology is present in a situation which isn't explicit, which is often unconscious.

ML: Denied, split off . . .

AV: The problem occurs when it *is* denied, split off . . .

ML: Exactly. I prefer to know that I acted as a feminist, and not simply for the good of the patient or whatever. Obviously the patient (mentioned above) had the possibility of going either way.

AV: In those days there were many analysts who did not question anything, who considered the splits from the APA as forms of acting-out.

ML: I think this question must be looked at in each specific case, in each analysis. Coming back to my own experience, which at this level is all I have to give you, I took care not to take on new analysands because I could see what was coming, from the time I initiated *Cuestionamos* and even earlier on, from the time I again became involved in politics. When I left the APA, my analysands also left. But this dynamic operates in reverse as well. It is possible that my candidates would have left the APA in any case, and I after them. It's difficult to tell. I remember that only one analysis was interrupted; it was the re-analysis of a training analyst who was 'on the other side', and who was very pained by the split and broke off her analysis.

AV: The question of acting-out isn't just about the particular case of each patient. When you presented your paper on 'Marxism and psychoanalysis' at the 1971 Congress, I remember that in the discussion there was an exchange with Hanna Segal on the issue of acting-out. And it seemed to me there was a very important point, which was insufficiently emphasized, related to ideology and *Cuestionamos*. But I don't know if this is your view.

ML: I think I answered Hanna Segal rather badly or not at all. And, what's more, we were friends. I felt it was difficult for me to answer, or more complicated for me to answer. Did the splits involve acting-out? Well, yes, logically so. But I must add something from what I saw about the APA members who left with me: it was an acting-out to the extent that the patient had the fantasy of being a favourite child, of being involved n the same thing, of supporting me, of living together in a small organization, to be like me. All these were fantasies, conscious and realistic ones in that situation. Effectively, links were forged which hadn't yet been forged in the APA. But what happens with a trainee generally? You always have this problem. For the training analysts who remained within the APA, their candidates had a similar fantasy of adapting to the analysts, and a similar acting-out occurred when they became associate members. They had no option but the acting-out provided by the training institution, particularly in those days.

AV: Sure. In other words, there is an acting-out under the umbrella of the Establishment, and an opposite situation in the break with it.

ML: Both of them are acting-out situations. As I believe was said by Wilhelm Stekel (contemporary of Freud) about a purely therapeutic analysis, if the patient finishes before resolving the transference – and of course the transference is never totally resolved – the patient will never see the analyst again anyway, so it doesn't matter so much. If the analysis has been done well, the patient progresses. However, in a training analysis the transference is never resolved, with the aggravating factor that, if you both stay in the same institution, the ex-trainee has a certain power over you, because tomorrow he can vote. The day after tomorrow he may compete with you. Perhaps he will support you, when you want to attain the presidency, for example, or perhaps he will vote against you: either way an acting-out of the transference. As the transference isn't resolved in a therapeutic analysis, it is even less so in a training analysis.

AV: Does this mean that ideology is always present in the institution and in analysis – within the analytic situation and outside it?

ML: Yes, outside it as well. And it is perpetuated and reinforced with greater consequences through the vote. The vote is very important inside any association – much more in the APA than in Plataforma, which was dissolved after eight or ten months, and, well, now we (ex-Plataforma members) are friends.

AV: Let's return to my original question. Why *Cuestionamos* in Argentina, at that time?

ML: Because of the pre-revolutionary situation there, and because we were also in the period of France 1968, the Vietnam issue, and our 'Cordobazo' (the uprising in Córdoba on 29 May 1969).

AV: Yes, there was a wider social context, a political situation motivating these events. What was the institutional context?

ML: The institutional context was expressed more clearly by the Documento group, which initially tried to reform the APA from within, after the Plataforma group had left the APA. Documento wanted the associate members to have voting rights, so that members who completed their training would automatically become training analysts. Although Documento made no formal protest about the great expense of analysis, there was implicit criticism; that issue was more prominent at the Rome Congress, not so much in Argentina.

AV: I understand that a general strike there was also a catalyst, but even beforehand there were dissensions within the APA.

ML: There were areas of discontent, for example, when COPAL (Consejo de las Organizaciones Psicoanalíticas de America Latina) was to meet in Brazil during the dictatorship there. The theme was to be 'violence'. We received a message from Brazil asking us to change the theme, which the APA changed to 'New Currents in Psychoanalysis'. Part of the APA, especially the younger, more radicalized members, said that this change was wrong. In their view one shouldn't go to a country to take part in a psychoanalytic congress, which supposedly involves a commitment to tell the truth, if you have to change the theme. They said, 'If we can't stick to our theme, much less tell the truth – without our colleagues over there running risks, which of course we don't want – then the venue must be changed.' There were several tense APA meetings where the voting decided in favour of going to Brazil and abandoning the theme of violence. So we were intimidated. There were many situations like that.

AV: That is to say, the APA's prevailing attitude was 'Don't get involved', which is also an ideological attitude.

ML: Yes, it means maintaining the status quo, leaving things as they are. This is very clear in a letter from Jorge Mom, the APA President, to Emilio Rodrigué, the FAP (Federation of Argentinian Psychiatrists) President: 'One must not perturb the candidate in his internal process, with reality.' What is this about reality?

AV: This attitude of 'not perturbing the candidate with reality' can also be seen as an acting-out.

ML: Of course.

AV: So, what do we question *for*?

ML: For a very concrete reason: to have a place to publish our ideas about psychoanalysis. When we question, this will lead us to think, to do something new, to create something new. In this respect we have failed considerably. Isn't that so? There are very few written works from that period, just two volumes of *Cuestionamos* and an occasional paper here and there.

AV: Given that there are few works from that period, was the questioning process interrupted, denied? Or was there insufficient understanding of the process being experienced?

ML: I regret that I haven't been able to read and study all the documentation from that period, but I want to outline what happened in Argentina. After the Plataforma and Documento splits from the APA, there was an experience of separation. Obviously this left people shaken, but the APA went on as if nothing had happened; they changed their membership roster and that was it. Later on the APA suffered a further separation from the APDEBA (Buenos Aires Psychoanalytical Association), and both were cowed by the terrible military dictatorship (1976–83), which is understandable. Thus it happened that a Congress of the APAL was inaugurated and presided over by a general representing the dictatorship. The Congress became totally compliant.

AV: The equivalent in Nazi Germany would be . . . ?

ML: Hitler sending Goering. He wouldn't have gone himself; he would have sent Goering to inaugurate the Congress. The APAL Congress took place during the hard years of Argentina's dictatorship, with the motto of 'non-involvement', which of course was both an allegiance to the state and a survival strategy. But now, in the 1980s, with the widely-known democracy that we have in Argentina, do you know what the APA did? In 1986 it organized a congress on the consequences of the violence and repression, and on the analysts' denial of reality. This time they invited President Alfonsín, who didn't attend. The congress was a modest symposium at the San Martín Theatre. And it was sponsored by Dr Vincente Galli, an APA member who was also National Director of Mental Health in the new democratic government. Janine Puget told me that only half the APA members attended the congress. A symposium where half the APA doesn't attend is non-existent! But it happened with this one.

AV: The printed programme says, 'The 25th Symposium of the Argentinian Psychoanalytical Association', entitled 'The Malaise in our Culture'. And the symposium headings are '1. What is the priority of the psychoanalyst? 2. Social violence. 3. Terrorism. 4. State terrorism. 5. Nuclear war.'

ML: Aren't we quick in Argentina? Quicker than the Germans? (She suggests a contrast with post-war Germany's reluctance to reappraise their Nazi-era practices.)

AV: Yes! Well, Argentina has always been characterized by that magnetic quality . . .

ML: And being on the ball. In fact, while the APA symposium was taking place (18–20 December 1986 in Buenos Aires), there was a demonstration against the Punto Final Law (which sets a statute of limitations on newly brought charges of human rights violations from the dictatorship period). Some sessions at the symposium were rescheduled so that members could take part in the demonstrations, while others weren't. Which means that they were in contact with reality and their ideology was clearly expressed.

AV: So fifteen years after *Cuestionamos* we find that a series of views, positions and ideological changes began to manifest themselves.

ML: Yes. And as another viewpoint on facing reality, Janine Puget says

'Reality must be included; we can no longer play at not doing so.' And of course we can't play at this any longer. Once a follower of Lacan said that for him reality was something imaginary, non-existent, when he was analysing patients; and a woman replied by asking, 'If someone comes to your consulting room and removes a person by force, is this reality removing him or an imaginary reality or what?' (This refers to situations which actually occurred under the 1976–83 dictatorship in Argentina.)

AV: How do you view the 1986 APA symposium, the space created for people's dissent to be expressed? Does this have something to do with what developed from the late 1960s?

ML: Yes, I'd say that this is the result of many people of good faith who admit that under the dictatorship they split themselves off, they repressed things, they became dissociated, employed all the defence mechanisms they had. Others did so more out of opportunism. The speed with which this reappraisal occurred means that the discussion engendered by Plataforma and Documento must have survived in some way all these years.

AV: Because *Cuestionamos* is very alive in the mind of anyone who works as a psychotherapist or psychoanalyst in Argentina.

ML: Yes, at least for those who attended the 1986 symposium in Buenos Aires, though not the very young ones. It went against the grain of many members because speakers cited pertinent papers from *Cuestionamos* by authors who are no longer APA members.

AV: Were there some psychoanalysts who eventually returned to the APA?

ML: Many.

AV: Did some return with a changed attitude towards the institution?

ML: Some people returned; others wished to do so but were not accepted. I was told – though I don't know the accuracy of this claim – that APA and APDEBA don't accept those who left as a group (Plataforma or Documento) but do accept those who left even a few days later. This means these members couldn't or didn't take a decision as speedily. If the latter wished to return they would be accepted, and some did return.

AV: Do you think this is part of an institution's narcissistic wound?

ML: Yes, yes.

AV: What did *Cuestionamos* teach you during these years?

ML: I am very happy to have done *Cuestionamos*, that is, to have taken the initiative to compile it, because my contribution is no greater than that of the others, but I feel it was important and I congratulate myself for having conceived this idea, as it provided a testimony for an historical moment.

AV: And what lessons are there for you and for others – both positive and negative, in relation to *Cuestionamos* and in relation to the last fifteen years – of a terrible dictatorship?

ML: It did me good, much good, to leave the APA at that time. And I learned things, I went through things I could never have experienced on the inside. And I am also pleased that, because of my political activity of the time, I *had* to leave Argentina and didn't have to endure the dictatorship remaining silent, in fear, humiliation, impotence. A terrible situation, eh? When it is said that some people reproach those who remained, I always defend those who remained, and I say they had much more courage than those who left. Well, we left, and were able to benefit from this. Unlike those who remained shut in – this is called internal exile, much worse than external exile.

AV: When will you write a paper on internal exile?

ML: (laughing) I no longer write about . . .

AV: But internal exile is very significant.

ML: But neither you nor I have experienced it!

AV: No. Perhaps I have, a bit. It is a mental attitude where we hide our ideology.

ML: I experienced that all my years in the APA, please note. For me it was precisely a matter of coming out of my internal exile: to be able to speak about what I think publicly (while it was possible in Argentina), to write what I think, and later, abroad. Now for the others, I think everyone gained, in a certain sense. I have contact with many people in Argentina who returned from exile. All of them have been enriched by the experience. Although it is difficult to discern whether they were enriched by leaving APA, or because this exit from the APA – a political one – made them more political and led them to exile. Now, where there exists disillusionment but also change is in the fact that when we left, we left as defined Marxists, Freudo-Marxists. I believe none of us now are fixed on that: we are much more pragmatic. For example, we ask about Nicaragua, 'How can one be useful to Nicaragua, with certain psychoanalytic concepts?' We don't ask, 'Let us see whether Nicaragua is Marxist and how we connect theoretically as Marxist psychoanalysts?'; we are not interested in that kind of question, which has lost much of its appeal.

AV: In all this, there is a position which considers psychoanalysis in its social application with a particular ideology. The most difficult issue would be: What happens to psychoanalysis with the Marxist ideology?

ML: I don't know if it is in relation to Marxist ideology, or rather to the country in which you live. Even according to Freud, psychoanalysis sup-posedly questions the official ideology or takes an oppositional stance. However, when we visited Cuba, what most caught our attention as Marxist psychologists is that psychologists' work there is syntonic with the state. I am often asked this kind of question about Nicaragua, where our aim is not to set the individual against the state. Now, please note that an oppositional stance was the original idea of psychoanalysis. If we take a look at the APA Congress inaugurated by a general, or the relationship between the Establishment and psychoanalysis in the USA, or anywhere, we can say that psychoanalysis everywhere has lost its manner of questioning the official ideology.

AV: So you see in psychoanalysis an attitude which the individual ought to have in questioning himself and the context in which he lives.

ML: Yes, it's complex. For example, in Zurich I am always told that psychoanalysis in itself is subversive. And I say, 'If I look at analysts and analysands I would doubt this a bit.' Or one could say that the majority of analyses are a failure because one doesn't see subversiveness in people. Although in Zurich there are a few subversive analysts and a parallel organization which originated in Plataforma, for example.

If I am asked what analysis is for, beyond transforming symptoms, I always say 'in order not to lie to oneself any more'. And I think that's as far as it goes. If I go to Nicaragua I think I am not lying to myself, although I know of the existing contradictions. I try to weigh things up and say, despite the contradictions, that I am in favour of the Sandinista Revolution, because the positive far outweighs the negative. And one could say the same of Cuba if one were working there.

AV: If you were working there, you might say that Cuba is different from Nicaragua, because at present its reality is much more solid. There is a precarious situation in Nicaragua at the moment. Would you think individual analysis would be possible in Cuba at the present time?

ML: No, I don't think so, but for other reasons: because economically – more in time than in money – it is almost unfeasible. We are going to have a second meeting there, requested by Fidel Castro, called 'a meeting between Marxist psychologists and Latin American psychoanalysts'. If Cuba is well disposed to the introduction of psychoanalysis there, my main question will be: 'How will its application and training be feasible?' The application is not so difficult – it will be applied psychoanalysis – but the training could be problematic. (After Marie Langer presented this talk, entitled 'Psicoanálisis sin divan', she was invited to join Cuba's Academy of Sciences.)

AV: But there is also a historical difference, because, when Cuba emerged in the historical context of its revolution, then Cuba developed its mental health programme and health care in general, according to prescriptive beliefs of that period. Nicaragua has the possibility of emerging differently, because over twenty years separates it from the Cuban Revolution.

ML: Yes, Nicaragua has the great advantage in lacking a strong psychiatric tradition. When the followers of Franco Basaglia in Europe ask me, 'How many psychiatric hospitals in Nicaragua have been able to close?', I say (laughing) 'None, because there is only one, and it is already half empty. What more can you ask for? Two hundred and fifty beds for an entire country is not an excess of psychiatric authority.'

AV: So this gives greater flexibility.

ML: Of course!

AV: So let's look at Cuba. What has changed in Cuba for them to reognize psychoanalysis? Is your presence an asset?

ML: When I attended the congress of intellectuals there, it began with an opening towards Christianity. In the inaugural session at the huge Palace of Conventions, at the top table were Fidel and his entourage, all in uniform; there was also the permanent commission of intellectuals, to which I now have the honour of belonging, along with García Márquez the author, and Friar Betto the Brazilian theologian. Fidel's book about Christianity and liberation theology was distributed among the audience. So I believe that they are determined to open up Cuba, to abandon the past rigidity and suspicion that if this or that comes into the country, then culturally it would be catastrophic.

When Fidel said, 'We are going to bring in psychoanalysis. Yes, let's have this congress,' he sent me to the Minister of Culture, Armando Hart. He introduced me to Roberto Fernandel, director of the Casa de las Americas (publishing house), by telling me he hoped I would give a lecture at the Casa (which became 'Psicoanálisis sin divan'). I felt embarrassed, not only because of the importance they were conferring on me, but because I felt unwell, from my undiagnosed cancer. Fernandel said, 'When years ago I brought a Nicaraguan priest as juror on the commission of the Casa de las Americas, people were annoyed with me and asked, "What is this, bringing a priest?"!' The priest was Ernesto Cardenal (who later became Minister of Culture in the Sandinista government). When Maria Langer went modestly to Cuba as a tourist, she came in through the back door. But now she has come in, together with psychoanalysis, through the main door . . . and as a Jew as well (laughing). The Cubans joke, 'Now we invite the Catholics – and you.'

AV: This made a profound impression on people in Europe as well, because it implies a great change. Has it a lot to do with you as a person?

ML: No, no. It has nothing to do with me. I was merely the person adequate for the job.

AV: So, yes, it does have something to do with your stance, your path.

ML: Possibly. Just as Friar Betto was the appropriate person (to introduce liberation theology to Cuba) . . . but it could have been Ernesto Cardenal or Méndez. Now Cuba will hold a congress for Spanish-speaking people on Marxist psychology and psychoanalysis in February 1988. That's why I can't go to Tepotzlán (a rural village she frequented) for the weekend, because tomorrow we have a meeting of the Mexican commission for the congress. It is planned as an encounter between Marxist psychologists and Latin American psychoanalysts, 'Latin American' mainly because of the language. It will be held in Havana, at the Congress of Conventions, which has the facilities for simultaneous translations.

AV: Let us return to a previous question. Fifteen years further on, what do you think about the others who also formed part of the *Cuestionamos* project?

ML: Most of them continued working along similar lines. At the first congress in Cuba, I realized that this was something that people from Plataforma and Documento had finally achieved. Before, we had dreamed of such an event, but it had seemed impossible. Now, when I visited Buenos Aires, I learned that in August 1985 there was a Congress of Alternative Psychiatry (called 'International Encounter'), full of people from Plataforma and Documento who had never left Buenos Aires, or who had left and returned, or who were there on a holiday visit. It was beautiful, an encounter of people dear to me. It was a congress about the application of psychoanalysis to human rights.

AV: I see more clearly the relationship to Latin America, because of the shared historical path, which is still an open wound. What is the importance of *Cuestionamos* in Europe?

ML: I think it will be important precisely because in Europe now people are looking at these problems, although fortunately Europeans are far away from them, historically and geographically. At a recent International Psychoanalytical Congress in Hamburg, there was a presentation of all the material known as 'The Catalogue' on the repression that has occurred recently in Latin America. In France a book will be published in which Latin American analysts describe what happened to them during the repression, and Argentinian analysts have spoken about this at a congress there. Thanks to such a bloody dictatorship, people now speak of Freud's desolation (his concept of Thanatos) faced with the fact that the First World War had been possible, that man is so evil, although he always has been. Now we seem to react with confusion and stupor when confronted with social perversion: torture, state terrorism, sexual-sadistic perversion, etc. There is a great desire to study this, to understand this; there is the whole dimension of the human being in relation to the social, the political, the state.

AV: So our perplexity leads us to study these phenomena such as perversion, state terrorism, and the possiblity of nuclear war, which could lead to the destruction of the world?

ML: And the need to *understand*, because this is our aim.

AV: A final question, then. From your standpoint, what would be the future and function of psychoanalysis?

ML: The future of psychoanalysis is one thing. More important is the application of psychoanalytic concepts to other therapeutic systems, easier ones, briefer ones, reachable ones, economic ones (in time and money).

As for the function of psychoanalysis, there are two: the medical function, exercised for years through the psychologist or whomever, and the search for truth. What truth? That of understanding in order to make known, to divulge, to burrow like ants, to become more capable of preventing catastrophe – state terrorism, or the great catastrophe, nuclear holocaust.

AV: If you were interviewing Marie Langer, what question would you ask her?

ML: In Nicaragua, which do I care about most: introducing psychoanalysis, or that Nicaragua live in peace (laughter)? Answer: That Nicaragua live in peace.

Interview conducted in Mexico City, January 1987
Edited with assistance from Margaret Hooks and Les Levidow

LAST WORDS

THE LANGERS were and are a clan. Since the death of Maximo, which took place exactly fifteen years ago today, the family (Tomás, Martín, Ana and Veronica, the children in chronological order, and from time to time Gucki, the 'tante' who died in 1979, the daughters-in-law and the grandchildren) frequently gathered together around Marie, at the prompt, regular lunches and dinners in a large apartment in Calle Juncal near the Botanic Gardens, or in the weekend country house, built largely by Maximo and Marie about thirty years ago in Escobar, a small village near Buenos Aires.

The children grew up in the Juncal apartment. (The Buenos Aires custom is that a house or a neighbourhood identifies a person for the rest of their lives.) It was there that Marie attended to her patients for twenty-eight years.

Veronica frequently recounts an erroneous but comical recollection from the first months of her life: that of receiving her mother's breast in the ten minutes between each patient; Ana tells the joke that only once, when the house was on fire, did Mimi leave her consulting room before the end of the fifty-minute analytic hour. I was only in the Juncal apartment for a week and only once in the consulting room. On that occasion I was impressed by a feature which I have since verified as characteristic of Marie: a frugal comfort in which there is never one detail too many. The divan, the desk covered with glass under which photographs of family members swarmed like living organisms, the floor-to-ceiling bookshelves, the armchair, a couple of chairs, a Picasso rug . . . The window facing the street occupied all of the wall which Marie turned her back to while she was working: a long balcony on which some plants grew (I remember a Crown of Christ with its paradoxical little flowers like drops of blood among the thorns) communicated with various of the other rooms, a situation the children made use of to spy on the consultation or, as adults, to verify whether or not their mother was busy without breaking the rule of 'no interruptions'.

But the Juncal apartment, when I knew it, was also the administrative headquarters of the Argentinian Federation of Psychiatrists, of which Marie was then President. In a room that occasionally served as a sewing room or guest bedroom, the office of the FAP was overwhelmed with correspondence, notices, support and rejections. Friends and colleagues, generally friend/colleagues, arrived at midday – which in Buenos Aires is about one in the afternoon – for lunch, or in the evening for dinner.

During the week, private practice, lunches, dinners with family or friends, political meetings, unpaid work at the hospital, teaching, occupied the entire day. At the weekends, Escobar and the whole family: to swim exhaustingly, even at the onset of winter, to ride the enormous horses of the Argentinian pampa (which once caused her a very serious fracture) for various hours; to share the ritual barbecue, to talk to the children, the children of the children, and the daughters-in-law. Beyond – or closer to? – her occupation as psychoanalyst, and the occupation is often that which gets in the way, Mimi is a very unusual conversationalist: always attentive to the problems of others and never failing to share hers. It is probable that half-jokingly, half in earnest, the children would complain of the undeferrable and exacting work of their mother, but all agreed that with Mimi one could talk about absolutely 'everything'. I still do not know of any child who can say this about his mother. I have never spied on her work, but I know that psychoanalysts of her age are solemn and very often intolerable; perhaps this is one of the distinctive characteristics of Mimi: the absence of solemnity . . . But an essential part of the activity at Escobar was the long walks in solitude: there always came a moment when the commotion made her leave the group and walk by herself for a long while . . .

At that time the international airport at Ezeiza was like a bus terminal on the point of being deserted. On many occasions I waited for visitors there; on many occasions I felt this same melancholy that the Tepehuanes station produced in me, where the train arrived like at the world's end. Semi-deserted with its one narrow soulless corridor – it has changed, they say – where a small disturbance would suddenly occur when an aeroplane deigned to land or take off, immediately returning the place to a provincial calm afterwards . . . On 6 September 1974, I was a protagonist in one of those small disturbances. In an act of absolute irresponsibility, as though we had thrown our fate to the wind, Ana and I had got married three days before and were leaving Argentina. I said that the Langers are, were, a clan; like all clans, they suffer for being such. Now one of the members of that clan was leaving, perhaps for ever.

In the terminology of Pichon Riviere, my family is schizoid; Ana's is epileptoid. I am not familiar with the theory that sustains these concepts, I only know that our families are in fact radically different: the Langers tend (tended) towards union and suffer (suffered) terribly as a result of separation; we, however, tolerate entire years of separation without any great display of sorrow. On that occasion in Ezeiza, everybody cried except me. In an already-old habit, I denied it all and thought the drama was pure exaggeration: that when all was said and done we were not going to the other side of the world. (Today I am convinced that we went to the other side of the world.) I remember that when once we were on the plane and Ana was feeling depressed, out of pure foolhardiness I said: 'You'll see, they'll be coming to visit you within three months. You can't be apart.' It was a silly assertion that turned out to be a premonition.

At that time Marie made me apprehensive, but many people and things made me and make me apprehensive. Ana and I had decided to get married after knowing each other for only two weeks. Marie's doubts about this marriage were expressed in an excessive rejection of form ('I can't understand why you want to get married when you can live together without any obligations'), which was perfectly in keeping with her reputation as a liberal. Not out of conformity, but from an overwhelming respect for individual freedom bordering on utopian socialism, Marie could not deny permission for our wedding; nor could she stop inquiring as to the nature of this person that for once and for all was taking her daughter to a far-away country. In the week prior to the wedding, I felt that she wanted to work out who I was; she pursued my words, my glances and my actions (this paranoia is chronic).

We got married in the house of Fernando Ulloa. The entire membership of Argentinian psychoanalysis was at the reception. Mimi insisted on introducing me to Emilio Rodrigué because he might be able to help me publish a novel I was then writing. Predictably Rodrigué did not comprehend anything – fortunately, because it was a forgettable and forgotten novel. I mention these details because in them I see another of Marie's characteristics: a preoccupation with the intellectual 'achievements' of family members. Tomás is a brilliant doctor, Martín a brilliant engineer, Ana a brilliant paediatrician; Veronica gave up becoming a brilliant doctor and is now on the way to becoming a brilliant actress. By contagion, the husbands and wives of her children are, at least, academics or university graduates.

We arrived in Mexico with nothing. We survived thanks to the generosity of Frida Zmud, who lent us her apartment, and Andrés Caso, who gave me a job at the Public Works Ministry. The Argentinian situation deteriorated day by day. López Rega and Isabel Perón adopted terrorist methods; the victims of assassination and torture rapidly began to appear among groups of intellectuals. Much later I knew that our concern for Marie coincided precisely with a conspiracy. From the moment that the 'Triple A' began 'to concern itself with her health', it was as if we had known it all along. Ana called Buenos Aires at the same time as the family was trying to convince Marie that she should come here. To this day, I cannot forget the anguish of Ana who had to talk in allusions to visits and intense longings, for fear that the telephone was tapped.

A few days after this call and less than three months after our wedding in Buenos Aires, Marie landed in Mexico accompanied by Armando Bauleo. We waited in the absolute confusion of the international lounge at the airport. Ana was still anxious that they might have been detained before they boarded the plane. (Had the remains of Silvio Frondizi not been found precisely on the road to Ezeiza?) At last we could see an agitated Mimi and almost heard the loud laugh of Armando, which could rise above the din of any airport. From then on, the scene was one now familiar to me: Mimi totally agitated, fearing the immigration officers' displeasure at her having forgotten some document, always anticipating the loss of a suitcase, passing through customs, coming out of the passage at the end of her tether and, finally, lighting the tranquillizing cigarette once inside the car. Nevertheless, she leaves the country two or three times a year.

Thanks to the hypomania of Armando Bauleo, the first few days were almost agreeable. We cooked ravioli and drank wine, going out to the airport to look for new exiles and listening to the records of Chavela Vargas. It was not unusual in those days to arrive at the apartment and find Nacha Guevara and Favero, Martha Bianchi, Luis Brandoni, her melancholy husband (Norman and Marie Brisky would arrive later) and many other less well-known Argentinians. The majority visited Marie in search of consolation, explanation and interpretation, and she was able to offer all in spite of her own depression. Another of her paradoxical features: the strength, impassiveness, in the face of situations that disconcert others; the uneasiness when faced with administrative matters that others usually deal with without anxiety.

Marie recalls her response to a reproach at the time for her having come to Mexico: 'Maybe I left ahead of time, but without any doubt I'd have had to go in the long run anyway.' For my part, I remember a morning when Ana and I were leaving for the weekend and Marie was staying alone in our apartment. Ana went into the room where Mimi was sleeping to say good-bye; as I passed by I saw, through the crack in the open door, Marie's face covered in tears. I felt very bad and asked Ana to invite her along to Taxco, but she didn't want to come. I thought she was crying because of being alone, of being old, of having left Argentina . . .

Today, six years later, I know that that morning she was crying over her weakness at having let herself be coaxed to go on a journey she was not convinced of; I know that at the meeting where the family persuaded her to leave for Mexico, Mimi knew two things: that the idea of dying like Frondizi did not bother her, and that she would not have been able to stand up to torture. To stay on in Buenos Aires once she knew that her name was at the top of a list of those condemned by the Argentinian Anti-Communist Alliance was to stay on to find out which alternative fate would bring her: instant death or torture.

Her insistence on trying to join the Communist Party in Barcelona in 1936, when she had no document accrediting her as a member of the Austrian Communist Party, and the providential move to the Aragón front that would save her from being accused of espionage and subsequent death by firing squad, is something more than an entertaining anecdote. Marie often says that the clandestinity of the Austrian Communists since long before the war taught her to detect danger, but the very fact that within that clandestinity she was responsible for the security of the Central Committee – she will say it was only because of the security of the bourgeois environment her house in Vienna provided – is revealing in itself. I can easily imagine her taking the Secretary General of the Party across the Czechoslovakian border *incognito* and I can see her being much more preoccupied by having forgotten to buy cigarettes than by the situation itself . . . Leaving for Spain and the Civil War saved her from persecution and prison; being transferred to the front saved her from being shot in Barcelona; going to Paris to buy materials for the hospital in Murcia saved her from who-knows-what fate after the defeat of the Republic; leaving Czechoslovakia for Uruguay (when everyone else believed in the Schuschnigg plebiscite) saved her from the Nazis, from the Anschluss, from the camps and from death. Leaving Argentina had to have saved her from the 'Triple A'. And when I think of other things, it seems that a last-minute act, the one last attempt that others would not make, a caution that anyone else would neglect has always allowed her to obtain the document that would have been denied someone else, the book that was out of print, the aeroplane ticket that was not available.

I understand that many people call this type of character obsessive. The recklessness and indolence of the Mexican are mortal enemies of these characteristics. How many times have I resisted that (to me) seemingly excessive attention to detail which I would have easily underestimated and as a result lost so many opportunities.

Marie Langer is my mother-in-law . . . and my friend. In six years of being close to her, I have idealized and de-idealized her, quarrelled with and become reconciled with her. We have learned to co-exist: I, to take her obsessiveness with a grain of salt; she to take my 'autism' in the same way. ('Carajo!' she said to me just a few days ago, 'when am I going to meet your parents?' In six years I have never tried to arrange even one meeting for my parents and Mimi to get to know each other.) We have comfortable roles now: she is inept at practical things and I attempt to help her as much as I can; I am a loafer and forgetful, she motivates me and reminds me of my commitments. Of course I am convinced that it is impossible to maintain a desired equilibrium between these two attitudes, and working on this book has put our intentions to be tolerant and understanding to the test. She – is it the profession? – thinks that we should talk about everything; as a good autistic person, I give everything, of course! The result is misunderstanding and ridiculous resentment. But we are good people: we are willing to forget it and to go on liking each other.

Why am I co-author of this book? Marie has mentioned virtually every-thing and I am not thinking of repeating the story; I will only mention some of my motivations and refute some of Mimi and Enrique's arguments. I have been various people's ghost writer; I have written dozens of speeches that I have never given; I have put together articles that others have signed; I have edited theses that others have presented, and never written my own; I have done translations that others were paid for . . . Ten years of psychoanalysis with different therapists authorizes me to say that I have listened to all possible interpretations of this behaviour. Invisibility is my strength and showing myself is so painful for me that I do so with enormous timidity. Still nobody has discovered the pleasure I experience in spying – the 'refined pleasure' that exists in the divining of the thoughts of the other.

Working on these texts that you, tired reader, will have already read, and transforming them into the life of Marie Langer told in the first person, have constituted a great enthusiasm which can only be judged by those who have committed the same sins of vanity as I have, and repented – it is precisely these sins that Mimi has not committed.

The cultural background of her daughter Ana, my wife, leaves me cold. I was interested in writing this book for two reasons which I will try to shed light on. Proust says – note, no less a figure than Proust – that every life can be material for a novel (and it is well known that to Gide, the life of Proust, recounted in *Du côté de chez Swann*, seemed irrelevant) which presupposes that every life is interesting, which I believe to the letter. The life of my mother-in-law already seemed interesting to me in and of itself, that is, without having been written. So writing it turned out to be a real challenge and today I cannot feel anything other than that I was not up to this challenge for two reasons: one, I am not Proust (which I do not regret); two, one had to submit oneself strictly to a programme, my mother-in-law's life, which is no novel. I would add a third reason for my deficiency, but this is insignificant: there was no time, it was always a rush, a rush to write the drafts, to clean them up, to correct them . . . Could it be that this sensation was due to my mother-in-law's obsession, or to my never-ending justifications? These allow me to exclaim: 'Oh, what I could have done if it hadn't been so much of a rush.' The truth is that the poor manuscript did not know a good night's sleep that would allow it to get up the following day with its head cleared and with two medium-strong coffees sit down to work, to add things, to erase things.

This was one of the reasons that led me to insist with Mimi that this book should be written when she believed that the best thing was to forget about the whole affair. The other, Mimi, is the tenderness you arouse in me; it's what I love about you. It's what allowed me to see you move from disillusionment to enthusiasm, to the desire that your life would be told, that your book would come out. Was it worth it?

Clarifications: We were never a team. I have seen Enrique very few times, and never for work. He will agree that we never had the slightest interest in working together. Teams are formed by the choice of their members (except, of course, for football teams and then it's the owners who have the right to choose). This trio was never in tune – not, in my opinion, for the reasons Marie gives (that each of us had in mind another book and other readers). I know for certain that Enrique wanted another book; I wanted precisely this one. My readers are not those who are interested in history or literature (I don't know if at this stage I am interested in history and literature in this measure) and neither is my generation. Marie says that I am interested in the 'human', and at the risk of resorting to sentimentalism I'd say that yes, the 'human' is what interests me in this book and that this includes the 'scientific' discussions (psychoanalysis is still fighting to become a science). I believe that the astronomer as well as the historian, or the biologist as well as the man of letters could have a *vital* interest in the life and thought of Marie Langer. As far as my generation . . . I think that no one in Mexico who is around thirty-five knows which generation they belong to – that of the children of those who migrated from the provinces, that of the academics, the unemployed, the bureaucrats? That of 1968? As a writer, they tell me, I am already a 'disgruntled old man', so . . . All these groups, generations, sectors, or whatever they are could be interested in reading this book. I recommend it to them.

More clarifications: Mimi tells me that I am not interested in the political line of this book (my poor silence is already guilt enough)! Naturally I am interested in the political line of this book! I am not very interested in the psychoanalytic anecdote. I am interested still less in the detailed discussion that attempts to place psychoanalysis in the area of revolution or conservatism. (Part of this discussion as well as the language that is used, appears to me, like fashions, to be transient.) But who could deny the importance of theory, of praxis, as Armando Bauleo proposes it or as you have carried it out? I am not, nor could I be, a Stalinist. I believe that you still have vestiges of the Communist attitude of the 1930s, Mimi, and I cannot share it. To you the Comintern appears heroic; to me it cannot stop appearing horrible. Do you think that is why the politics of the book don't interest me?

In the end I achieved what I wanted: to conceal myself in the last pages of the book, and to catch the tired reader in order to perpetuate my ghost fantasies. But there are two people whom I do not want to become ghosts along with myself, despite the fact that one of them is dead. In the same way that Enrique and I are co-authors, so was Veronica Langer, by making the first tape recordings of her mother's life. And Horacio (I regret so much that I cannot even write his complete name), who enriched the manuscript so substantially and corrected and reorganized fundamental parts of it. I dedicate the little, or lot of, work that went into producing this book to Horacio (Skornik), whom I loved so much.

JAIME DEL PALACIO
28 December 1980

Left to right: Max (Marie's husband), Marie, Leopold Glas (Marie's father), Gucki (Marie's sister), Ana, Tomas, Martin (three of Marie's children), Argentina, 1953

APPENDIX: Documents from Argentina

DECLARATION OF THE PLATAFORMA GROUP TO MENTAL HEALTH WORKERS

The undersigned psychoanalysts who constitute the Argentinian Plataforma Group, member of the Plataforma International movement, have decided to make public their separation from the International Psychoanalytical Association and its Argentinian affiliate.

This decision is the result of prior consideration and is crucial for those of us who have taken it, since it annuls our membership in an institution that some of us helped create and in which we have invested many years of our lives, learning, teaching, researching and practising psychoanalysis.

We are aware that our withdrawal transcends us as psychoanalysts and even as individuals and has a significance that extends to a much broader context than scientific-institutional life. In order to explain our motives and intentions we turn to mental health workers, and our colleagues amongst them. With this communiqué, with scientific work and through the tasks of teaching, research and treatment, we hope to give all sectors a clear image of our identity. To this end we will publish a preliminary plan of our activities and organizational structure which will outline the method of joining our movement.

We believe that Freud's work, psychoanalysis, caused a revolution in the social sciences with its specific contribution to scientific knowledge and that this breakthrough, in spite of its relative autonomy, is and was determined by the socio-economic and political context. We understand, as we outline below, that psychoanalysis has been distorted and arrested, and that in order for it to take an innovative and evolutionary direction once more it requires the essential contribution of other sciences as well as a distinct and explicit social role, unavoidable at this point in history.

Our discipline provides the knowledge of the unconscious determinants that rule mankind's life, but, just the same, as a group of articulated social practices it is also governed by other determining factors: fundamentally the system of economic production and the political structure. Such relations generate systems of belief in individuals about the place they occupy in society, producing class ideologies. These are then partial registers of the reality of social practices destined to orientate and justify all practice. To be consistent with these concepts compels us to understand that scientific practice, inextricably linked to our lifestyle and the institutional organization we belong to, is equally conditioned and ideologized in all aspects by its insertion in the system, being merely a peculiarity of the institutions that combine and sustain it.

The reason for our withdrawal is disagreement with the psychoanalytic societal organization at all levels: theoretical, technical, didactic, investigative and economic; but here we want to emphasize one that is decisive, the ideological. On this level, this confrontation and the demands for concrete action that accompany it are insurmountable and in opposition to the overall ideology of the Institution (APA). We want to make clear that as a group or individuals we are not motivated by any intentions of a quasi-reformist or intra-institutional rivalry nature and that the criticisms that follow do not allude to individuals, many of whom we esteem and from whom we received or whom we provided with psychoanalytical training. For our part, we have been repeatedly criticized by those who maintain that we are negative or irrelevant, as well as by those who reproach us for not having assumed before it was necessary what we were striving towards from the beginning, a mature position. For now we will not concern ourselves with critics who out of passivity or pacts with the system attempt to obstruct us.

We hold that this separation, the product of a long and difficult process, is indispensable and cannot be silenced or dismissed, since we openly declare ourselves partial to a qualitatively and quantitatively different role within the national and Latin American social, economic and political process. As scientists and professionals we have the intention of putting our knowledge at the service of ideologies which uncompromisingly question the system, which in our country is characterized by the handing over of the national resources to the large monopolies and the repressing of all political activity that attempts to rebel against it. On the contary, we declare ourselves committed to all the combative sectors of the population which in the process of national liberation struggle for the advent of a socialist homeland.

In the institutional model, being as it is a submissive participant in this order, psychoanalytic thought has become distorted and static, paradoxically, because the organization was created with the mission of defending and cultivating it. This paralysis is essentially a result of the policy carried out by the directors, whose effect, beyond the good intentions of those who are also scientifically and emotionally sterilized by their role, is increasingly to consolidate the hierarchical stratification destined to maintain the economic privilege of those who are at the top of the pyramid. This in turn indoctrinates those at the bottom who aspire to reach the peak of power. We will mention some facts which demonstrate that this announcement is more than just a mere declaration, and which will permit the evaluation of the ideological pacts that are established between science and the system – links between the institutional structure and the ideology of the dominant class, which are expressed in this model of scientific practice:

—The Argentinian Psychoanalytical Association is at present composed of 367 individuals of whom 194 belong as members of the Institution (APA) and the rest to the Institute of Psychoanalysis as graduates and candidates. This sector has no legal access to institutional policy, nor can it receive in-depth information about the same under the pretext of protecting the analytical setting. On the other hand, of the total number of members accepted by the Institution, only the 79 full members have a voice and vote in the important decisions. Of the remainder, the 116 associate members have a voice but not the power to take part in decisions. Even within the ruling minority, the most important subgroups exclude the rest through quasi-legal manipulations.

—In the Institute of Psychoanalysis a similar situation exists. There is a Teaching Committee which is the maximum authority of the pedagogical organization. It is composed of full members who in turn belong to the same minority that rules the destiny of the Institution. There is also a Professors' Committee, where only full professors and associates vote and who in the majority belong to the previously mentioned group. In the face of this concentration of power, and to illustrate the disequilibrium, we would point out that a body of delegates representing the students is heard through their intermediary on the Teaching Committee but only with regard to circumstantial pedagogical restructuring with little innovative or scientific content or opposition to the relations of power.

—Suffice it to emphasize that a psychoanalytic candidate finds himself forced to allocate between forty and fifty work–study–money hours per week to his training, which means he either renounces all other vital activity for a period of four years or carries it out during his leisure time at the cost of his physical and mental health. In the final instance, it is the patients who pay for this unnatural overload and it is surprising to see how the candidates, in spite of this exacting regimen, find a way of using the virtually non-existent time remaining them in order to raise their standard of living, imitating the patterns of consumerism of the upper echelons of the Institution.

This vertical order, in which hierarchical authority does not necessarily coincide with a higher scientific level but with seniority and bureaucratic experience, has a clearly visible effect. It not only perverts the Institution's specific function, the promotion of the theoretical–technical development of psychoanalysis – the exploring of concepts, the exchange of knowledge with other sciences, the undertaking of new methods and areas of application, the trying out of innovative forms of teaching, etc. – but also replaces it with the search for prestige, status and economic achievements.

Other voices have already risen in protest against this 'lack of democracy' in the Institution and demanded a supposedly possible restructuring.

But this lack of liberality is not the key point in the break that separates us from the Institution. We are aware that the administrative verticality and paternalism is precisely typical of liberal organizations, whose great staying power is the result of a certain capacity they display for making concessions. We are not ignorant of the fact that these characteristics of the institutional model are indicative of the need of the socio-politico-economic system to support itself on the pillars represented by a prestigious and monopolistic scientific body of knowledge that is controlled for its specific production through the patterns and ideology that the same system provides for its perpetuation in other areas.

What essentially divides us is that these models of societal functioning, in addition to the effects mentioned, isolate the different groups from each other with respect to internal policy, and the institution from reality with respect to the external. They gradually encase psychoanalysts, with their acquiescence in their long wait for a promotion, in the bastion of a strictly apolitical and asocial profession. This painful condition is rationalized with the criteria of the 'valuable neutrality' of the scientist, supposedly possible and necessary, which is part of a utopian concept that includes deluded hopes for social change to which we cannot contribute as people because we are engrossed in professionalism, nor as psychoanalysts because any attempt in that regard is accused of being an 'ethical violation' and 'mixing science and politics'.

That's how we were trained and that's how we've trained others. We are on the way to becoming and to making others psychoanalysts, uniting with those who wish to collaborate with a position akin to ours. We want to practise true psychoanalysis. This is a decision which commits us in work and in denunciation together with other scientists and professionals who understand that their science cannot and must not be used to build an isolating barrier which alienates it from social reality or from its theoretical instrument, thus converting it into a mystifying and mystified tool at the service of the status quo. For us, from now on, psychoanalysis is not the official Psychoanalytical Institution. Psychoanalysis is wherever psychoanalysts may be, understanding 'being' as a clear definition that has no connection to an isolated and isolating science, but rather with a science committed to the multiple realities it attempts to study and transform.

DECLARATION OF THE DOCUMENTO GROUP

We are psychoanalysts who have resigned from our position as members of the Argentinian Psychoanalytical Association (APA) and the International Psychoanalytical Association. The object of the present declaration is to establish the reasons that drove us to such a decision which, although being made concrete at this point, must be understood as part of a process marked by the crisis in which psychoanalysis, and the Institution which until today appeared to represent it, finds itself. This crisis is qualitatively different from previous ones. In order to be able to understand it, it must be referred to within the socio-economic context in which it takes place, for which we consider our criticism of the APA as inseparable from a minimum political project in which the incorporation of psychoanalysis is expressed in a different context. Our disagreement with the APA is fundamental and commits us to an evaluation which also includes ourselves, and obliges us to redefine our role as professionals in a specific field – psychoanalysis – in the process of transforming our society. Our resignation forms part of an overall project in which we will attempt to give coherence to each of our actions.

The criticism of the APA that the Documento Group puts forth is not directed at individuals in particular, but at the Institution itself, and it would be biased and superficial if it were understood as being directly solely at a professional organization which simply 'functioned badly'. In fact, the APA is consistent with a social system which reproduces, with its particular characteristics, its relations of exploitation, its privileges and its methods of distorting and represssing any critical thought.

The APA has come to constitute an entity that struggles for the monopolistic control of psychoanalysis. Through belonging to it and achieving status within it, it assures its members participation in the system of privilege a monopoly implies. This monopolistic intention of the APA with respect to the remainder of mental health professionals, to which all the members of the entity contribute, is reflected in its internal structure, in that a reduced number of persons retain, both formally and effectively, the totality of political power. This power is exercised not only in the restriction of the vote to a minority group, but in a more subtle and effective manner through the teaching system. In this way, an institutional pyramid is created in which the hierarchies are fixed in a way that makes it impossible to alter a basic fact: the ideological instrumentation of psychoanalysis at the service of the dominant classes of our society. But the fact that the members of the APA as a body share the benefits that the Institution bestows does not eliminate the fact that, in order to continue to maintain its hegemony, the minority which exercises power within the same must resort to the censorship of any expression that tends towards real change. From the instant one presents oneself at the interviews for admission to the APA until the point one becomes a training analyst member, the highest political position within the organization, all participation in the activities of the Institution is utilized as an indicator of the degree of adherence to the norms and ideas imposed by the dominant group. This has led to an organization that without further intellectual demands permits the progress of all those who accept the rules of the game. In this way the conditions have been created that make difficult an authentic questioning of the supposed basics of the theory and practice of psychoanalysis, emphasizing instead secondary developments and formal details of technique. It turned out to be less risky to make partial contributions to already accepted positions than to expose oneself to the consequences of dissidence. Self-censorship thus complemented open coercion, contributing to the maintenance of repression. What should have been scientific work was converted into the mere means of rising within the bureaucratic pyramid. Here we have one of the factors that has contributed to the scientific stagnation of psychoanalysis.

In addition, the dominant orientation of the APA consists in separating psychoanalysis from the rest of the scientific disciplines, thus converting it into a type of super-science sufficient unto itself which attempts to expound to the others, as such giving way to a veritable epistemological deformation under the pretext of preserving the supposed purity of psychoanalysis. This narrow concept on the theoretical level corresponds to an equally limited practice: the multiple applications of psychoanalytic theory in fields of activity distinct from individual psychoanalysis, which in the interplay between praxis and theory would have permitted the opening up of new development perspectives for the latter, have not been explored.

The social value of psychoanalysis is not supplied by the few individuals it can treat but in the presenting of a body of theory, whose elaboration would allow for the creation of therapeutic instruments for increasingly large groups of the population. What is more, from the point of view of mental health, psychoanalysts should recognize its present limitations in order to provide a solution to the problem of the great masses of the population.

Given all of the above, we believe that the solution does not rest in proposing formal modifications to an Institution whose possibilities of change on the scientific and ideological plane are limited by its role in society.

Our resignation must be contextualized in relation to the present point in the psychoanalytic movement intimately linked to existing conditions in our country. The departure of the Plataforma Group, which also acted within the APA, constituted a political event which contributed to accentuating an already existing polarization within the psychoanalytic movement, a polarization exemplified by our consecutive actions within the institution. In view of the new open configuration, our rupture with the APA points to the strengthening of the broad movement of individuals and groups which, beyond their tactical and circumstancial differences, attempt to rescue psychoanalysis and put it at the service of a shared goal: the advent of a socialist society.

At the national level, our decision is located within the process of the sharpening of the existing contradictions between the sectors which hold economic and political power and the ever-growing masses of the population. In addition to the structural crisis at the economic–political level, caused by the unresolved problems of a country dependent upon the big monopolies, is a current situation that leaves a narrow margin of play for the traditional schemes of the oppressing classes. This has meant that the forms of repression have acquired unusual violence. The dominant classes increasingly put ideological pressures on all levels of scientific work: the only science acceptable is that which upon denying the socio-economic determinants places itself, consciously or unconsciously, at the service of the maintenance of the system. The tendency is to crystallize academic structures that fulfil this aim. In spite of certain recognizable human and scientific values, the APA is an example of the consequences of the capture of a scientific theory, revolutionary in its origins, by a system which restricts all demystifying thought. Our role as professionals in a socio-political structure with these characteristics makes any attempt at autonomy in our praxis utopian. We reject the fallacy of neutrality posited as a *desideratum* for the scientist, since we believe that apoliticism is nothing more than an endorsement of the system, full of political significance.

It is clear to us that in withdrawing from the APA we are only at the starting point of a task and action which will be what will finally give real meaning to this declaration.

NOTES ON CONTRIBUTORS

Jaime del Palacio is a Mexican writer who has published two novels, as well as various articles in Mexican publications. He is married to Marie Langer's eldest daughter, Ana.

Enrique Guinsberg is an Argentinian psychologist specializing in the area of mass communication media. A political exile, he now lives in Mexico, where he teaches at the Autonomous Metropolitan University in Mexico City.

Nancy Caro Hollander is Professor of Latin American History and Feminist Studies at the California State University, Dominguez Hills, as well as a candidate in training at the Psychoanalytic Center of California. She has translated Marie Langer's *Maternity and Sexuality* (Virago, forthcoming) and is writing a biography of her.

Margaret Hooks, an Irish journalist and writer, has been writing on Mexico and Central America since 1983 for various publications, including the *Guardian* and *The Irish Times*. She first met Marie Langer in Mexico in 1979 and is currently working on a collection of interviews conducted with her between 1980 and 1987.

Manuel Martinez, a poet, works as a civil servant in MINSA, Nicaragua's Ministry of Health.

Arturo Varchevker, originally from Argentina, is a Member of the Institute of Psycho-Analysis, London. He is also co-ordinator of the UK branch of the Internationalist Mental Health Support Group, and regularly works with the group that Marie Langer helped set up in Nicaragua.

BIBLIOGRAPHY

Achard de Marie, L. *et al.* (1971) 'Crisis social y situación analítica', in M. Langer, ed. *Cuestionamos* 1.

Badinter, E. (1980) L'amour en plus, *histoire de l'amour maternel, XVII–XX. siècle.* Paris: Flammarion. (*Die Mutterliebe: Geschichte eines Gefühls vom 17. Jahrhundert bis heute.* Munich: dvt, 1984.)

Baremblitt, G. (1974) *El concepto de realidad en psicoanálisis.* Buenos Aires: Editorial Socianálisis.

Basaglia, F. (1980) 'La mujer y la locura', in S. Marcos, ed. *Antipsiquiatría y política.* Mexico: Extemporaneos.

Bauleo, A. and Langer, M. (1971) 'Prólogo', in M. Langer, ed. *Cuestionamos* 1.

——(1974) 'Quel che pensiamo di quel che voi pensate della psicoanálisi', *Psicoterapia e Scienze Umane* 3. Milan.

Bettelheim, B. (1969) *Children of the Dream.* New York: Macmillan.

Bion, W. (1967) 'Notes on memory and desire', *Psychoanalytic Forum* 2: 272–3, 279–80.

Bleger, J. (1971) 'Psicoanálisis y marxismo', in M. Langer, ed. *Cuestionamos* 1.

Bornemann, E. (1975) *Das Patriarchat: Ursprung und Zukunft unseres Gesellschaftssystems.* Frankfurt: Fischer.

Castel, R. (1976) *Psychoanalyse und gesellschaftliche Macht.* Königstein: Athenäum. (*El psicoanalismo, el orden psicoanalítico y el poder.* Mexico: Siglo XXI, 1980.)

Davin, A. (1978) 'Imperialism and motherhood', *History Workshop Journal* 5:9–66.

Eckstein, R. (1969) 'Psychoanalysis and social crisis', *Bulletin of the Menninger Clinic* 33:333–45.

Engels, F. (1986) *Origin of the Family, Private Property and the State*. Harmondsworth: Penguin.

Freud, S. (1900) *The Interpretation of Dreams*, in James Strachey, ed. *The Standard Edition of the Complete Psychological Works of Sigmund Freud*, 24 vols. London: Hogarth, 1953–73. vols 4–5.

——(1905) 'My views on the part played by sexuality in the aetiology of the neuroses'. *S.E.* 7, pp. 269–79.

——(1910) 'Five lectures on psycho-analysis'. *S.E.* 11, pp. 9–55.

——(1912) *Totem and Taboo. S.E.* 13, pp. 1–16.

——(1913) 'On beginning the treatment'. *S.E.* 12, pp. 121–44.

——(1916–17) *Introductory Lectures on Psycho-Analysis. S.E.* 15–16.

——(1918) 'Lines of advance in psycho-analytic therapy'. *S.E.* 17, pp. 159–68.

——(1920) *Beyond the Pleasure Principle. S.E.* 18, pp. 7–64.

——(1921) *Group Psychology and the Analysis of the Ego. S.E.* 18, pp. 69–143.

——(1926) *The Question of Lay Analysis. S.E.* 20, pp. 177–258.

——(1927) *The Future of an Illusion. S.E.* 21, pp. 1–56.

——(1930) *Civilization and its Discontents. S.E.* 21, pp. 64–145.

——(1931) 'Female sexuality'. *S.E.* 21, pp. 221–43.

——(1933) 'Why war?' (Letter to Einstein). *S.E.* 22, pp. 203–15.

——(1937) 'Analysis terminable and interminable'. *S.E.* 23, pp. 216–53.

Fromm, E. (1981) 'Das freudianische Modell des Menschen und seine gesellschaftlichen Determinanten', in *GA* 8. Munich: dtv.

Gordon, L. (1978) 'Maternità volontaria', *NUOVA dwf* 6/7. Rome.

Greenson, R.R. (1981) *Technique and Practice of Psychoanalysis*. London: Hogarth.

Greffrath, M. (1979) *Die Zerstörung einer Zukunft: Gespräche mit emigrierten Sozialwissenschaftlern*. Reinbek bei Hamburg: Rowohlt.

Grinberg, L., Langer, M. and Rodrigué, E. (1956) *Psicoterapia del grupo. (Psychoanalytische Gruppentherapie*. Munich: Kindler, 1971).

Guinsberg, E. (1973) *Sociedad, salud y enfermedad mental*. Buenos Aires: Editor de America Latina; Mexico: Universidad Autónoma de Puebla, 1976.

——(1979) 'Freud y Marx, delincuentes ideológicos', *Cuadernos de Marcha* 3, julio–agosto. Mexico.

Jacques, E. (1955) 'Social systems as defence against persecutory and depressive anxiety', in M. Klein, ed. *New Directions in Psycho-Analysis*. London: Tavistock.

Klein, M. (1957) *Envy and Gratitude*. New York: Basic; London: Hogarth, 1975.

——(1975) *Love, Guilt and Reparation and Other Papers*. London: Hogarth.

Kurnitzky, H. (1974) *Die Triebstruktur des Geldes: Ein Beitrag zur Theorie der Weiblichkeit*. Berlin: Wagenbach.

Lacan, J. (1980) *Ecrits: A Selection*. London: Tavistock.

Langer, M. (1951) *Maternidad y sexo: Estudio psicoanalítico y psicosomático*. Buenos Aires: Paidós.

——(1959) 'Ideología y idealizacíon', *Revista de Psicoanálisis* 16(4). Buenos Aires.

——(1971) 'Psicoanálisis y/o revolución social', in M. Langer, ed. *Cuestionamos 1*.

Langer, M., ed. (1971, 1973) *Cuestionamos 1; Cuestionamos 2*. Buenos Aires: Granica Editor.

——(1984) Interview with Nancy Caro Hollander.

——(1985) 'National sovereignty and mental health', paper presented to the Encounter of Intellectuals for the Sovereignty of the People of our Americas, Havana, December.

——(1985) 'Psicoanálisis sin divan' paper presented to Cuba's Academy of Sciences, Havana, December. ('Psychoanalysis without the couch', *Free Associations* 15: 60–66, 1989).

——(1986) Interview with Nancy Caro Hollander.

——(n.d.) 'La vejez, mi vejez', *Fem*. Mexico.

Langer, M. and Maldonado, I. (1983) 'Nicaragua libre', unpublished.

Langer, M. and Siniego, A. (1977) 'Psychoanalyse, lutte de classes et santé mentale', in *Réseau Alternative à la Psychiatrie*. Paris: Union Général D'Editions.

Langer, M., Siniego, A. and Ulloa, F. (1979) 'Institutionelle, Gruppen-Analyse in der Arbeiterklasse', in E.H. Englert, ed. *Die Verarmung der Psyche*. Frankfurt/New York: Campus Verlag.

Laplanche, J. and Pontalis, J.-B. (1967) *The Language of Psycho-Analysis*. London: Hogarth; New York: Norton, 1973.

Larguía, I. (1980) 'El sector más explotado de la historia', *Fem* 4(15). Mexico.

Leclaire, S. (1977) *Matan a un niño*. Buenos Aires: Amorrortu.

Lema, V.Z. (1976) *Conversaciones con Enrique Pichon Riviere, sobre el arte y la locura*. Buenos Aires: Timerman Editores.

Liberman, D., Ferschtut, G. and Sor, D. (1961) 'El contrato analítico', *Revista de Psicoanálisis* 1. Buenos Aires.

Marx, K. (1964) *Precapitalist Economic Formations*. London: Lawrence & Wishart.

Masters, W.H. and Johnson, V.E. (1980) *Human Sexual Response*. London/ New York: Bantam.

Ministerio de Salud (1981) *Manual de normas de organización y funciones de psicología en salud*. Managua: Departamento de Psicología, División Nacional de Atención Medica.

Mitchell, J. (1976) *Psychoanalysis and Feminism*. Harmondsworth: Penguin.

Moeller-Gambaroff, M. (1977) *Emanzipation macht Angst*. Berlin: Kursbuch Verlag.

Ortiz, M.F. (1979) 'La salud mental en Nicaragua', paper presented at the 11th Congress of APAL, 4–10 November.

Puget, J. (1988) 'Social violence and psychoanalysis in Argentina', *Free Associations* 13:84–140.

Racker, H. (1968) *Transference and Counter-Transference*. London: Hogarth.

Reich, W. (1970) *The Mass Psychology of Fascism*. New York: Simon & Schuster.

Rodrigué, E. (1977) *El paciente de las 50.000 horas*. Madrid: Fundamentos.

Roudy, Y. (1980) *La mujer, una marginada*. Bogotá: Editorial Pluma. (*La femme en marge*. Paris: Flammarion, 1982.)

Roustang, F. (1982) *Dire Mastery*. Baltimore: Johns Hopkins University Press.

Schneider, M. (1973) *Neurosis and Civilization: A Marxist/Freudian Synthesis*. New York: Seabury.

Sternberg, F. (1972) 'Marxismo y represión', *Marxismo, psicoanálisis y sexpol* 1. Buenos Aires: Granica.

Sturgeon, T. (1986) *More Than Human*. London: Gollancz.

Suárez, V. (1978) 'Vicisitudes del movimiento psicoanalítico argentino', in V. Suárez, ed., *Razón, locura y sociedad*. Mexico: Siglo XXI.

Usandivaras, R. (1968) 'Comunicación terapéutica y clase social', *Psiquiatría Social* 2. Buenos Aires: Centro Editor de América Latina.

INDEX

This first edition of
From Vienna to Managua: Journey of a Psychoanalyst
was finished in May 1989.

It was set in 10/13 Erhardt Roman
on a Linotron 202
and printed on a Miller TP41
on to 80 g/m² vol. 18 book wove.

The book was commissioned by Robert M. Young,
edited by Les Levidow,
copy-edited by Gillian Wilce,
designed by Martin Klopstock,
and produced by Martin Klopstock and Selina O'Grady
for Free Association Books.